Elizabeth's THIRD GRADE BOOKIET!!

The HomeBase Big Book
of
Third Grade
Skill Practice

HomeBase Learning
Nashville, TN

Acknowledgment:
Many thanks
to Charlotte Poulos
and Laurie Grupé
whose adapted exercises
are included in this book.

Written by Imogene Forte and Marjorie Frank
Illustrated by Kathleen Bullock
Cover by Geoffrey Brittingham
Edited by Jennifer J. Streams

ISBN 978-0-86530-971-5

2   3   4   5   6   7   8   9   10   10   09   08   07

PRINTED IN THE UNITED STATES OF AMERICA

TABLE OF CONTENTS

Language, Writing, & Usage Exercises

Social Studies

Social Studies Exercises

Map Skills & Geography Exercises

Geometry, Measurement, & Graphing Exercises

Math Computation & Problem Solving Exercises

INTRODUCTION

Do basic skills have to be boring? Absolutely not! Mastery of basic skills provides the foundation for exciting learning opportunities for students. Content relevant to their everyday life is fascinating stuff! Kids love learning about topics such as galaxies and glaciers, thunderstorms and timelines, continents and chemicals, tarantulas and tornadoes, poems and plateaus, elephants and encyclopedias, mixtures and mummies, antonyms and Antarctica, and more. Using these topics and carefully-designed practice they develop basic skills which enable them to ponder, process, grow, and achieve school success.

Acquiring, polishing, and using basic skills and content is a cause for celebration—not an exercise in drudgery. *The HomeBase Big Book of Third Grade Skill Practice* invites students to sharpen their abilities in the essentials of language arts.

As you examine *The HomeBase Big Book of Third Grade Skill Practice*, you will see that it is filled with attractive age-appropriate student exercises. These pages are no ordinary worksheets! *The HomeBase Big Book of Third Grade Skill Practice* contains hundreds of inventive and inviting ready-to-use lessons based on a captivating theme that invites the student to join an adventure, solve a puzzle, pursue a mystery, or tackle a problem. Additionally, each illustrated exercise provides diverse tools for reinforcement and extension of basic and higher-order thinking skills.

The HomeBase Big Book of Third Grade Skill Practice contains the following components:

- **A clear, sequential list of skills for eight different content areas**
  Checklists of skills begin each content section. These lists correlate with the exercises, identifying page numbers where specific skills can be practiced. Students can chart their progress by checking off each skill as it is mastered.

- **Over 300 pages of student exercises**
  Each exercise page:
  - . . . addresses a specific basic skill or content area.
  - . . . presents tasks that grab the attention and curiosity of students.
  - . . . contains clear directions to the student.
  - . . . asks students to use, remember, and practice a basic skill.
  - . . . challenges students to think creatively and analytically.
  - . . . requires students to apply the skill to real situations or content.
  - . . . takes students on learning adventures with a variety of delightful characters!

- **A ready-to-use assessment tool**
  Six skills tests, one for each content area, follow each series of exercises. The tests are presented in parts corresponding to the skills lists. Designed to be used as pre- or post-tests, individual parts of these tests can be given to students at separate times, if needed.

- **Complete answer keys**
  Easy-to-find-and-use answer keys for all exercises and skills tests follow each section.

HOW TO USE THIS BOOK:

The exercises contained in *The HomeBase Big Book of Third Grade Skill Practice* are to be used with adult assistance. The adult may serve as a guide to ensure the student understands the directions and questions.

The HomeBase Big Book of Third Grade Skill Practice is designed to be used in many diverse ways. Its use will vary according to the needs of the students and the structure of the learning environment.

The skills checklists may be used as:

    . . . record-keeping tools to track individual skills mastery;

    . . . planning guides for instruction; and

    . . . a place for students to proudly check off accomplishments.

Each exercise page may be used as:

    . . . a pre-test or check to see how well a student has mastered a skill;

    . . . one of many resources or exercises for teaching a skill;

    . . . a way to practice or polish a skill that has been taught;

    . . . a review of a skill taught earlier;

    . . . reinforcement of a single basic skill, skills cluster, or content base;

    . . . a preview to help identify instructional needs; and

    . . . an assessment for a skill that a student has practiced.

The exercises are flexibly designed for presentation in many formats and settings. They are useful for individual instruction or independent work. They can also be used under the direction of an adult with small groups.

The skills tests may be used as:

    . . . pre-tests to gauge instructional or placement needs;

    . . . information sources to help adjust instruction; and

    . . . post-tests to review student mastery of skills and content areas.

The HomeBase Big Book of Third Grade Skill Practice is not intended to be a complete curriculum or textbook. It is a collection of inventive exercises to sharpen skills and provide students and parents with tools for reinforcing concepts and skills, and for identifying areas that need additional attention. This book offers a delightful assortment of tasks that give students just the practice they need—and to get that practice in a manner that is not boring.

As students take on the challenges of the enticing adventures in this book, they will increase their comfort level with the use of fundamental reading, writing, and language skills and concepts. Watching your student check off the sharpened skills is cause for celebration!

LANGUAGE ARTS

Skills Exercises
Grade Three

Reading Spelling Vocabulary Grammar Writing

SKILLS CHECKLIST
READING

✔	SKILL	PAGE(S)
	Find the main idea of a passage	22, 23
	Find information on a map	24, 25, 35
	Read to find details	24, 25, 29, 30
	Follow written directions	26–28
	Make inferences about a passage	29, 30, 48, 49
	Match a story to a picture	31
	Read to find information	31–39
	Answer questions after reading a passage	31–39
	Find information on a chart	32
	Read titles to gain information	40
	Read to determine cause and effect	41, 42
	Identify sequence of events in a passage	43, 44
	Put words and sentences in proper sequence	43, 44
	Supply missing information for a passage	45
	Gain information from captions; match captions to pictures	46
	Determine author's purpose for writing a selection	47
	Give personal response to a passage	47, 50–55, 57
	Make predictions after reading a passage	50, 51
	Make an analysis of characters	55
	Distinguish fact from opinion in a passage	56
	Draw conclusions after reading a passage	57
	Identify exaggerations in a passage	58
	Complete similes	59
	Use context to decide word meaning	60, 61, 65
	Determine word meanings	60–68
	Recognize synonyms and antonyms	62, 67
	Complete analogies	66
	Identify words with multiple meanings	68
	Recognize and appreciate alliterative words and sentences	69

SKILLS CHECKLIST
SPELLING

✔	SKILL	PAGE(S)
	Correctly spell words with confusing initial blends: *gh, ph*	70
	Correctly spell words with double vowels	71
	Correctly spell words with special vowel combinations	72–75
	Correctly spell words with special endings	76, 77
	Correctly spell words with *y* and *ey* endings	78
	Correctly spell words with silent letters	79
	Correctly spell plural nouns	80, 81
	Correctly spell verbs in the past tense	82, 83
	Correctly spell verbs with ing endings	84
	Correctly spell comparative adjectives (*er* and *est* endings)	85
	Correctly spell words with prefixes	86
	Correctly spell words with suffixes	87
	Distinguish among words that sound alike: homonyms	88, 89
	Identify words spelled correctly	89
	Identify, spell, and form compound words	90, 91
	Spell contractions correctly	92
	Distinguish between words that are easily confused with one another	93
	Identify words spelled incorrectly	93–95
	Identify and correct incorrect spelling in written pieces	94, 95

SKILLS CHECKLIST
LANGUAGE, WRITING, & USAGE

✔	SKILL	PAGE(S)
	Identify and write verbs	96
	Identify and write adjectives (describing words)	97, 98
	Add *er* and *est* to adjectives to make comparisons	98
	Identify and use adverbs	99
	Recognize and correct run-on sentences	100
	Identify, capitalize, and punctuate exclamations	101, 104, 107
	Identify subjects and predicates	102, 103
	Identify and correct punctuation errors	104, 105, 107
	Identify, capitalize, and punctuate questions	104, 105, 107
	Identify, capitalize, and punctuate statements	104, 105, 107
	Capitalize words in sentences	104, 107
	Distinguish among statements, questions, and exclamations	104, 107
	Identify, write, and capitalize proper nouns	104, 107
	Identify different punctuation marks and their uses	105
	Choose effective, interesting words for writing	106
	Create good titles for written selections	108, 109
	Express original ideas clearly in writing	108–113
	Generate and organize ideas for writing	108–113
	Create good questions	110
	Use collected ideas to create a written piece	111
	Write a short letter and envelope	111
	Write clear directions	112, 113
	Eliminate excess ideas in a written piece	114, 115

A Big Mix-Up

Aunt Frannie is retiring from the Pick-up and Go Travel Agency after thirty years. Yesterday her friends gave a big party to celebrate her retirement. In the excitement of the good wishes and good-byes, the tags on her retirement gifts were mixed up. Help her find the labels in the word find puzzle. Circle each word as you find it and then write it in the correct sentence.

GOODBYE, FRANNIE

s	m	l	a	d	o	w	v	a	b	s
j	o	u	r	n	a	l	o	u	i	d
m	f	t	e	l	e	p	h	o	n	e
l	u	y	m	g	v	i	r	j	o	g
i	c	b	r	t	d	l	s	k	c	a
f	a	m	p	r	a	l	c	v	u	g
x	m	i	h	z	t	o	q	u	l	g
w	e	p	w	f	l	w	p	j	a	u
c	r	t	k	c	a	n	v	z	r	l
n	a	h	m	v	s	h	o	e	s	o

1. Aunt Frannie loved the sturdy hiking
   _shoe_s.

2. The _ _ g _ _ g _ her boss gave her will hold everything Aunt Frannie could possibly want to pack.

3. Only her friend Bess would know how much she loved to rest her head on a soft p _illow_.

4. A favorite client sent an _ t _ _ _ _ so that she would never be without a map.

5. The fancy _ _ _ _ c _ has a second hand and an extra loud alarm.

6. Aunt Frannie couldn't believe her eyes when she took the powerful b _inoculars_ out of the classy leather case.

7. The perfect retirement gift, of course, is a _Journal_ for recording the marvelous events of the golden years ahead.

8. The c _amera_ complete with _fil_ m, will help Aunt Frannie capture the sites and scenes along the way.

9. Aunt Frannie will never be stranded now that she has her own portable _telephone_.

Name ___Elizabeth Lee___

Mail From Far-off Places

Aunt Frannie has friends and relatives all over the world. The mailman has just arrived with a lot of letters and packages for her.

As she reads her mail, Frannie starts to dream about faraway places. Soon she'll start looking at maps and visiting the travel agency!

Read each letter she has opened. Write the main idea of each letter.

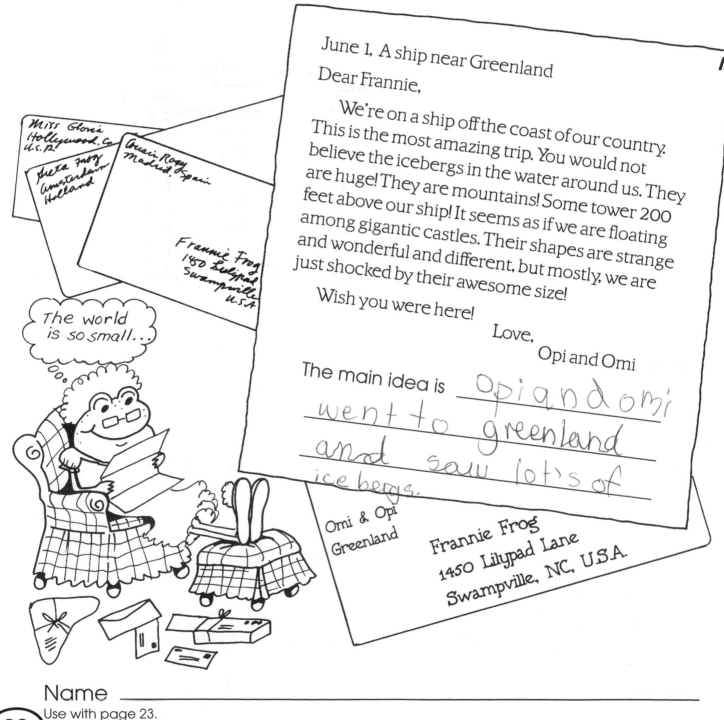

June 1, A ship near Greenland

Dear Frannie,

We're on a ship off the coast of our country. This is the most amazing trip. You would not believe the icebergs in the water around us. They are huge! They are mountains! Some tower 200 feet above our ship! It seems as if we are floating among gigantic castles. Their shapes are strange and wonderful and different, but mostly, we are just shocked by their awesome size!

Wish you were here!

Love,
Opi and Omi

The main idea is _Opi and omi went to greenland and saw lots of ice bergs._

Omi & Opi
Greenland

Frannie Frog
1450 Lilypad Lane
Swampville, NC, U.S.A.

June 14, China

Dear Frannie,

I think you'll like this picture of a giant panda. Today, I'm off hiking with a group that's searching for the panda. We know these bears sleep in trees during the day, so we are looking in the bamboo forests. So far, we have had no luck. We have looked for 3 days. I am so anxious to see at least one! Most of all, I want to see some panda cubs.

Wish me luck!

Love, Gonzo

The main idea is _Gonzo was searching for the panda she found none._

2.

3.

Madrid, Spain
June 25

Dear Aunt Frannie,

You wanted to hear about the bullfight, didn't you? I'm not sure you will like what you hear! It was so dreadful. I was frightened most of the time. It seemed so cruel to stab the bull and make him angry. The bull-fighter had a lot of skill, but he was badly injured. I closed my eyes most of the time, because it was so awful. The crowd cheered. They loved it! I won't ever watch one again.

Love, Roxy

The main idea is

Roxy went to a bullfight she said it was so dreadful.

4. Australia, June 19

Dear Frannie,

Here's a surprise for you—a boomerang from Australia. It will not be easy to use. I thought I could just toss it, and it would come right back to me. Wow! Was I ever wrong! It was so hard to learn. I had to practice for about a year, but it is so much fun! Maybe you'll learn faster than I did. Have fun!

Cousin Rudy

The main idea is _Cousin Rudy gave frannie a boomerang from Australia._

Name _Elizabeth_

It's a Big World Out There

Aunt Frannie has caught the travel bug. Her Travel Wish List is growing longer. Today, she has started putting pins on a world map to mark some places she would like to visit.

Read the Wish List and the map to answer the questions on page 25.

Travel Wish List

Grand Canyon
Sahara Desert
Bermuda Triangle
Alaska & Canada
African Jungle
Everglades Swamp
Loch Ness – Scotland
The Great Pyramids
Paris, France
Great Wall of China
Hollywood
Music City–Nashville
Angel Falls
Australia's Outback
Amazon Rain Forest
Submarine Ride
India & Italy
Antarctica
Siberia
The Himalayas

North America

South America

Flippity-doo-da! Pack my bags! I'm going on a worldwide trip!

It's a Big World Out There, cont.

EUROPE

ASIA

AFRICA

AUSTRALIA

I'm going shopping for some new duds!

1. How many pins has she put on Africa? __3__
2. How many pins are on South America? __2__
3. How many pins are in the ocean? __2__
4. What desert would she like to see? __Sahara__ ~~Desert~~ Desert
5. What does she want to see in Scotland? __loch ness__
6. What ride would she like to take? __Submarine ride__
7. What does she want to see in China? __Great wall of china__
8. What swamp does she want to visit? __everglades__

ANTARCTICA

Name __Elizabeth Lee__

Off to the Travel Shop

There's a good travel shop at the mall where Aunt Frannie went to buy things for her trip. Read about her shopping trip below. Use a marker or crayon to draw the path she took to the travel shop.

1. First, Frannie bought hiking boots at the shoe store.

2. Next, she got a new calendar to keep track of her travels.

3. Frannie bought two pairs of good sunglasses at the Sunglass Hut.

4. She stopped for a big box of popcorn.

5. Frannie went to the jewelry store for a waterproof diving watch.

6. Next, she shopped for Bermuda shorts at the Shirts & Shorts Shop.

7. She bought toys to take to nieces and nephews in China.

8. She got hungry for some pizza, so she headed to the food court.

9. Finally, she bought luggage and other supplies at the travel shop.

Name _____

Where Are the Backpacks?

Oops! The travel shop is not ready for customers yet. Some merchandise needs to be put on the shelves. Follow the directions to finish putting out the supplies.

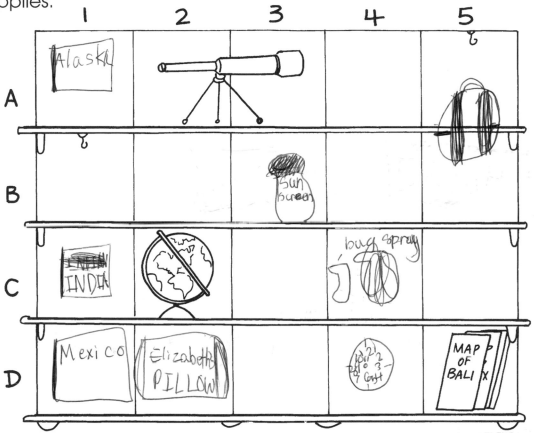

Draw these things on the grid:

1. Draw a backpack hanging in A, 5 and B, 5.
2. Draw a travel book on India in C, 1.
3. Draw a travel book on Alaska in A, 1.
4. Draw a travel book about Mexico in D, 1.
5. Draw a travel clock in D, 4.
6. Draw a travel pillow in D, 2.
7. Draw some bug spray in C, 4.
8. Draw some sunscreen lotion in B, 3.

Name _____Elizabeth_____

Baggage Confusion

There's trouble on the baggage carousel. Tags and labels have fallen off suitcases everywhere.

Follow the directions to get things back to normal.

1. Draw a sticker for Brazil on Maria's luggage.

2. Write Percy Penguin's name on the tag of the bag with the Australia sticker.

3. The bag with the China sticker needs Lu Sing's name on the tag.

4. Draw a sticker for Hawaii on Chester's luggage.

5. Write Frannie Frog's name on the bag with the Malibu sticker.

6. The bag with the Nashville sticker needs a tag for Dolly Dimples.

Name _____

Read to Follow Directions

Ticket Mix-Up

Oh, no! Frannie has just discovered that she has the wrong ticket! She needs a ticket to Mexico. Straighten out this ticket mix-up. Read the information on the tickets to finish the sentences and questions below.

1. The yacht ticket belongs to Jenny Jinx. Write her name on it.

2. Waldo is traveling to Texas. How will he get there? __Hot Air BALLOON__

3. The plane ticket to Singapore belongs to __George Gonzo__

4. Will Zeke travel to Greenland by plane? __~~No~~ I DontKNow__

5. Find Mrs. Smuggs' ticket. Where is she going? __Las Vegas__

6. Where is Frank Frog headed? ~~Fort~~ __Peru__

7. Bart is going to the Super Bowl. How is he traveling? By __Car__

8. Find Frannie's ticket. How is she traveling to Mexico?

   By __Airplane__

Ed's Budget Airline ONE WAY To: **Singapore**
Name: *George Gonzo*

Arlene's **A-1** *Airline*
One Way Ticket To: **Mexico** Frannie

Bart Biggins

Bubba's Blimp Rides

OVERLAND BUS CO.
Name: **Mrs. Smuggs**
Destination: **Las Vegas**

DUCHESS CRUISE LINES
EMBARKING FOR: **Greenland**
Name: *Zeke Zucker*

Sam's HOT AIR Balloon Trips
Name: *Waldo Waldorf*
TO: WALDO **TEXAS**

Yancy's Yacht Rides
Sailing For: **JAMAICA** Jenny JINX

SOUTH AMERICAN RAIL ROAD EXCURSION TRIP TO PERU
Name: *Frank Frog*

Name __Elizabeth__

The Great Taco Mystery

There are 500 tortillas missing from Cousin Pepito's Taco Stand in the little Mexican town of Las Truchas! They were stolen some time between 6:00 and 8:30 A.M. Boot-like footprints were found at the stand. Read the clues to help him solve the crime.

Clue #1

Santos works at the Las Truchas Motel from midnight to 9:00 A.M. He has greasy fingers. He says it is from maple sugar candy.

Clue #2

Candita has drips of something greasy on her skirt and pieces of lettuce stuck in her teeth. She left home at 8:00 A.M. It takes 40 minutes to drive into Las Truchas.

Clue #3

Pedro says he was sleeping until 10:00 A.M. His boots have crunchy crumbs stuck to them. He has a large sack in his truck. It has crunchy crumbs in it.

Where are those tacos?

Taco Stand

Who do you think stole the tacos?
Candita

Why do you think so? because she had grease all over

What do you think he or she did with the tacos? Ate them of course

Name _____

Read for Details • Inference

Cruising Through the Rain Forest

Cousin Felix has convinced Frannie to join him on an Amazon River cruise through the rain forest.

Look at the picture. Then read the story. Circle words or phrases in the story that do not match the picture.

Cruising along with the Alligators

Oh, what a lovely, rainy day! Frannie has her camera out to take pictures from the jungle cruise boat. She is just arriving in Amazonia to stay at the Raindrop Resort. Her boat will stop near Bill's Boat Rentals where there are four boats for rent. Five other little boats are floating nearby on the river, and a lazy gorilla is enjoying a float on the cool water. "Look at those alligators snoozing in the hammocks," she says to Cousin Felix. She is excited to see the little café, because she's very hungry from her trip. She thinks she will join the two black panthers at the café table. Frannie is happy to get off the boat and enjoy a cool drink. "I love this place!" she exclaimed. "It's too bad there are no umbrellas at the café to protect us from the hot sun."

Name ___Elizabeth   Lee_____

Record Setters

"I want to visit the coldest spot, the longest cave, the hottest desert, and the tallest waterfall in the world!"

Read the chart to help Frannie find information about some of these places.

WORLD RECORD SETTERS

Place	Location	Length	Cost
Longest Cave	Mammoth Cave Kentucky	4 days	$1200
Largest Desert	Sahara Desert North Africa	1 week	$3500
Biggest Island	Greenland	2 days	$800
Highest Waterfall	Angel Falls Venezuela	3 days	$1000
Tallest Building	Petronas Towers Malaysia	3 days	$1000
Coldest Town	Norlisk Russia	9 days	$4200

1. Which trip costs the most? _Norlisk Russia_

2. How long is the trip to the Sahara Desert? _1 week._

3. What is the biggest island? _Greenland_

4. In what country is the coldest town? _Norlisk Russia_

5. What is the tallest building? _Petronas towers Malaysia_

6. How long is the trip to the highest waterfall? _3 days_

7. How much does it cost to get to the longest cave? _4 days_

8. Which trip takes the longest? _Norlisk Russia_

Name _____

The Big Drop

Finally! After a long, muddy bus ride from Brazil to Venezuela, Frannie can set her eyes on something she has dreamed of seeing all her life—the world's tallest waterfall!

A Lucky Discovery

In 1933, an American named James Angel went to Venezuela. He landed his small plane to look for gold, but his plane would not take off again. He had to walk a long way back to a city. On the way, he was lucky enough to discover the world's tallest waterfall. It was named after him. It's called Angel Falls. He never did get his plane back. It wasn't rescued until 37 years later! This was after he had died.

World's TOP 10 Waterfalls

Angel Falls . . . Venezuela
Tugela . . . South Africa
Utigard . . . Norway
Mongefossen . . . Norway
Yosemite . . . United States
Ostre Mardola . . . Norway
Tyssestrengane . . . Norway
Cuquenan . . . Venezuela
Sutherland . . . New Zealand
Kjellfossen . . . Norway

3212 feet

ANGEL FALLS BUS LINE

1. How many of the world's top ten highest falls are in Norway? ___5___
2. Which country has two of the top ten waterfalls? __Venezuela__
3. The tallest waterfall in the U.S. is 2425 feet high. What is it? __Yosemite__
4. Which waterfall is in South Africa? __tugela__
5. Which waterfall is in New Zealand? __Sutherland__
6. What was James Angel looking for in Venezuela? __gold__
7. In which year was his plane found? (Use your math skills!) __1970__

Name _____

Special Permission Required

It's good that Cousin Maxie is a scientist. Otherwise Frannie might not be able to visit the Galapagos Islands. Visitors are allowed only with special permission. Take some bug spray, Frannie! The mosquitoes are huge!

The Galapagos Islands

They are called "the end of the world." The nine Galapagos Islands are located in the Pacific Ocean several hundred miles west of Ecuador. The Islands are covered with many volcanic craters from volcanoes that blew their tops. What is so special about these islands? When scientists first came here, they found plants and animals that were different from those anywhere else in the world. The islands are filled with giant land iguanas, interesting birds, and giant turtles. Sea iguanas and sea lions fill the waters around the island. Very few people live on the islands, which are owned by Ecuador. They've been turned into a national park and wildlife sanctuary.

1. The Galapagos Islands are in the ___Pacific___ Ocean.
2. Who owns the islands? ___few people owned by ecuador___
3. What is unusual about the animals there? ___Sea Iguanas, and sea lions.___
4. Name an animal Frannie will see on the islands. ___sea lion___
5. How many people live on the islands? ___Few___
6. What two kinds of iguanas can be found? ___SEA Iguana and Giant land Iguanas.___
7. What caused the craters? ___I don't know___

Name _____

Not on a Yacht!

Is there a stowaway on board the *Princess Frog* yacht? Mysterious things keep happening on Frannie's cruise. Use the map of the yacht and the clues to find the mysterious passenger. *(A stowaway is a passenger that did not pay and had to sneak on board!)*

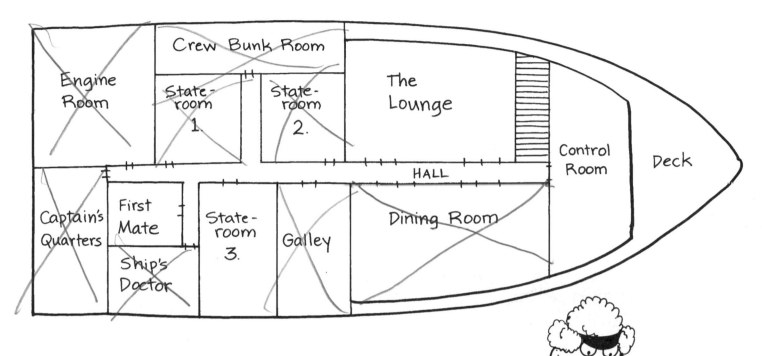

1. The visitor is not in the dining room.

2. The visitor is very small.

3. The visitor is not in the doctor's room.

4. The visitor loves to nibble scraps of food.

5. The visitor is not in the first mate's quarters.

6. The visitor has a tail.

7. The visitor is in a room that is next to stateroom 3.

8. Where is the visitor? ___Galley___

9. What or whom do you think the visitor is? ___A crocodile___

_____

Name _____ Elizabeth Lee _____

Streaks Across the Sky

What's that flaming streak that Frannie is watching from the deck of the ship? Read the passage below to find out. Then answer the questions.

What's That Flash in the Sky?

A flaming streak flashes across the sky!

Now it's gone! Did you see it? What was it?

On many nights, blazing trails of light can be seen across the dark sky. These are really small chunks of matter from outer space burning up in Earth's atmosphere. Before the chunks enter Earth's atmosphere, they are called meteoroids. As soon as they enter the atmosphere, they become meteors.

Most meteors burn up before they reach Earth's surface. Some meteors are so large that they fall all the way to Earth before they burn up entirely. If one does hit Earth, it becomes a meteorite. Thousands of meteoroids enter Earth's atmosphere every year, but only about 500 reach Earth.

1. What are the chunks called after they enter the atmosphere? _____

2. What are they called before they enter the atmosphere? _____

3. What are they called when they hit Earth? _____

4. What happens to most meteors? _____

5. About how many meteorites reach Earth each year? _____

6. What word is used to describe the trails of light? _____

7. Where do meteoroids come from? _____

8. How many meteoroids enter the atmosphere each year? _____

Name _____

Strange Events at Sea

It's brave of Frannie to sail this way across the Atlantic Ocean. She's headed right through the Bermuda Triangle!

Finish the puzzle with information from the paragraph about the Bermuda Triangle.

DISAPPEARED!

The Bermuda Triangle is an area in the Atlantic Ocean shaped like a triangle. It is found between the Southern United States coast, the island of Bermuda, and a group of islands called the Greater Antilles. For over 100 years, people have reported strange happenings in this place. It is said that over 70 ships and airplanes have disappeared in this area, but no one has ever found any wrecked boats or planes or any other proof that anything has happened!

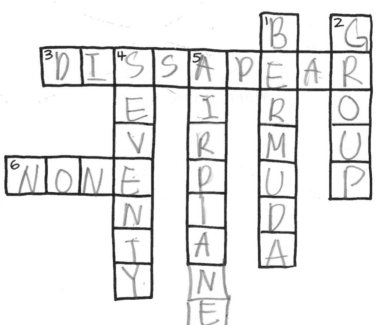

1. The mysterious area is the ___Bermuda___ Triangle.

2. There is no ___Group___ of any of the rumors.

3. People say that things ___Dissapear___ in the Bermuda Triangle.

4. How many ships and planes are missing? ___Seventy___

5. What is supposed to have disappeared? ___Airplane___

6. How many wrecked planes or ships have been found? ___None___

Name _____

A Stop at the Pastry Shop

Ahhh, Paris! There's nothing like a morning visit to the pastry shop on a Paris corner. Gaze at the Eiffel Tower while you enjoy a whipped cream cake (or two)!

francs

chocolate éclair — 15

caramel cream — 10

strawberry crêpe — 15

cheese pastry — 14

whipped cream cake — 25

French bread — 13

cinnamon bun — 10

apple tart — 14

lemon custard — 11

mocha crêpe — 15

Wheeeec

Oui.

Answer these questions about what's on today's menu.

1. How much would two cinnamon buns cost?
   20 dollars

2. What is the most expensive item on the menu? _Whipped cream cake_

3. What two kinds of crêpes could Frannie try?
   Strawberry crêpe
   and _mocha crêpe_

4. Which is more expensive, two éclairs or three lemon custards?
   Three lemon custards

5. What is more expensive than a crêpe?
   whipped cream cake

6. What costs the same as a cinnamon bun?
   Caramel cream

7. How much would an apple tart and a cheese pastry cost? _28_

8. Which item from the menu do you think Frannie will like best?
   whipped cream cake

Name _____

Keeping Watch for Nessie

Great Uncle Fergus McFrog recites a poem for Aunt Frannie while they're out sightseeing on the famous Loch Ness.

The sailors say it's down there,
Hidden, lurking, deep,
Waiting in murky waters,
Waiting, but not asleep.

The Loch Ness Monster they call it—
Thirty feet long, at least.
Many say they have seen it,
But no one can catch the beast.

No ship is safe from danger,
From the coils of this monstrous snake.
No ship can escape when it rises
From the bottom of the Scottish lake.

Wait in the foggy darkness.
Watch from the ship's front rail.
Look in the black, cold waters.
Look! Do you see that tail?

Beautiful, Fergus! What an imagination.

1. Write three words used to describe the waters of the lake.
   beautiful _cool_ _fantastic_

2. How long do they say the monster is? _Thirty feet long_

3. What word in the first verse means "waiting"? _but not asleep_

4. Where does the monster live? _The scottish lake_

5. Where is this lake? _Scottish lake_

6. What does the word "foggy" describe? _darkness_

7. Do you think the Loch Ness Monster is real? _Yes_ No.

Name _Elizabeth M_

A Midnight Visitor to the Castle

Someone is sneaking into the library of Zamalot Castle deep in a forest in Germany. Who could it be?

The visitor notices that the names of the authors are missing from the books.

Read each book title, and decide which author matches the book. The clues are hidden in the authors' names. Write the number of the book next to the author's name.

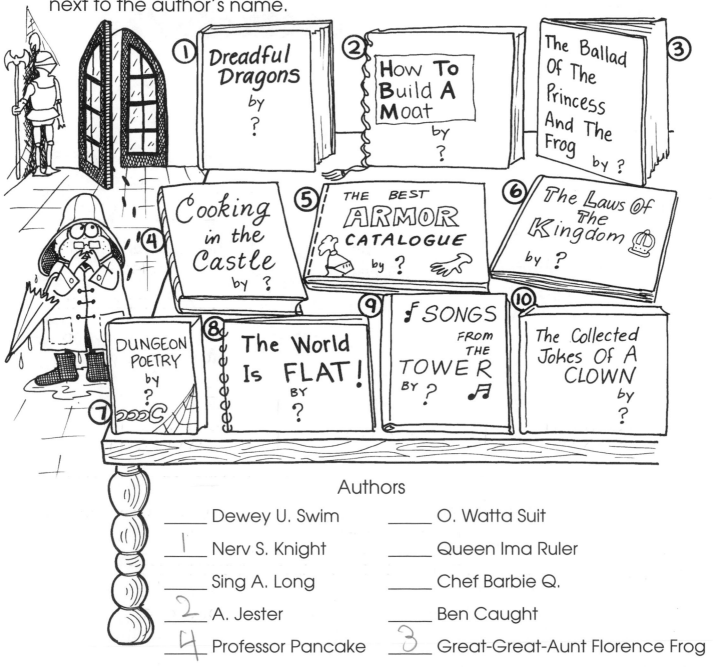

① Dreadful Dragons by ?

② How To Build A Moat by ?

③ The Ballad Of The Princess And The Frog by ?

④ Cooking in the Castle by ?

⑤ THE BEST ARMOR CATALOGUE by ?

⑥ The Laws Of The Kingdom by ?

⑦ DUNGEON POETRY by ?

⑧ The World Is FLAT! BY ?

⑨ SONGS FROM THE TOWER BY ?

⑩ The Collected Jokes Of A CLOWN by ?

Authors

____ Dewey U. Swim		____ O. Watta Suit
1 Nerv S. Knight		____ Queen Ima Ruler
____ Sing A. Long		____ Chef Barbie Q.
2 A. Jester		____ Ben Caught
4 Professor Pancake		3 Great-Great-Aunt Florence Frog

Name _____

What Caused the Blisters?

Third cousin Gerta von Frog is taking Frannie on a stroll through the famous tulip gardens of Holland. Unfortunately, Frannie has terrible blisters on her feet. What caused the blisters?

Here are some things that happened while Frannie was in Holland.

Find the causes and effects that match, and you will find out about the blisters! Color each pair the same color to show what caused each event below. Use a different color for each of the six pairs.

CAUSES

Frannie bought some new wooden shoes.
The hotel ran out of apples.
Another tourist sat on Frannie's camera.
The tulip gardens are in full bloom.
The bus to Amsterdam had a flat tire.
Frannie ate four pounds of Dutch chocolate.

EFFECTS

Frannie arrived late at her hotel.	Thousands of visitors have come to Holland.
The chef baked berry pies.	Frannie had huge blisters on her toes.
Frannie spent two days in bed sick.	Frannie had no pictures of Holland.

Name _____

Headlines From Italy

A. Italia Press
TRAVELERS STRANDED

1. The airport was fogged in.
2. People had to stay in hotels.
3. Some suitcases were lost.

B. La Roma Times
TOWER FALLS ON TOURIST

1. An earthquake shook the Tower of Pisa.
2. The tourist sneezed.
3. A tourist stood by the tower.

To catch up on the news, Frannie stopped by a newsstand in the city of Pisa, Italy. Did she find some interesting headlines?

Read the headline on each newspaper. Then write the number of the statement that shows what probably caused that headline to be written.

A. 1
B. 1
C. 3

D. 2
E. 2
F. 2

C. Florence Daily
ART TREASURES STOLEN

1. The paintings were fakes.
2. A thief was caught.
3. No one locked the museum door.

D. Venice Daily
GONDOLA CAPSIZES

1. A tourist rocked the boat.
2. Many people got wet.
3. A sea monster made huge waves.

Pardon me Senora,...

Do you have the Swampville Gazette?

Sorry!

Can you tell me where to get a pizza?

News-stand

E. Venice News
OPERA SINGER HITS HIGHEST NOTE

1. A bee stung her as she sang.
2. She wore a new costume.
3. She had a sore throat.

F. Pisa Gazette
SPAGHETTI-EATER HOSPITALIZED

1. A new restaurant opened.
2. He ate too much in an eating contest.
3. The hospital was hit by a tornado.

Name _____

Such Nonsense!

While Frannie was visiting Limerick, Ireland, she had such fun reading all the limericks written by Edward Lear. He was a famous writer of limericks. He even wrote a book of limericks called *The Book of Nonsense*.

Three of these limericks are a bit mixed-up! Unscramble them.

Number the lines in the correct order. Then enjoy reading them.

There was a Young Lady whose chin
Resembled the point of a pin;
So she had it made sharp
And purchased a harp,
And played several tunes with her chin.

B.

____Who was horribly bored by a Bee;
____He replied, "Yes, it does!
____When they said, "Does it buzz?"
____It's a regular brute of a Bee."
____There was an Old Man in a tree,

A.

____When the door squeezed her flat,
____Who casually sat in a doorway;
____There was a Young Lady of Norway
____She exclaimed, "What of that?"
____This courageous Young Lady of Norway.

C.

____Have all built their nests in my beard."
____There was an Old Man with a beard,
____Two Owls and a Hen,
____Four Larks and a Wren,
____Who said, "It is just as I feared!

Name _____

Scrambled Phone Conversations

When Frannie called Cousin Toad, there was a bad phone connection. Toad got everything all mixed-up. Then he called Uncle Hopper to tell him about Frannie's call, and he got things more mixed-up!

For both phone calls, number the sentences in the right order.

Frannie called Cousin Toad back home in Swampville.

☐	**Guess what? I'm in Tanzania, Africa!**
☐	**Good-bye, Cousin!**
☐	**I went on a safari.**
☐	**I took lots of pictures of the mountain.**
☐	**Hello! I want to speak to Toad.**
☐	**I'll send you some shots.**
☐	**The safari went near Mt. Kilimanjaro.**

Cousin Toad called Uncle Hopper about Frannie's phone call.

☐	**First she went to Dan and Zia's.**
☐	**Have you heard about Aunt Frannie?**
☐	**She wore a sari there!**
☐	**Hello, Uncle Hopper.**
☐	**Good-bye, Uncle!**
☐	**Then she rode a killer banjaro.**
☐	**And she's sending the jackpot tomorrow.**

Name _____

Sequence

Trouble in the Jungle

Oh, no! It looks as if Frannie has stumbled across a big problem on her visit to the African jungle. Read the story, and fill in the parts that are missing with a word or phrase. Make sure your story matches the picture.

Oh, No!

She was having a nice tour of _____ , listening to the chattering of the birds and monkeys. Then she heard _____ . When she peeked through the tall plants to see what was happening, she saw that _____ over a fire. Then she realized that those frogs were her nephews! She _____ , screaming and waving her arms. They had to stop! She never thought a minute about her own safety. She just knew that she had to _____ . Well, wasn't Frannie surprised when she learned what was really going on? Her nephews were not really in any _____ . They were just playing a part in a jungle movie. They were pretending to get cooked. They were even getting paid for it!

Name _____

Missing Captions

A photo album is a good way to remember a trip. Frannie has forgotten to put the captions with her pictures from Africa. Help her do that before she forgets what happened on this trip. Draw a line from each caption to the matching picture. She forgot to write one caption. Write it for her and match it to the right picture.

We visited the Hippo Mud Spa.

I took a quick dip in Lake Makat.

I flew over Ngorongoro Crater

I camped in the fig trees near the Lerai Forest.

I liked Ed, my elephant guide.

Name _____

Read Captions

Curious About Mummies

What a shock to come face-to-face with a mummy! Aunt Frannie got a big surprise when she visited the pyramids in Egypt. She learned that one of her distant relatives actually lived there a long, long time ago!

HOW TO MAKE A MUMMY

People are very curious about mummies. Did you ever wonder how they are made?

Mummies are bodies that have been preserved. Long ago, Egyptians made mummies of their rich kings (called pharaohs) and rulers. First, the body was preserved with spices. After about 70 days, the body was wrapped in cloth. Usually the mummy was put into a wooden case or wrapped in cloth made stiff with glue. The Egyptians wrote and painted things about the person's life on the outside of the case. Often they painted a mask on the end of the case. Sometimes people made mummies of animals that had special meaning, especially cats.

It's my great-great-great-great-great-great great Uncle Pharaoh!

Why do you think the author wrote this?

_____

_____

_____

Name _____

Author's Purpose

Who's Going to Tahiti?

Fog has closed down the airport. Not one plane can leave for hours!
Aunt Frannie is keeping herself busy by trying to guess where the other
passengers are going. Read the clues to find out who is going to Tahiti.

Write the name of the place where each passenger is going
above his or her head.

1. The passenger between the lizard and the porcupine is
   going to Spain.

2. The prickliest passenger is going to Germany.

3. The smallest traveler is going to Peru.

4. The elephant is definitely not going to Tahiti.

5. The passenger with the baby is going to Australia.

6. The passenger with the longest nose is going to Omaha.

7. Aunt Frannie is not going to Tahiti.

8. Who is going to Tahiti? _____

Name _____

Who Owns the Helicopter?

One of these vehicles is waiting to take Aunt Frannie to the train station in Siberia. The other vehicles are waiting for other passengers. Read the clues to figure out which one is for Frannie. While you're looking for that, figure out who owns the helicopter!

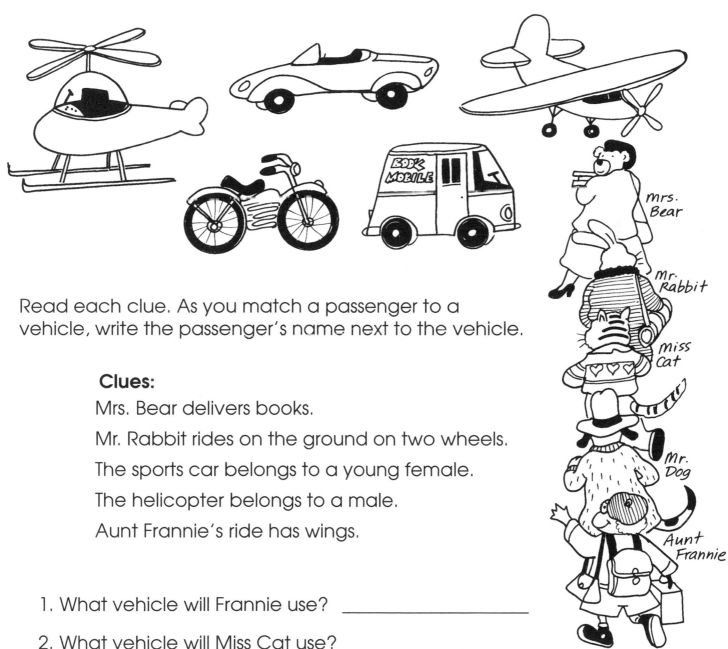

Read each clue. As you match a passenger to a vehicle, write the passenger's name next to the vehicle.

Clues:

Mrs. Bear delivers books.

Mr. Rabbit rides on the ground on two wheels.

The sports car belongs to a young female.

The helicopter belongs to a male.

Aunt Frannie's ride has wings.

1. What vehicle will Frannie use? _____

2. What vehicle will Miss Cat use? _____

3. Who owns the helicopter? _____

Name _____

The Night Train

On a snowy night, passengers are making a long trip across Siberia in northern Russia. Frannie has a feeling that this will be an unusual trip. Read about Frannie's strange train ride.

The night is very stormy as the train speeds across the open fields of Siberia. Snow is piling up on the railroad tracks. Sometimes the train moves very slowly through the snow. Twice the train has had to stop to wait for snow to be shoveled from the tracks.

The passengers have settled down for a long ride. Aunt Frannie notices a mysterious passenger walking down the aisle. He has a very lumpy overcoat. Frannie has a feeling that there is something very strange about him. He is moving slowly and looking over his shoulder often. He keeps his hands in his pockets.

Suddenly, the train screeches to a halt with a loud "THUD!" The lights go out. Passengers scream!

Tell what you think will have happened when the lights come back on.

_____

_____

_____

Name _____

Dear Diary

The Himalayas are the highest mountains in the world. Aunt Frannie cannot wait to get up into those mountains and climb!

Read some of the things she has written in her diary. Write her diary entry for the day of the climb. What did she write that day?

Sunday, July 4
Dear Diary,
I have finally arrived in Nepal. This country is full of huge mountains. I am glad for the mountain-climbing trips I have taken before. This one will be hard. Today we bought supplies for the climb on Thursday.

Wednesday, July 6
Dear Diary,
Tomorrow we climb! The local people have been warning us about the Yeti. The Yeti is known as the Abominable Snowman. They say this monster lives in the mountains and harms climbers. I don't really believe there is an Abominable Snowman!

Thursday, July 7

uh oh!

Name _____

Music for a Snake

In India, Frannie gets a chance to join a snake charmer as he tries to get the snake to dance. What a huge and amazing animal! Frannie never thought she would be playing music for a snake!

Read the shape poem about the snake. Then tell what you think about the poem.

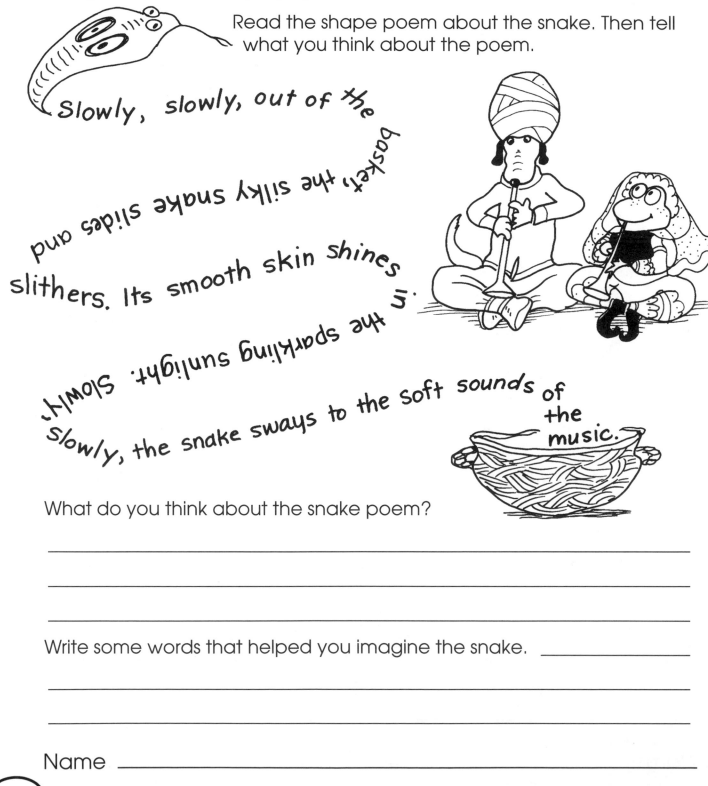

Slowly, slowly, out of the basket, the silky snake slides and slithers. Its smooth skin shines in the sparkling sunlight. Slowly, slowly, the snake sways to the soft sounds of the music.

What do you think about the snake poem?

_____

_____

_____

Write some words that helped you imagine the snake. _____

_____

_____

Name _____

What's Your Fortune?

How many relatives does Frannie have in China? She's having dinner tonight with all of them. They are all looking forward to the end of the dinner, because they all love to eat fortune cookies.

Read the fortunes from the cookies. Then choose fortunes for Frannie and yourself.

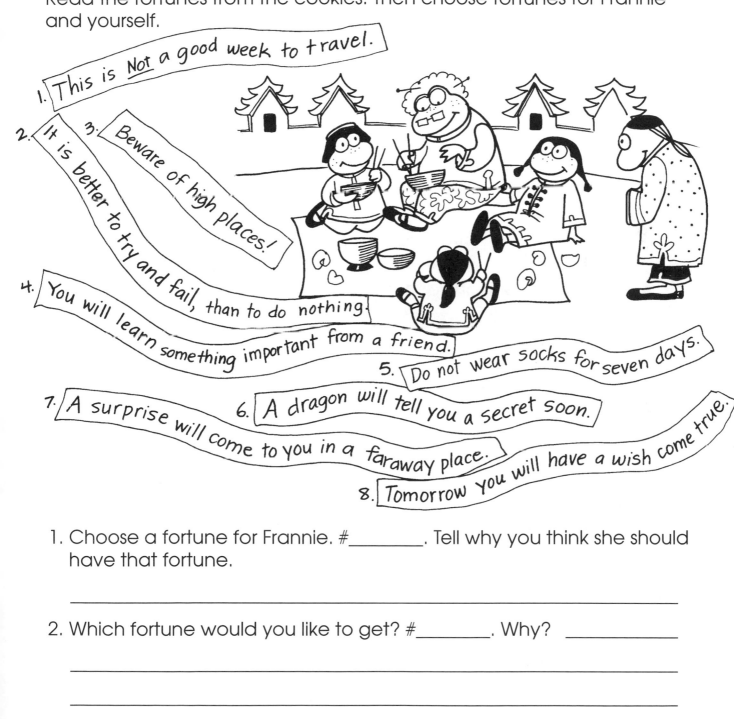

1. This is <u>Not</u> a good week to travel.

2. It is better to try and fail, than to do nothing.

3. Beware of high places!

4. You will learn something important from a friend.

5. Do not wear socks for seven days.

6. A dragon will tell you a secret soon.

7. A surprise will come to you in a faraway place.

8. Tomorrow you will have a wish come true.

1. Choose a fortune for Frannie. #_____. Tell why you think she should have that fortune.

_____

2. Which fortune would you like to get? #_____. Why? _____

_____

_____

Name _____

Would You Go There?

Not many people travel to Antarctica. Would you? Frannie couldn't stay away. She has always wanted to see this cold, far-off continent. Now that her good friend Penelope Penguin is working in Antarctica, she has a good excuse to visit. Read some facts about Antarctica, and decide if it's a good place for Frannie to be.

CHILLY ANTARCTICA

· **It is covered with a sheet of ice.**

· **The ice sheet is thousands of feet thick.**

· It is the coldest place on Earth.

· **No people live there permanently.**

· It is too cold for plants to live.

· It is the windiest place on Earth.

· **The cold is so extreme that it is dangerous.**

· **The average temperature is 70° below zero.**

· **The lowest temperature is 128° below zero.**

Should Frannie stay here a long time? Would you visit this place? Tell what you think!

_____

_____

_____

_____

_____

_____

_____

_____

Name _____

Relatives on the Reef

The Great Barrier Reef off the coast of Australia is the largest coral reef in the world—1250 miles long! It is a great place for diving and snorkeling. Read the snorkelers' thoughts below. How would you describe their feelings?

Write the number of the snorkeler that matches each word.

____ helpful ____ frightened ____ selfish

____ excited ____ bored ____ grumpy

Name _____

Opinions From Hawaii

These postcards are ready to send to relatives and friends back in the USA. Frannie has written facts and opinions about her visit to Hawaii. Can you tell which are which?

Read each postcard. Find the sentences or phrases that show Frannie's opinions. Circle them in red. Circle facts in blue.

1.
Dear Frankie,
Hawaii is wonderful. You should have seen me at my hula lesson! It lasted one hour. I sure did like silly-looking, but I was pretty the grass skirt! The food here is wonderful. They serve meals all day. See you in September.
Love, Aunt Fran

Frankie Frog
1111 Hwy 66
Ashland, OR
97520

2.
Dear Mandy,
My hotel is a bit dumpy. I think it is also overpriced. It costs $100 a day because it is on the beach. The hotel staff is not friendly, and there are too many mosquitoes! The beach is the best part!
Love, Aunt Frannie

Mandy Froglegs
4100 Mud Lane
Swampville, NC
01007

3.
Dear Sammy,
Today I took a helicopter tour over the volcanoes of Hawaii. There are many active volcanoes in Hawaii. It is amazing! The tour lasted 3 hours. The helicopter pilot was from Singapore. I thought the view was beautiful.
Love, Aunt Frannie

Sammy Leaper
20 River Rd
Green River, CA
94221

Name _____

First to Fly

The Frog family has a history of setting records in the air. Some of Frannie's relatives have been the first frogs to take flights in balloons. On her hot air balloon ride, she's telling her nephew Felix a little bit about the family's past adventures.

Read the labels on the balloons. Then answer the questions.

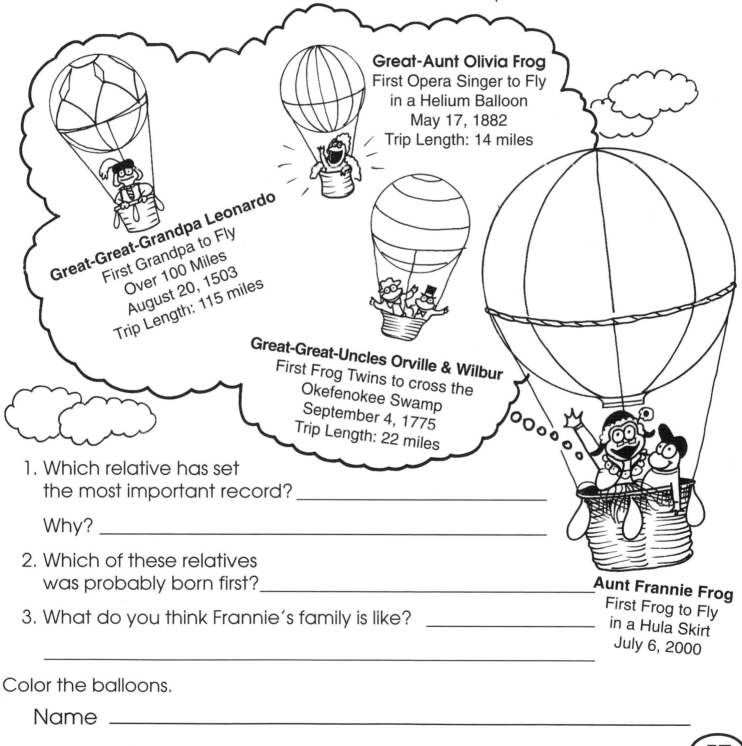

Great-Aunt Olivia Frog
First Opera Singer to Fly
in a Helium Balloon
May 17, 1882
Trip Length: 14 miles

Great-Great-Grandpa Leonardo
First Grandpa to Fly
Over 100 Miles
August 20, 1503
Trip Length: 115 miles

Great-Great-Uncles Orville & Wilbur
First Frog Twins to cross the
Okefenokee Swamp
September 4, 1775
Trip Length: 22 miles

Aunt Frannie Frog
First Frog to Fly
in a Hula Skirt
July 6, 2000

1. Which relative has set
   the most important record? _____

   Why? _____

2. Which of these relatives
   was probably born first?_____

3. What do you think Frannie's family is like? _____
   _____

Color the balloons.

Name _____

Tall Tales From the Arctic

The plane was not supposed to land here! Frannie was on her way to Alaska, but the plane got a bit lost and ended up much farther north.

She can't believe how cold it is! Read the tall tale she wrote later about her stop in the Arctic. Look for her exaggerations.

A Tall, Tall Tale

It's a wonder I survived one day in the arctic. It was so cold that my nose turned into an icicle the minute I stepped off the plane. My fingers became long ice cubes and broke right off. As I walked away from the plane, my shadow froze to the side of the plane and couldn't follow me. When I sneezed, the drops of mist turned to snowflakes and dropped to the ground. The plane landed very near to a farm where a farmer was milking cows in a barn. It was so cold that the milk came out of the cow as ice cream. I tried to say "hello" to the farmer, but the words froze before they reached him. I picked up a stick to help me walk through the snow back to the plane. Later, when it got warm inside the plane, the stick thawed out and crawled away. It was a snake! I was sure glad to leave that cold place!

SPUT
SPUT

An **exaggeration** is telling more about something than is actually true.

1. Draw a circle around every statement in the tale that is an exaggeration.

2. Write one exaggeration of your own about the cold.

_____

_____

_____

_____

_____

Name _____

A Great Fishing Story

Fishing is a good topic for great stories. Often people stretch the truth a bit when they talk about the fish they caught. A fishing story is best when the writer uses phrases that compare things to each other. Finish each of these similes that Frannie started. You can use the ideas here or create your own! (A **simile** is a comparison between two things that are not alike. It uses the words *like* or *as*.)

Writing Starters

- an apartment building
- running a marathon
- a fighting tiger
- climbing a mountain
- a speeding train
- crushed icebergs
- wrestling an alligator
- a mad dog

- fireworks
- a bull
- a tiger
- iron
- a blimp
- lightning
- a tunnel
- black coffee
- a school bus
- a beachball
- the moon

- a whale
- a racing stallion

The fish that got away was as big as _____

The first fish I caught was as fat as_____

Catching that 100-pound fish was like_____

The river was rushing as fast as _____

The night was as dark as _____

The water was cold like _____

The moon was as bright as _____

The fish fought like _____

That fish was tough like _____

Name _____

Similes

Safety on the Slopes

When Frannie stopped for a visit in Canada, her friend Mortimer insisted that she learn how to ski.

Make sure you read the rules for skiers.

Then answer the questions about the words on the sign.

RULES FOR SKIERS

1. Ski safely at all times.
2. Be courteous to other skiers.
3. Rowdy skiers will be banned from the hill.
4. Don't deposit food or refuse on the slope.
5. Watch out for beginning skiers.
6. Don't feed the snowbirds.
7. Please don't ski into or under the sign.
8. No loud shrieking or bad language.

1. What word on the sign means "acting wild"? _____

2. What does "courteous" mean in Rule #2? _____

3. What word in Rule #4 means "trash"? _____

4. What does "banned" mean in Rule #3? _____

5. What word on the sign means "shouting"? _____

6. If the word "leave" had been used, what word would it replace? _____

Name _____

Letter From the Lodge

Frannie has a little extra time for writing letters. Read the letter she's writing to her friend Abigail. Then answer the questions about her letter.

Mt. Whistler Ski Lodge
Whistler, Canada

Dear Abigail,
I should not have listened to that stubborn Mortimer! He insisted that I must learn to ski. Well, I made a good effort, but you know how clumsy I am! The trees were too massive and too close together. The skis were too slick. Now, look at me! What a monstrous mess I am! Here I am, all droopy and lonely in the lodge. My leg is wrapped up with ghostly white fabric. To walk, I have to use two sticks that look like wishbones. I am sorry to repeat myself, but I will. I should not have listened to Mortimer!
Love,
Your ailing friend, Frannie

1. Which word means "strongly stated"? _____

2. Which word means "slippery"? _____

3. Which words mean "huge"? _____

4. How does she describe her mood? _____

5. How does she describe her crutches? _____

6. What word means "sick" or "not doing well"? _____

7. What words are used to describe the fabric around her leg? _____

Name _____

A Famous Sidewalk

Frannie couldn't wait to get to Hollywood to visit her movie star friend, Gloria Frogarella.

Now Gloria has taken Frannie to see the famous Hollywood Walkway of the Stars.

Look at the words in each star. If the star contains a pair of synonyms, color the star gold.

wild savage

rapid speedy

difficult simple

prevent stop

simple easy

rough smooth

destroy ruin

never often

weary tired

ugly beautiful

frighten scare

steal rob

Name _____

Where Would You Find It?

Do you know what a gorge is?

Where would you find one?

Frannie is visiting the largest gorge in the world—the Grand Canyon. It is a deep valley cut through stone by the rushing Colorado River. It is 277 miles long!

Circle the answer that tells where you would find each of these.

Where would you find . . .

1. . . . a glacier?
   a. in the Arctic
   b. in the desert
   c. in your freezer

2. . . . a baboon?
   a. on an iceberg
   b. in the jungle
   c. in your shoe

3. . . . a synonym?
   a. in a story
   b. in your soup
   c. on a spider

4. . . . a carousel?
   a. on a map
   b. at a fair
   c. in a bathroom

5. . . . a zucchini?
   a. in a shoe store
   b. in a post office
   c. in a garden

6. . . . a peninsula?
   a. on a map
   b. in your lunch
   c. at a hospital

7. . . . an omelette?
   a. in a swimming pool
   b. on a plate
   c. in a jewelry store

8. . . . a hearth?
   a. near a fireplace
   b. in a sandwich
   c. in a sink

9. . . . a sum?
   a. in a car engine
   b. in a math problem
   c. in a birdcage

10. . . . a vessel?
    a. in a tool box
    b. in your body
    c. in a milkshake

Name _____

What Would You Do With It?

What would you do with a lasso? At a Dude Ranch in Texas, Frannie and her twin sister Freeda are learning what to do with a lasso.

Circle the answers that tell what you would do with these other things!

What would you do with . . .

1. . . . a spatula?
   a. put it in the bank
   b. flip a pancake with it
   c. eat it

2. . . . a blimp?
   a. ride in it
   b. spend it
   c. swim in it

3. . . . a treasure?
   a. swallow it
   b. take a bath in it
   c. hide it

4. . . . a trophy?
   a. put it on a shelf
   b. cook it
   c. spread it on toast

5. . . . a forecast?
   a. put it in a toolbox
   b. listen to it
   c. dance with it

6. . . . a casserole?
   a. bake it
   b. bury it
   c. study it

7. . . . a vitamin?
   a. copy it
   b. rearrange it
   c. swallow it

8. . . . marmalade?
   a. rent it
   b. spread it on toast
   c. write it down

9. . . . an antique?
   a. give it a bath
   b. treasure it
   c. munch on it

Name _____

Word Meaning

Welcome to Music City, USA!

Cousin Twila Crocker wrote a song about Nashville. Frannie is lucky enough to get there just in time to hear Twila perform at the Grand Ole Opry!

Read Twila's song.

Then answer the questions about some of her words.

Grab your gal, and grab your man.
Have some fun with a band.
The Country Music Hall of Fame
Has more stars than you can name!

The Grand Ole Opry—you must see
When you come to Tennessee.
Come on in, reserve a seat.
The music makes you tap your feet!

Join right in! Grab your guitar!
You might get to be a star!
You could try to write a song.
The whole gang will sing along.

Take a seat and sit a while.
Country music makes you smile.
Listen all you want—it's free!
Why don't you stay in Tennessee?

Write words from the song to complete these problems.

Write a word that means . . .

1. take hold of _____

2. great _____

3. save _____

4. group _____

5. entire _____

Write the opposite for each word . . .

6. less _____

7. city _____

8. give _____

9. leave _____

10. frown _____

Name _____

Bumper Stickers in New York

What interesting bumper stickers Frannie is seeing in New York City! Each pair of bumper stickers compares one set of things to another. All the bumpers today have half of a bumper sticker. Each pair of bumper stickers compares one set of things to another. Draw lines to match the two halves.

Example:

Stop is to go . . . as up is to down.

Hungry is to eating

Lawyer is to courtroom

Fingers are to typing

Grumpy is to happy

Monkeys is to monkey

Cold is to freezing

as feet are to climbing.

as nervous is to relaxed.

as mice is to mouse.

as doctor is to hospital.

as warm is to hot.

as tired is to sleeping.

Name _____

A Strange Weather Report

Wilbur is the new weather reporter for a big TV station in Minnesota. Tonight he is so nervous that he is getting the report mixed-up. He keeps saying the opposite of what he means to say!

Circle all the wrong words in Wilbur's report. Then write the correct word (the opposite) on one of the lines.

TELE-PROMPTER

Bad evening, folks!

Welcome to the station that gives you the worst, most incomplete weather report in town. I came in late today and worked easily to get none of the latest facts about the weather. I'll tell you about the weather today, and then sooner, I won't give you the forecast for yesterday. Today, it was warm and sunny. It was cold and sunny at midnight, with a temperature of 85°. Tomorrow it will be hot again all night until evening. Then the weather will warm, with temperatures dropping below 50°.

Well, that's it for now, folks. Enjoy this terrible weather today. Please don't tune in again tomorrow. We'll have less weather for you!

WEATHERFROG
WILBUR
WI-FROG Ch. 50
NEWS AT 11:00

Name _____

Welcome Back!

All the friends and neighbors in Swampville are happy to have Frannie back home. When they say "welcome back," they are using one meaning of the word **back.** It has other meanings, too. Maybe Frannie has a tired **back,** or maybe she needs to **back** her car out of the driveway!

Each sentence shows one meaning of the word in bold type.
Write a sentence that shows a different meaning of the word.

1. This brick is **light** to carry.

_____

2. I need a **saw** to cut this board.

_____

3. I ate a **quarter** of your pizza.

_____

4. I **can** do this hard math.

_____

5. What do you **mean** by that?

_____

6. I got a good part in the **play.**

_____

7. Don't peel **bark** off that tree!

_____

8. **Duck,** or you'll hit your head!

_____

Name _____

What a Way to Wander the World!

"What a way to wander the world!"
Frannie says to her friends.

"I've seen slithering snakes, creepy castles, and dazzling disappearances!"

Frannie is using sentences with **alliteration.**

She puts words together that begin with the same consonant sounds.

Read the silly sentences in her journal. In each sentence, circle the sounds that are the same.

Frannie's Silly Sentences

1. Sid's sister searched seven Siberian cities for six Saturdays.

2. Fat frogs find fun at the Fudge Factory in Frankfort.

3. Chew chunky chocolates and tasty truffles in a Paris café.

4. Polly picked a pyramid as the place to plant her petunias.

5. I sniffed and sneezed for seventeen seconds.

6. You can't catch a cough or a cougar in Canada.

7. Which way do you wish to walk in Wichita?

8. You'll never need knickers in Nashville!

9. Texas Todd climbed ten tall towers.

10. Homer Hamster hurried home to Hollywood.

Name _____

Confusing Pairs

Ralph and Fulbright like to hop on the rocks in this rushing stream.
To help them, you need to finish the spelling words with the letters *ph* or *gh*.
Be careful, because *ph* and *gh* often make the same sound.

Ralph will only step on words with the letters *ph*. Color these stones RED.
Fulbright only steps on words with the letters *gh*. Color these stones BLUE.

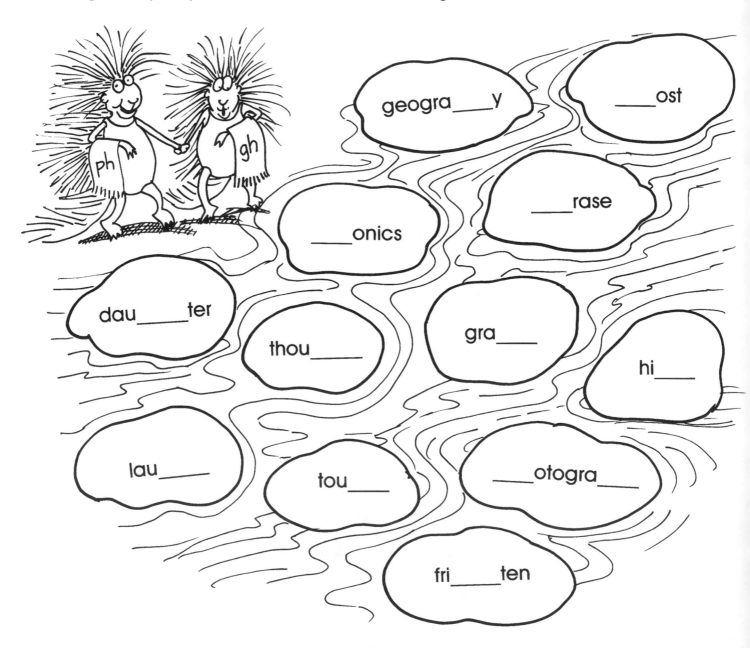

geogra____y

____ost

____onics

____rase

dau____ter

gra____

thou____

hi____

lau____

tou____

____otogra____

fri____ten

Name _____

Twice the Trouble

Mr. Moose is seeing double today.
All the words on his eye test are missing their vowels.
He can see them. Can you?
Write the missing vowels.

EYE CHART

OO oo oo EE EE EE

1. aftern _____ n

2. br _____ ze

3. d _____ rknob

4. fr _____ zer

5. kn _____

6. oversl _____ p

7. g _____ se

8. outd _____ rs

9. ch _____ sy

10. dr _____ l

11. r _____ ster

12. squ _____ ze

13. bl _____ m

14. f _____ lish

15. sp _____ ch

16. c _____ l

17. st _____ p

18. qu _____ n

19. racc _____ n

20. bab _____ n

21. t _____ th

22. p _____ k

23. l _____ se

24. cart _____ n

25. sch _____ l

26. ball _____ n

27. coc _____ n

Name _____

Double Vowels

Vowels to Shout About

When he reached the top of this tough mountain, Chester shouted with joy!

Chester got to the top by following a path of words with the vowel pair *ou*.

Which words need the letters *ou* to be spelled correctly?

Fill in the blanks which need *ou*.

Then use a red marker to connect them.

This will show the path that Chester used to climb the mountain.

Yahoo!

sc___t

y___rs

sh___ld   h___se

r___nd   br___k

f___rful

sh___t

b___ght   w___ther   bl___se

s___nd   th___ght

r___sonable   m___th

cl___n   gr___nd   arg___ment

s___son

c___sin   f___ntain   p___son

ab___t   gr___n   rep___t

Name _____

Special Vowel Combinations (ou)

Vowels to Boast About

Coach Roach loves to boast about his winning track team.
He also loves to use words with vowels that sound like the vowels in his name.
Read all the words on the track and field where his team practices.

Circle the words in which the vowel combination *oa* makes the same sound as it does in Coach's name.

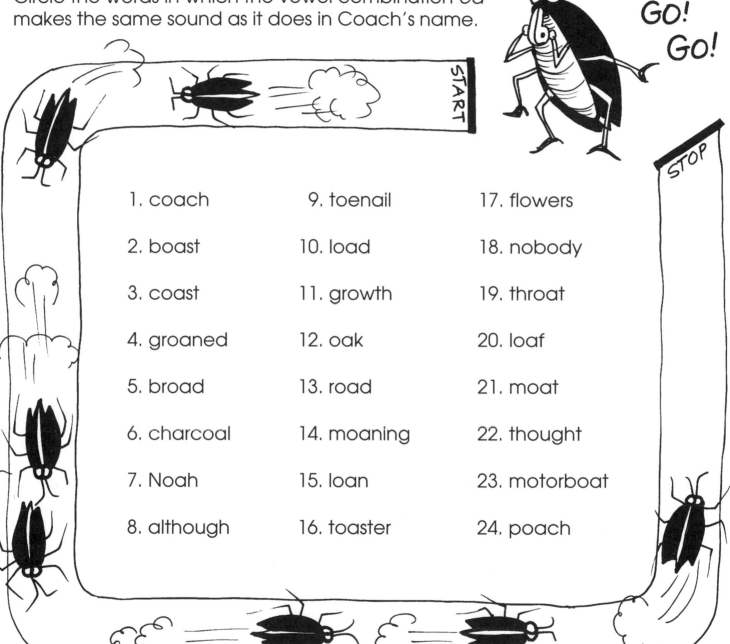

GO! GO! GO!

START

STOP

1. coach
2. boast
3. coast
4. groaned
5. broad
6. charcoal
7. Noah
8. although

9. toenail
10. load
11. growth
12. oak
13. road
14. moaning
15. loan
16. toaster

17. flowers
18. nobody
19. throat
20. loaf
21. moat
22. thought
23. motorboat
24. poach

Name _____

Vowels to Treasure

The map will help Felix find a buried treasure, if he can keep his vowels straight!

Follow the clues to draw a trail straight to the treasure.

Remember this: the trail goes ONLY to words with an *ea* vowel combination.

Look on the map for a word to match each clue.

Clue #1
    Begin at Cape Fear

Clue #2
    NE to opposite of late

Clue #3
    E to hair on chin

Clue #4
    NW to opposite of hard

Clue #5
    NE to looking hard

Clue #6
    SE to robbing

Clue #7
    W to a food

Clue #8
    N to summer & winter

Clue #9
    S to a wiggly animal

Clue #10
    SE to Use your lungs!

Clue # 11
    SE to rainy or sunny

Clue # 12
    N to a sandy place

Dig here for the treasure!

Mark the spot with X.

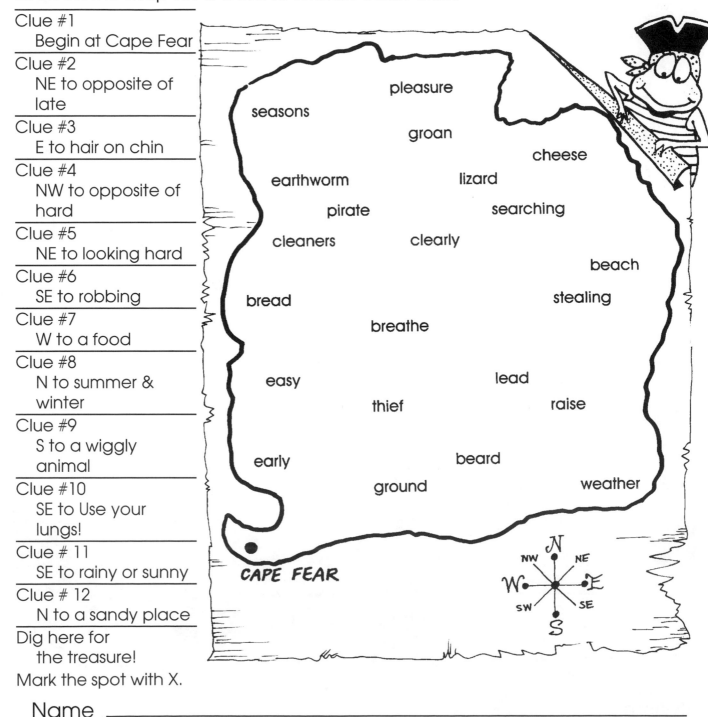

Name _____

Vowels To Puzzle Over

Francie has a good reason to avoid this giant!
However, there isn't a reason to avoid these vowel pairs.
All the words in the puzzle contain one of these pairs.
The vowels are already in the puzzle. Follow the clues to finish the words!

CLUES
Down
1. It's____ , it's pouring!
2. your mother's sister
3. letters and cards
4. sticky stuff
6. bothersome sounds
8. opposite of smile
10. clothing for swimming
11. dirt in the ground
12. color of ocean

Across
4. huge creature
5. houses and schools
7. sharp end of a pencil
9. to lift up
13. a river does this
14. end of a dog

Name _____

Special Vowel Combinations (ai, au, ia, ui, oi, ue, ow)

Star Power

Lila LeFrog is a singer. Lester Beaker is an actor.

The endings on *singer* and *actor* sound the same, but are not spelled the same.

An ending with this sound can be spelled with *er, or*, or *ar*.

Write the correct ending for each word on Lila and Lester's stage.

La-la-la-la
La-la-la

To be, or not to be.

1. col_____

2. rul_____

3. tow_____

4. liv_____

5. winn_____

6. doct_____

7. summ_____

8. od_____

9. doll_____

10. raz_____

11. teach_____

12. coll_____

13. mot_____

14. flav_____

15. ladd_____

16. sol_____

17. maj_____

18. riv_____

19. moth_____

20. fav_____

21. vot_____

22. nev_____

23. socc_____

24. tract_____

Name _____

Special Endings (er, or, ar)

Words to Recycle

To Gretta's surprise, today the dumpster is full of words instead of food!

They were thrown into the trash because they have the wrong endings.

Help her get them out of the trash and recycle them by spelling them correctly. Follow the directions below.

1. Write the words that should end in *age*. Spell them correctly.

   _____

2. Write the words that should end in *adge*. Spell them correctly.

   _____

3. Write the words that should end in *edge*. Spell them correctly.

   _____

4. Write the word that should end in *idge*. Spell it correctly.

   _____

5. Write the words that should end in *udge*. Spell them correctly.

   _____

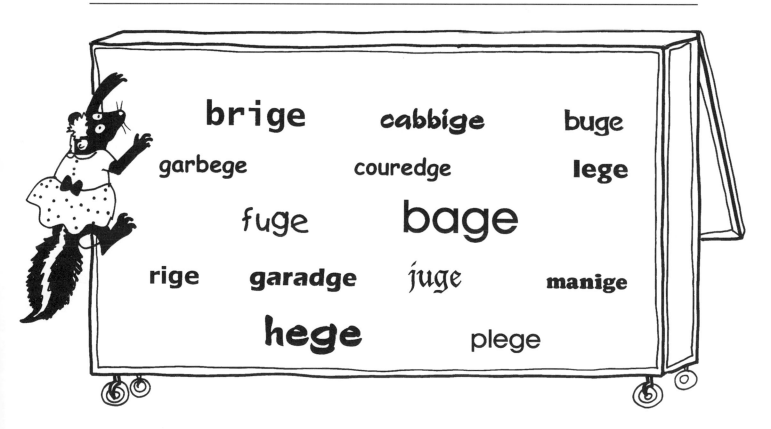

brige   cabbige   buge

garbege   couredge   lege

fuge   bage

rige   garadge   juge   manige

hege   plege

Name _____

Wise About Ys

Are you wise about words that end in *y*?

Some words end in *y*. Some end in *ey*. In both kinds, the sound is the same.

Wilbur thinks he knows the right endings for all these words. Do you?

Write the correct ending.

Color the starbursts: yellow for *y* and purple for *ey*.

1. donk__

2. penn__

3. likel__

4. lad___

5. reall__

6. monk__

7. mon___

8. ic___

9. cit__

10. cheer__

11. tin__

12. hon__

13. sill__

14. turk__

15. speed__

16. vall___

17. berr__

18. cop__

Name _____

Straight to the Hive

All of Bruno's bees are buzzing as they head for the hive.

However, some of the letters in the path are NOT making any sound.

The bee path has many words that contain one or more silent letters.

Read the words. CROSS OUT any words that do NOT have a silent letter.

kneel
thumb
knot
rhyme
wrap
wrong
cave
never
knife
liver
bridge
honest
halo
dough
knight
sword
wishes
cola
combing
doorknob
stretch
ghost
gasping
crumb
wrote
lamb
slippery
limbs
knuckle
tassle
climb
whine
knees
whisper
shape
lumpy
laugh

Name _____

Plenty of Balloons

Each balloon in Buddy's bunch has a word that means ONE of something.
Make each word into a plural (more than one) by following the rule.
Each one you get right will help Buddy float even higher in the air.

If you added *s* to a word, color the balloon red, yellow, or blue.
If you added *es* to a word, color the balloon orange, purple, or green.

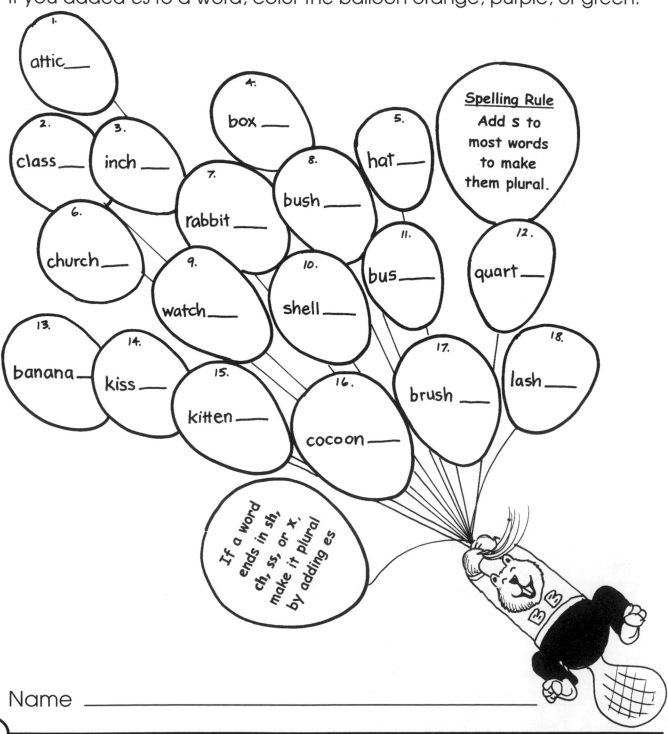

1. attic ___
2. class ___
3. inch ___
4. box ___
5. hat ___
6. church ___
7. rabbit ___
8. bush ___
11. bus ___
12. quart ___

Spelling Rule
Add **s** to most words to make them plural.

9. watch ___
10. shell ___
13. banana ___
14. kiss ___
15. kitten ___
16. cocoon ___
17. brush ___
18. lash ___

If a word ends in sh, ch, ss, or x, make it plural by adding es

Name _____

Plural Nouns

A Sky Full of Plurals

At the kite flying contest, three kites are left in the sky.
Each one has a spelling rule written on it.
Look at each word on the word list and decide which kite it matches.
Write the word in a plural form on one of the bows on
that kite. Spell it right!

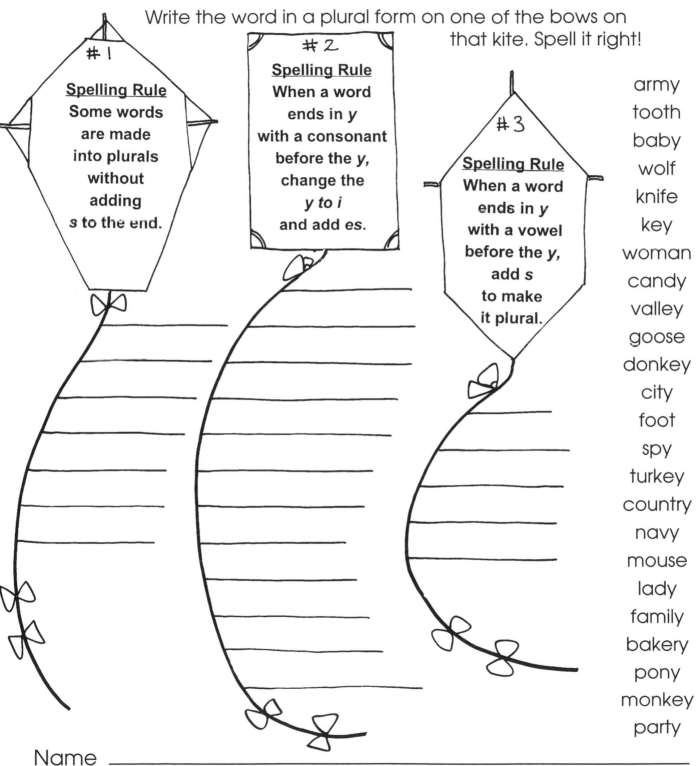

#1

Spelling Rule
Some words
are made
into plurals
without
adding
s to the end.

#2

Spelling Rule
When a word
ends in *y*
with a consonant
before the *y*,
change the
y to i
and add *es*.

#3

Spelling Rule
When a word
ends in *y*
with a vowel
before the *y*,
add *s*
to make
it plural.

army
tooth
baby
wolf
knife
key
woman
candy
valley
goose
donkey
city
foot
spy
turkey
country
navy
mouse
lady
family
bakery
pony
monkey
party

Name _____

Words from the Past

The Frogstone family had a very busy life many, many years ago.
Adding *ed* to the words will show that their activities happened in the past.
Follow the rules to write each word in the past tense.

SPELLING RULES

- **To change most words to past tense, add *ed*.**
- **If a word ends in *y* with a consonant before the *y*,
  change the *y to i* before adding *ed*. (*cry---cried*)**
- **If a word ends in a consonant with one vowel before it,
  double the consonant and add *ed*. (*sag--sagged*)**

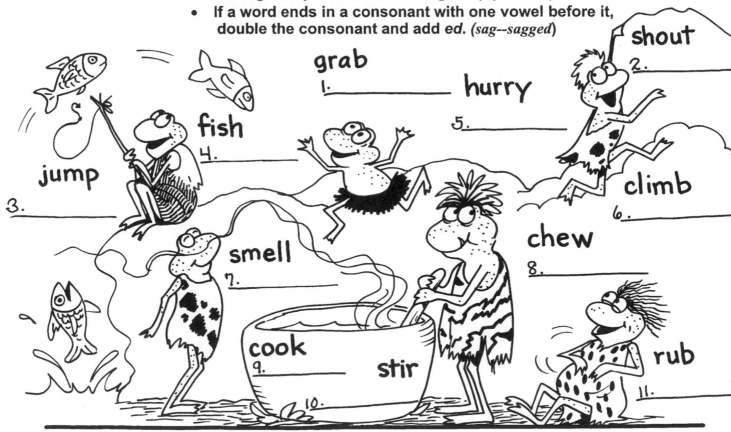

12. try _____

13. follow _____

14. wish _____

15. deny _____

16. sniff _____

17. worry _____

18. slip _____

19. rest _____

20. trim _____

21. rob _____

22. enjoy _____

23. laugh _____

Name _____

Verbs in the Past Tense

More Words from the Past

Change these present-day statements to the past tense.
This will show what Frederick Stonefrog and his pet dinosaur did a long, long time ago.
All of these are words that do not follow the usual rules for past tense.
Be careful about the spelling of the new words!

1. I slide down a rock. Many years ago, Frederick _____ down a rock.

2. I leave for school. Many years ago, Frederick _____ for school.

3. I keep busy. Many years ago, Frederick _____ busy.

4. I shake hands. Many years ago, Frederick _____ hands.

5. I bite my food. Many years ago, Frederick _____ his food.

6. I eat lunch. Many years ago, Frederick _____ lunch.

7. I choose to laugh. Many years ago, Frederick _____ to laugh.

8. I build a fort. Many years ago, Frederick _____ a fort.

9. I teach swimming. Many years ago, Frederick _____ swimming.

10. I catch a cold. Many years ago, Frederick _____ a cold.

11. I find a friend. Many years ago, Frederick _____ a friend.

12. I lose a tooth. Many years ago, Frederick _____ teeth.

13. I see the sky. Many years ago, Frederick _____ the sky.

14. I hide in a cave. Many years ago, Frederick _____ in a cave.

Name  _____

Endings that Swing

Jungle Jayne spends a lot of time swinging on vines and leaping between trees.

The words around her vines tell other things Jayne does.

Write each word again on the line below it, adding *ing* to each one.

Follow the rules to spell the words right.

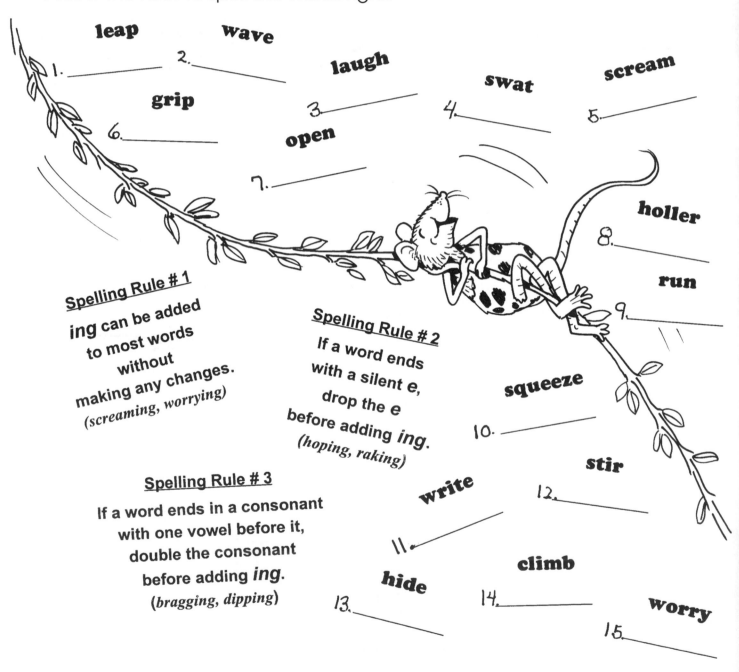

leap

wave

1. _____

2. _____

grip

laugh

swat

scream

3. _____

4. _____

5. _____

6. _____

open

7. _____

holler

8. _____

run

9. _____

Spelling Rule #1

ing can be added to most words without making any changes.

(screaming, worrying)

Spelling Rule #2

If a word ends with a silent e, drop the e before adding **ing**.

(hoping, raking)

squeeze

10. _____

Spelling Rule #3

If a word ends in a consonant with one vowel before it, double the consonant before adding **ing**.

(bragging, dipping)

write

11. _____

stir

12. _____

climb

hide

13. _____

14. _____

worry

15. _____

Name _____

Who's the Hungriest of All?

At the pancake-eating contest, Herbert is the hungriest!
The word hungry changes as the eaters are compared.
Follow the rules to add *er* and *est* to each of the words!

Spelling Rule
If a word ends in a consonant with one vowel before it, double the consonant before adding **er** or **est**.
(hotter, reddest)

Spelling Rule
When a word ends in *y*, change the *y* to *i* before adding **er** or **est**.
(friendlier, tiniest)

hungry   **hungrier**   **hungriest**

1. sweet   _____   _____
2. tasty   _____   _____
3. big   _____   _____
4. grumpy   _____   _____
5. full   _____   _____
6. great   _____   _____
7. sticky   _____   _____
8. hot   _____   _____
9. fluffy   _____   _____
10. tall   _____   _____

Name _____

Comparative Adjectives

Underwater Discoveries

The divers are discovering some lost prefixes sinking below the waves.
For each word below, find the matching prefix in the waves.
Add the prefix to make a new word. Write the whole word on the line.

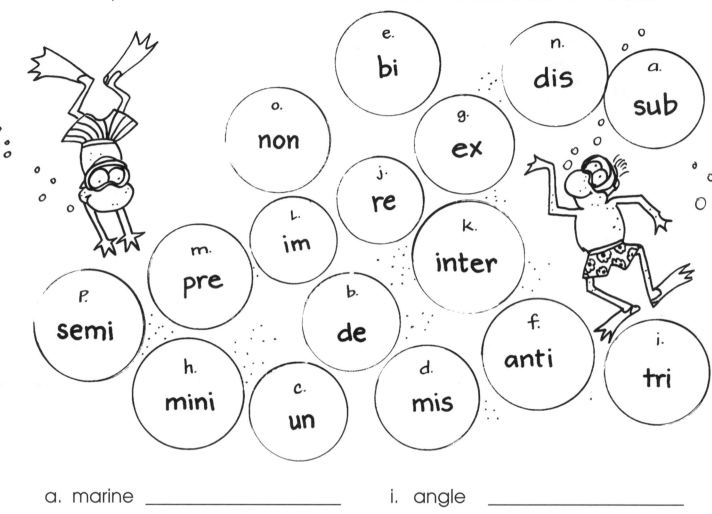

e. bi
n. dis
a. sub
o. non
g. ex
j. re
k. inter
l. im
m. pre
b. de
f. anti
i. tri
p. semi
h. mini
c. un
d. mis

a. marine _____
b. scribe _____
c. tie _____
d. take _____
e. cycle _____
f. germ _____
g. plain _____
h. van _____

i. angle _____
j. write _____
k. net _____
l. polite _____
m. view _____
n. obey _____
o. fat _____
p. circle _____

Name _____

Dangerous Waters

How will Felix ever get off this island? The water is full of danger!
The suffix *ous* means full of. Add *ous* to the word danger, and you have
a word that describes Felix's problem!

Add the suffix to each of these words to make a new word.
Follow the rules, so that you get the new word spelled right.

Spelling Rule
**When a word ends with a silent *e*,
drop the *e* before adding a suffix—
if the suffix begins with a vowel.**
(love + able = lovable)
(drive + en = driven)

Spelling Rule
**When a word ends in *y*,
change the *y* to *i*
before adding a suffix.**
(grumpy + er – grumpier)
(shaky + ness = shakiness)

1. scare + y = _____

2. act + or = _____

3. differ + ent = _____

4. tropic + al = _____

5. lone + ly = _____

6. care + less = _____

7. friendly + ness = _____

8. trouble + some = _____

9. fame + ous = _____

10. shiny + est = _____

11. fright + en = _____

12. like + able = _____

13. fancy + er = _____

14. self + ish = _____

15. forget + ful = _____

16. friend + ship = _____

Name _____

Sound-Alike Words

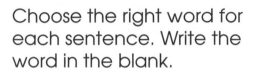

GACK!

Did Polly meet a *bare* with *bear* feet or a *bear* with *bare* feet?
Was it a dark, stormy *knight* or a dark, stormy *night*?

Homonyms are words that sound alike.

When you use a homonym, make sure to spell it right!

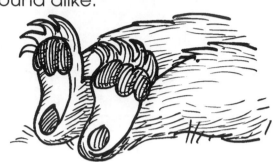

Choose the right word for each sentence. Write the word in the blank.

1. (choose, chews) Did you _____ to walk alone in the woods at night?

2. (pail, pale) She could barely see in the _____ moonlight.

3. (grown, groan) Polly let out a loud _____ when she saw the big bear.

4. (so, sew, sow) She was _____ frightened that she could not move.

5. (fir, fur) The bear was covered with shaggy brown _____ .

6. (see, sea) It's a good thing Polly can _____ well in the dark!

7. (toe, tow) Is the bear angry because he stubbed his _____ on a log?

8. (pause, paws) Did you see those sharp claws on the bear's _____ ?

9. (aunts, ants) The fallen log is covered with crawling _____ .

10. (sense, cents) That bear has a great _____ of smell.

11. (prince, prints) The bear followed her foot _____ through the woods.

12. (road, rode) Polly ran along a winding _____ through the forest.

13. (shoe, shoo) As she ran, she lost a _____ in the dark.

14. (berry, bury) The bear stopped to pick a juicy _____ from a bush.

Name _____

Homonym Mix-Up

It is easy to get mixed up about words that sound alike.
When Mildred wrote her story, she got many homonyms
confused with other words that sound the same.

Find all the words that are spelled wrong.
Circle them in red.
Then write the correct word on one of the lines.

My story happened on a night
when I was very board and wanted to do
something fun. My friend Cricket and I
decided we wood meat write at ate o'clock
to go on an adventure to the creak. I
meant to weight where I said I would,
but I did knot.

Instead, I took a shortcut threw the
prickly bushes to beet him there. This was
a bad idea. Cricket maid it to the creek,
but I never did.

My tale got tangled in the prickly
bushes and eye was trapped all knight.
Luckily, a pare of friendly mice came buy
and set me free—or I might still be their!

Mine is a long, sad tale.

Name _____

Two Words Make New Words

The words in Oscar's favorite pond are words that have a special talent. They can be combined with other words to make compound words.

water + falls = waterfalls   **under + water = underwater**

For each group of words below, find a word in the pond that makes compound words from ALL the words.

bed flash shoe band home any
sea sand finger rain water

A. _____ melon
   _____ falls
   _____ color
   _____ way
   _____ front

B. _____ nail
   _____ paint
   _____ print
   _____ tip

C. _____ bow
   _____ coat
   _____ drop
   _____ fall

D. _____ time
   _____ bug
   _____ room
   _____ spread
   _____ side

E. _____ box
   _____ bag
   _____ storm
   _____ pile

F. _____ lace
   horse _____
   _____ box
   snow _____

G. _____ body
   _____ thing
   _____ one
   _____ way
   _____ where

H. _____ shore
   _____ weed
   _____ shell
   _____ sick

I. _____ sick
   _____ work
   _____ made
   _____ grown

Name _____

Compound Words

Words with Fire

Bring some *firewood* to build a *campfire* in the *fireplace*!

Watch the *fireflies* and the *fireworks* by the *fireside*!

FIRE helps to make a lot of compound words!

What is the word that can make compound words for each of these groups?

Write that same word to make compounds from all the words in the line.

1. _____ mare over _____ _____ gown _____ time _____ light

2. camp _____ _____ side _____ doors knock _____ with _____

3. _____ fire _____ ground _____ site

4. sun _____ _____ house flash _____ day _____ _____ weight

5. _____ water _____ ground _____ line _____ pants

6. sun _____ _____ town _____ stairs _____ pour

7. _____ worm _____ store _____ case cook _____

8. _____ flake _____ man _____ ball _____ shoes

9. out _____ _____ step _____ bell _____ way

10. _____ light _____ down _____ burn _____ set _____ flower

Name _____

Catching Contractions

Cassie Crab has caught a net full of contractions today.
Some of them are not yet written in her net.
Write a contraction to match each word pair below.
Spell them right!

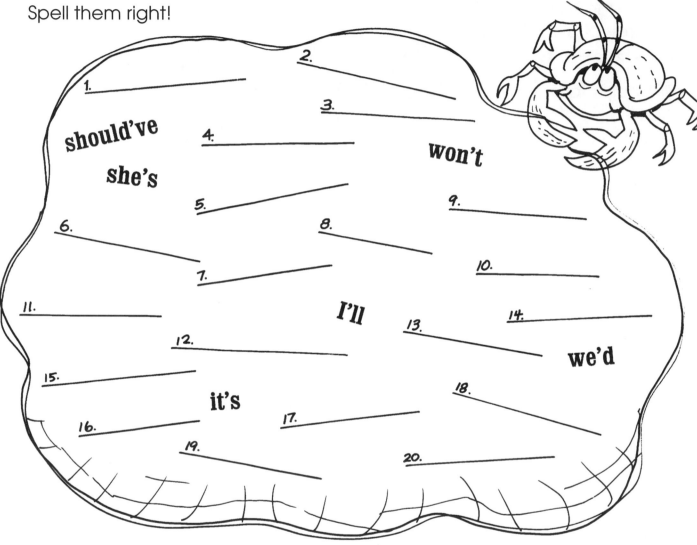

should've
she's
won't

1. _____
2. _____
3. _____
4. _____
5. _____
6. _____
7. _____
8. _____
9. _____
10. _____

I'll
we'd

11. _____
12. _____
13. _____
14. _____
15. _____
16. _____
17. _____
18. _____
19. _____
20. _____

it's

1. you are	6. were not	11. we would	16. you will
2. I have	7. who will	12. did not	17. they are
3. will not	8. was not	13. it will	18. cannot
4. she would	9. what is	14. could not	19. he will
5. let us	10. we are	15. that is	20. does not

Name _____

Confusing Words

A large pine cone hit Uncle Freddy on the head while he was napping.

This left Uncle Freddy very confused with his words. Every sentence he says has a wrong word.

Circle the wrong word. Write the correct word at the end of the sentence.

1. Witch day is it today, anyway?

2. The fresh air makes me so tried.

3. I like the quite afternoons in the forest.

4. I had tasty gooseberries for desert today.

5. It looks as if rainy whether is coming soon.

6. Please don't run away form me!

7. I have lost everything accept my head.

8. Can you crawl though that hollow log, Frankie?

9. I drank the whole cartoon of tasty cream.

10. Grandma Fox gave me her receipt for acorn stew.

11. Just look at those beautiful collars in the sunset!

12. Later today, I will write in my dairy.

1. _____
2. _____
3. _____
4. _____
5. _____
6. _____
7. _____
8. _____
9. _____
10. _____
11. _____
12. _____

Name _____

Words That Get Confused

Signs of Trouble

There's some trouble with the signs in the forest.
Bucky is having a hard time reading them because of the spelling errors.
Write the message from each sign for Bucky.
Use the lines below to write the messages. This time, spell all the words right.

1. _____

2. _____

3. _____

4. _____

5. _____

6. _____

7. _____

8. _____

Name _____

Correct Spelling Errors in Writing

Conversations After Dark

These raccoon conversations have many words spelled wrong.
Listen in on their "talk" and find the errors.
Write each sentence over. Correct the spelling as you work!

Name _____

Correct Spelling Errors in Writing

Take a Spin!

Rule 1
Add **ed** to most verbs to show past tense. If a verb ends in **e**, drop the **e** and add **ed**.

The Clown-around Kids were having great fun on the spinning teacups. Oops! When they finished, they were very dizzy.

Read the rules about forming the past tense of verbs (like *finished*). Write each verb in the past tense.

If you followed Rule 1, color the cup or saucer yellow.
If you followed Rule 2, color the cup or saucer green.

Rule 2
If a one-syllable word ends in a consonant with a vowel before it, double the consonant and add **ed**.

1. help
2. talk
3. leap
skip
trip
4. trim
beg
5. pop
6. crawl
yell
trot
jump

Name _____

The Big Game

An **adjective** describes a noun. It can tell color, size, shape, number, or what kind.

Tonight is the big night.
Zelda is the skeeball champion of the whole carnival!
She is undefeated for the whole year.
She needs 100 points to keep her lead.

10
10 20 50 20 10
10

Circle all the adjectives that describe the nouns in bold type in the sentences.

Every time you find an adjective, Zelda gets 10 points. Find out what Zelda will score tonight!

Points

_____ 1. Zelda wore her lucky purple **hat** to the big **game.**

_____ 2. She brought along six good **friends** to watch.

_____ 3. She chose new, striped **balls** for this important **game.**

_____ 4. The first **ball** had a nice, smooth, steady **path** down the middle.

_____ 5. Four noisy teenage **clowns** used the lane next to hers.

_____ 6. The second **ball** got the highest **score.**

_____ 7. She stopped for a big **treat** of pink cotton **candy.**

_____ 8. When the long **night** was over, did she have a winning **score?**

What was Zelda's score? _____

Name _____

Clowning Around

Add **er** to an adjective to compare two objects. Add **est** to compare more than two objects.

Polly   Molly   Lolly

"My hat is biggest," Molly brags.

"My shoes are bigger," hollers Polly.

"Well, my hair is longer!" says Lolly.

The Clown-around Sisters are comparing some things.

Write the correct form of each word to make their comparisons correct.

1. Polly's shoes are _____ than Molly's. (large)

2. Whose nose is the _____ of all? (big)

3. Polly is _____ than Molly (tall) but _____ than Lolly. (short)

4. Whose feet are _____ ? (large)

5. Whose hair is _____ than Polly's? (long)

6. Molly's hair is _____ than Lolly's. (short)

7. Which hat has the _____ brim? (wide)

8. "I'm glad my hat is the _____ ," says Polly. (little)

9. "My cheeks are not any _____ than yours!" says Molly. (red)

10. Who thinks that Polly has the _____ shoes? (silly)

Name _____

Comparative Adjectives

Adventures on the High Wire

Amazing! Henrietta can walk on a skinny wire high off the ground!

It is a long, long way down if she falls.

Will she stay on the wire? Find out!

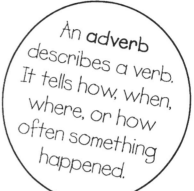

An **adverb** describes a verb. It tells how, when, where, or how often something happened.

As you read, circle the adverb in each sentence that tells the how, when, or where about the verb. The clue at the end of each sentence will help you.

1. Henrietta climbed slowly up the ladder to the wire. (Climbed how?)
2. She knew that she would start her act soon. (Would start when?)
3. She did not look down at the crowd. (Did not look where?)
4. Carefully, she stepped onto the wire. (Stepped how?)
5. She looked only ahead. (Looked where?)
6. She held on tightly to her umbrella. (Held how?)
7. She never felt nervous at the beginning. (Felt how often?)
8. She frequently felt nervous halfway across. (Felt how often?)
9. She began to breathe deeply to relax. (Breathed how?)
10. Soon she would reach the other side. (Would reach when?)
11. Suddenly she sneezed. (Sneezed how?)
12. She fell rapidly toward the ground. (Fell how?)
13. It was good that she landed safely in the net. (Landed how?)
14. "Tomorrow I will stay on the wire!" she said. (Will stay when?)

Name _____

Ribbons Around Run-Ons

The carnival has a show with acrobatic ribbon dancers. Rita and Rizzo are the best! It may look easy, but it is not! They leap over the ribbons while they do flips and amazing tricks. And the ribbons never get tangled!

A **run-on sentence** runs two complete sentences together.

Add a ribbon to one of the sticks each time you find a run-on sentence. Draw the ribbon from the stick around the run-on sentence. Then fix the sentence by putting in the right punctuation and capitals.

1. Rita and Rizzo can control twelve moving ribbons at once!

2. They leap over the ribbons they do somersaults under the ribbons.

3. These ribbon dancers are as talented as any other acrobats.

4. Can they twirl the ribbons from their toes can they close their eyes?

5. The audience was so surprised that their popcorn flew out of their hands.

6. Rita and Rizzo make ribbon hoops after that they jump through them.

7. The dancers surprised everyone they ate cotton candy while they danced.

8. Have you ever tried to do cartwheels while spinning ribbons with one hand?

Name _____

Watch out for Pirates!

Don't you love this ride! It's the best one at the carnival!
Watch out for pirates, the shark, and the plank!
Read all the things being said on the pirate ship.
Color all the bubbles that contain exclamations.

An exclamation shows strong feeling. It ends with a !

Save a bone for an old Sea Dog.

Ahoy, maties!

There's a ship on the horizon.

Look out below!

I am so scared of heights.

Shiver me timbers, I'm going to be sick!

Man overboard!!

Arrrrgggh! Don't make me jump!!

Wow! I found some pirate booty! Oh, boy!

Booty

Just take one more step.

Oh, no! I'm a goner!

Help me, Mommy!

CLOWN - AROUND PIRATE SHIP
OPEN 9 A.M. – 6 P.M.
Please do not feed the mechanical shark!

Name _____

Exclamations

In the Center Ring

The upside-down lady | rides on the wild stallion!

      subject   *predicate*

Someone | taught this bear to dance!

      subject   *predicate*

The **predicate** tells what the subject is or does.

The **subject** of a sentence tells whom or what the sentence is about.

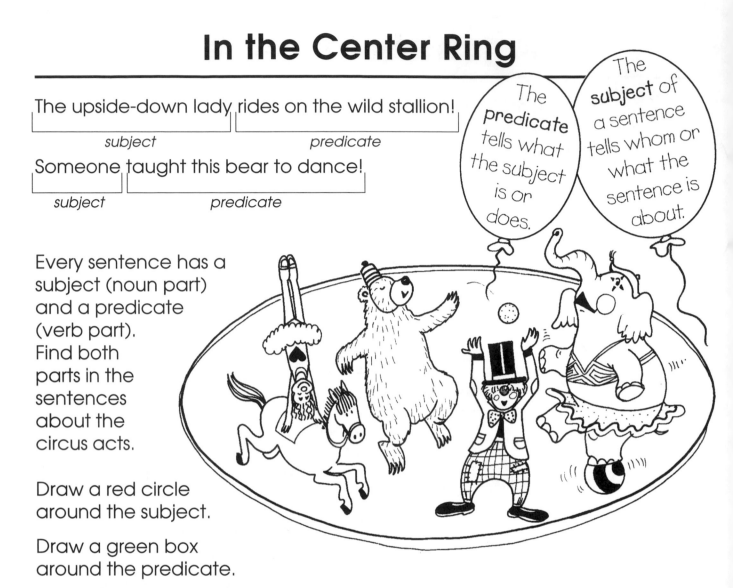

Every sentence has a subject (noun part) and a predicate (verb part). Find both parts in the sentences about the circus acts.

Draw a red circle around the subject.

Draw a green box around the predicate.

1. The balancing elephant is wearing a rather strange costume!
2. The clown juggles only one ball.
3. Only one bear was invited to be in the show today.
4. The other four elephants lost their costumes.
5. Ellie can stand on a ball with one foot for three minutes.
6. The galloping horse pays no attention to the lady on his back.
7. Clyde's pants need some more patches.
8. The audience wonders what is under the clown's hat.
9. A rather silly little hat sits on the bear's large head.
10. The center circus circle has four acts going on today.

Name _____

Sentence Parts

Seven Silly Seals

Would seven silly seals throw tomatoes at parties? You decide!
The seal and the elephant have lists of sentence parts.
Every noun part (subject) needs a verb part (predicate).
Use a separate piece of paper to write ten sentences.
Use one sentence part from each list to write your sentences!

Most sentences have a **subject** (noun part) and a **predicate** (verb part).

SUBJECTS

Seven silly seals

A nervous lion tamer

Fred the fire-eater

Four acrobats

Tina's pet snake

Four dancing bears

Elephants with wrinkles

The Clown-around Kids

The juggling brothers

Daring trapeze artists

Milton the Magnificent

Ten crazy monkeys

PREDICATES

swallows a sword!

ride prancing stallions.

stand on their heads.

eat French fried worms.

wear purple underwear.

blow bubbles in the bathtub.

gobbles red hot chili peppers.

tumble off the high wire.

looks in the lion's mouth.

tiptoe across a high wire.

leaps through a ring of fire.

throw tomatoes at parties.

Name _____

Mistakes on the Merry-Go-Round

It is hard to resist a ride on a good merry-go-round!

This one is a favorite spot for the Clown-around Kids.

The merry-go-round could use some decoration!

Follow the directions to give it some color!

Circle the letters that should be capitalized, and add the correct punctuation. After you fix each sentence, color part of the ride.

Color

poles

floor

elephant

giraffe

unicorn

zebra

roof

clowns

1. bubbles rides the giraffe on fridays and saturdays
2. do you like all that loud music
3. chester held onto a ring and rode standing up last jun
4. this ride has an elephant a giraffe and a unicorn
5. reach for the ring
6. ulysses likes to ride on the unicorn on tuesdays
7. is this carnival open on thanksgiving
8. does the carnival travel to chicago illinois

Name _____

Madame Mystery's Message

Look out below?
The trapeze clowns have a
tricky act, they do twists.
turns. and breath-taking flips,
Is there anything they are afraid
to do! They never fall? But
watch out when they add
the flying elephants
to their act,

What a pickle !

Madam Mystery finds a strange and mysterious message in her mystery ball. It is interesting, but it is hard to read because it has so many mistakes. Write the message here. Correct the punctuation mistakes!

_____

_____

_____

_____

_____

_____

Name _____

Tempt Your Taste Buds

Cookie does some wonderful cooking!
Read her descriptions of three tasty treats.
Look for words that are ordinary or a little bit dull. Circle these.
Try to think of a better word to replace each one.
Make the new word more interesting, clever, fun, or unusual!

.... and for breakfast, scrumptious apple-butterscotch-cinnamon-flapjack-fritters!

Sundae on a Stick

It's a nice change!
The tasty vanilla ice cream is topped with good chocolate and dipped in little, chunky nuts.
It is cold and refreshing!

Sweet Cotton Candy

Come and get your pink fluffs of sugar candy on a paper cone.
It tastes so great that you will hurry back for more.

Hot Dogs

Hot dogs! Hot dogs!
Walk over to the hot dog stand and get your warm dogs right now.
Cover them with mustard, ketchup, or relish.
Try some fresh onions.

Name _____

A Letter to Ulysses

Ulysses, the unicycle rider, rode his unicycle to the mailbox and found a letter from his clown friend, Pretzel, who lives far away.

When you read the letter from Pretzel, you will see that he made a lot of mistakes.

Fix all the mistakes. Circle the letters that should be capitalized, and add punctuation in the correct places!

dear ulysses

i miss your smiling face i would have written sooner but i've been tied up the life of a famous contortionist can be knotty did you hear my news i've added a trick to my act you should see me do a double loop with a knee twist

come and see me in florida
your clown pal
pretzel

Name _____

Titles to Talk About

Great stories happen every day at the carnival.
These carnival stories have all lost their titles!
Write a new title for each story
on these two pages (108 and 109.)

_____

Step right up!
See the greatest show on Earth!
See jugglers, lions, and tigers!
See clowns and fire-eaters!
The tricks will amaze you!

_____

Zina Zardoom has squeezed her big feet into this tiny little car. How can she drive it without crashing into the lion cage? Good luck, Zina!

_____

Hungry Harry gets carried away with the circus treats. He can't stop eating popcorn, candy, and ice cream. His favorite treat of all is gooey, sticky, sugary cotton candy!

Name _____

Use with page 109.

Writing: Titles

_____

Ellie is all dressed up for the big show. She has on her favorite hat and her favorite ruffle. She wears her striped socks for good luck. What trick will she do tonight?

_____

Jugglers Gino and Georgie delight the crowd with their tricks. Their best trick is juggling vegetables. They take bites out of the vegetables. Then they throw them into the audience!

_____

This tricky monkey can hop, leap, stand on his head, and turn flips. He can throw his hat into the audience right onto someone's head! Then he scampers up on the person's shoulders to snatch back his hat!

Name _____

Use with page 108.

Writing: Titles

A Chat with the Fire-Eater

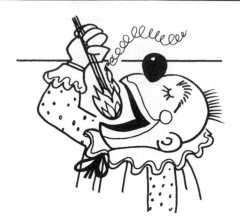

Have you ever seen someone eat fire?

Many carnivals have a person
who does just that!

What would you ask a fire-eater
if you could meet one?

Think of some questions you would ask
him or her.

1. _____

2. _____

3. _____

4. _____

5. _____

6. _____

7. _____

8. _____

Choose one of your questions. Tell how you
think the fire-eater might answer the question.

_____

_____

_____

Name _____

Writing: Interview Questions

A Letter From a Lion

Can you imagine a lion writing a letter? What would a lion say?

If Lester the Lion sent a letter to his friend, what do you think he would write?

Think about the things a lion does during a day. What might he hear, watch, wish, or think?

Write Lester's letter.

Dear Lillie,

Love,
Lester

Lester Lion
Clown-Around Circus

Lillie Lion
Happy Days Circus
Winter Camp, FL

Name _____

Writing: Letter

A Lion on the Loose!

There's a lion on the loose on the grounds of the carnival!
Look at the path the lion has taken to escape.
Write clear directions to tell the lion tamer how to follow the lion.
Use words such as *over, under, through, beside, across, behind, around, inside, in front of, north, south, east,* and *west.*

_____

_____

_____

_____

_____

_____

Name _____

Writing: Directions

Help for Handy

It's time for Handy to get ready to go to work. He wants to look dandy for the show. Help him decide how to get dressed. Write directions for Handy to tell him what to put on. Write your directions in order. Write complete sentences.

1. _____
2. _____
3. _____
4. _____
5. _____
6. _____

7. _____
8. _____
9. _____
10. _____
11. _____
12. _____

Name _____

Too Much of a Good Thing

The stories about the clowns at the carnival are full of good ideas, but every one of them has one idea too many!

Read each story on these two pages (pages 114 and 115).

Find the idea that is not needed in each story. Cross it out!

The Ticket Line

1. The Clown-around Kids have to wait in line to ride the Tilt-a-Whirl. It is their favorite ride, so they don't mind waiting.
After waiting for a long time, they reach the ticket window.
All the balloons fly into the air.
Zelda opens her purse and buys two tickets for everyone.
Then they enjoy a wild ride!

Ulysses Shows Off

2. Finally! Ulysses is ready to take the training wheels off his unicycle!
He has invited all his friends to watch him perform. He is happy to show off.
The monkey ate a bag of peanuts.
Ulysses rides around the center ring without a spill. At last he is a true unicycle performer!

Name _____

Use with page 115.

Writing: Eliminating Irrelevant Ideas

Too Much of a Good Thing, cont.

Luscious Lion Treats

3. It's time for a lion treat! Cookie Clown is cooking up a special treat for her friend Lester Lion. She starts with chopped liver and adds onions and baked beans. She stirs in a dozen eggs and cooks it all for twenty minutes. Cookie washed her dishes. When the stew is done, she will call up Lester and invite him to lunch!

Prizes for Silly Clowns

4. Today is the Silly Clown Contest. The Clown-around Kids get into their silliest costumes and perform their silliest tricks. Zeke stands on his head. Zelda squirts people with her squirt-gun flower. Bubbles does some backwards somersaults. Henrietta walks on the tightrope with a glass of water on her head. Chester visited the elephants yesterday. All the Clown-arounds are very silly. Everybody wins a prize!

Name _____

Use with page 114.

Writing: Eliminating Irrelevant Ideas

SOCIAL STUDIES

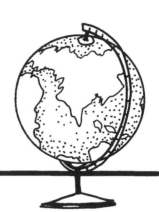

Skills Exercises
Grade Three

SKILLS CHECKLIST
SOCIAL STUDIES

✔	SKILL	PAGE(S)
	Locate and name some states and cities in the U.S.	120, 121
	Locate own city, state, and country on maps	120, 121, 125
	Recognize some U.S. states	120–125
	Use map skills to locate places and find information on maps	120–129, 142–144
	Make a map of your state, locating your town and other key features	125
	Recognize and locate some countries that are neighbors to the U.S.	126, 127
	Identify landforms on a map	128
	Locate countries, regions, oceans, and continents on a map or globe	129
	Locate some features and landmarks around the world	130
	Differentiate between cities, states, countries, and continents	131
	Identify current officials of local and federal governments	132
	Identify the three branches of government in the United States	132
	Identify and describe important American traditions, symbols, and holidays	133
	Explore traditions & symbols	134, 135
	Recognize & describe the American flag	136
	Read a timeline of historical events	137
	Identify key events in U.S. history	137, 138
	Identify some current events in own town or city	139
	Identify some important Americans and their accomplishments	140
	Describe some responsibilities of citizens	141
	Find information on a population chart	145

SKILLS CHECKLIST
MAP SKILLS & GEOGRAPHY

✔	SKILL	PAGE(S)
	Locate own home in the universe	146, 147
	Locate own country, home, and neighboring countries on a world map	146, 147, 155
	Place items on a map	147, 151, 166–168, 178
	Use maps to locate things and places	147, 152–162, 170–174, 176, 177
	Use a simple scale to determine distances on a map	148–150
	Identify and use a variety of maps	148–150, 152–162, 170–174
	Use maps to find information and answer questions	148–150, 160–174, 176, 177
	Recognize landforms on a map	151
	Identify poles, equator, and hemispheres on a map	152, 153
	Recognize and identify different kinds of maps	152, 153, 170–174
	Recognize continents and oceans on a world map	152–155
	Recognize boundaries on a map	155
	Identify some states on a U.S. map	157–159, 162
	Recognize names and shapes of some states in the U.S.	157–159, 162
	Identify and locate some cities and landmarks in the U.S.	158–162
	Compare locations on a map	158–162, 173, 176, 177
	Locate own state on a U.S. map	159
	Identify some major bodies of water and cities in the U.S.	160, 161
	Find information on charts	163, 164
	Find the location of objects located on a simple grid	165–169
	Follow directions to place objects on a grid	166–168
	Find information on a population map	170
	Find information on an environmental map	171
	Find information on a product map	172
	Find information on a rainfall map	173
	Find information on a road map	174
	Recognize a variety of geographic terms	175
	Use directions to locate things on a map	176, 177
	Identify directions on a map	176, 177
	Make simple maps	178

The Case of the Missing States

Something is missing from Mario's map! All the states that begin with **A, F, O,** and **T** are missing their names. Can you put them back?

Name _____

U.S. Map • Recognize States

1. Find your own state. Color it red.

2. The names of these cities are missing. Write their names where they belong:

        Chicago   New York   San Francisco   Miami

3. Find a state that touches the Atlantic Ocean. Color it green.

4. Find a state surrounded by the Pacific Ocean. Color it orange.

5. Draw a route for a train to travel from Bumble Bee to Owl's Head. Stop in these cities: Squirrel, Hungry Horse, Porcupine, Beaver Dam, Alligator, Monkey's Eyebrow, and Cowpens.

Name _____

Far-Out State Facts

Which state had the first pizza parlor?
Which state has "Yankee Doodle" as its state song?
Which state has the largest volcano?

You can find out right now—if you know the shapes of the states in the USA!

Look at the shape of each state below and find it on the map (page 123).

Color the state on the map, and then write its name on the line.

It has the world's largest flat-top mountain.

_____

The sun hits here first every morning.

_____

The state song is "Yankee Doodle."

_____

The first airplane ride happened here.

_____

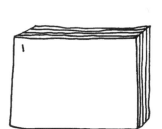

The Indianapolis 500 car race has its home here.

_____

The first pizza parlor started here in 1895.

_____

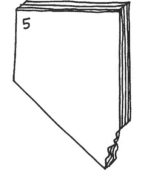

The state song is "Home, Home on the Range."

_____

The lightbulb was invented here.

_____

It has the most wild horses in the USA.

_____

It is the home of the largest active volcano.

_____

Name _____

Use with page 123.

U.S. Map • Recognize States

The United States

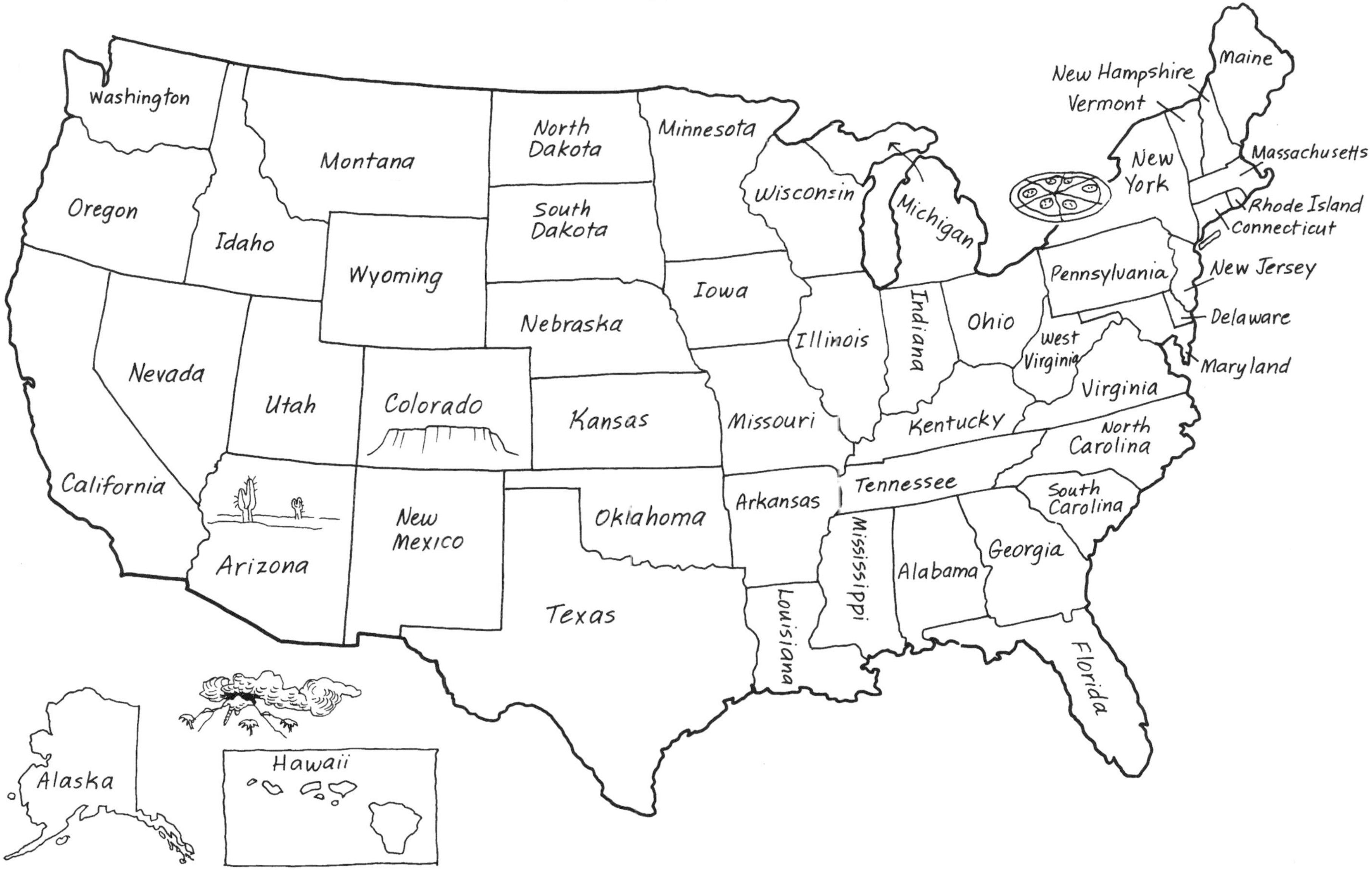

Name ______________________________

Amazing Alaska

Did you know that Alaska is the biggest and the coldest state?
Did you know that it contains the highest mountain in the United States?
Alaska is an amazing place full of forests, grizzly bears, beautiful lakes,
mountains, and glaciers.
Use the map to find out more about amazing Alaska!

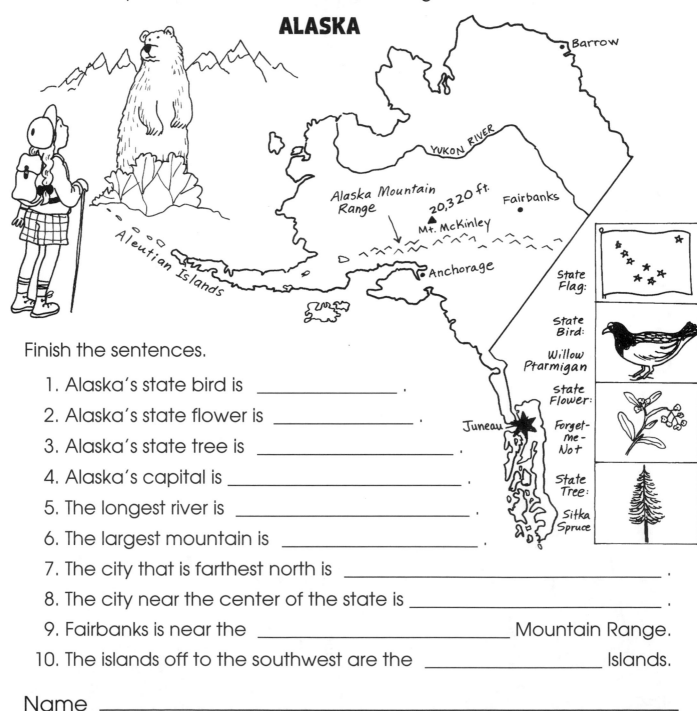

ALASKA

Barrow

YUKON RIVER

Alaska Mountain Range

20,320 ft.

Fairbanks

Mt. McKinley

Aleutian Islands

Anchorage

Juneau

State Flag:

State Bird:
Willow Ptarmigan

State Flower:
Forget-me-Not

State Tree:
Sitka Spruce

Finish the sentences.

1. Alaska's state bird is _____ .

2. Alaska's state flower is _____ .

3. Alaska's state tree is _____ .

4. Alaska's capital is _____ .

5. The longest river is _____ .

6. The largest mountain is _____ .

7. The city that is farthest north is _____ .

8. The city near the center of the state is _____ .

9. Fairbanks is near the _____ Mountain Range.

10. The islands off to the southwest are the _____ Islands.

Name _____

Your Amazing State

What is amazing about your state?

Does it have the highest bridge in the world, the first library, the only diamond mine in the USA, or the most people?

Every state in the USA has some amazing places, spaces, and facts to know about it. See what you can find out about your own state!

My state has the deepest lake in the U.S.A.!

1. Draw your state here.

2. Put your town or city on the map.

3. Put the capital city on the map.

4. Add other cities, a river, a mountain, or some other features of your state.

5. Find and draw the state symbols on the right.

6. Find out one amazing thing about your state. _____

State Flag:	State Bird:
State Flower:	State Tree:

Name _____

Where's the Party?

Roberto is headed to a party!

On his way, he is picking up food and other great stuff.

He is getting these things from the United States and its neighbors.

Read about each stop he makes, and look at the map on page 127.

Draw his route in red on the map as he travels to collect these things . . .

1. hats from his country, Panama

2. coconuts from Costa Rica

3. sugar cubes from Nicaragua

4. bananas from El Salvador and Honduras

5. flowers from the island country of Jamaica

6. tasty lobsters from Belize

7. bright-colored tablecloths from Guatemala

8. candy-filled piñatas from Mexico

9. pizza from San Francisco, California

10. fresh salmon from Alaska

11. hamburgers from Winnipeg, Canada

12. ice cubes from Greenland

13. French pastries from Quebec, Canada

14. clams from Boston, Massachusetts

15. key lime pie from Miami, Florida

16. musical instruments from Haiti

17. sugar cookies from Cuba

18. chocolates from the Bahamas

19. a camera from the Dominican Republic

20. At last! Roberto has arrived with all his stuff!

    The party is on the island that is farthest east.

    Where is the party? _____

Name _____

Use with page 127.

U.S. Neighbors

The United States & Its Neighbors

Alaska

Fairbanks

Greenland

Nuuk

Canada

Vancouver

Winnipeg

Quebec

Toronto

Boston

San Francisco

Denver

Chicago

New York City

United States of America

Washington, D.C.

Los Angeles

Dallas

Monterrey

Miami

Bahamas

Mexico

Cuba

Dominican Republic

Mexico City

Belize

Haiti

Puerto Rico

Jamaica

Honduras

Guatemala

Nicaragua

El Salvador

Costa Rica

Panama

Panama City

N
W   E
S

Name _____

Use with page 126.

U.S. Neighbors

A Map of Ups & Downs

Mario's class has made a map that shows the ups and downs on the Earth's surface. They put little flags on the map to show different landforms.

Do you know which landform is which?

Write the number from the correct flag next to the word for each landform.

bay ☐   island ☐   plain ☐

river ☐   lake ☐   beach ☐   valley ☐

peninsula ☐   mountain ☐   plateau ☐   ocean ☐

Name _____

Spin the Globe

Abby and Mario are spinning their globes to see where they stop.

When they stop, the kids are looking for the continents that are in different hemispheres. (A hemisphere is half of the Earth!)

Help them find the continents in each hemisphere. Look at both globes.

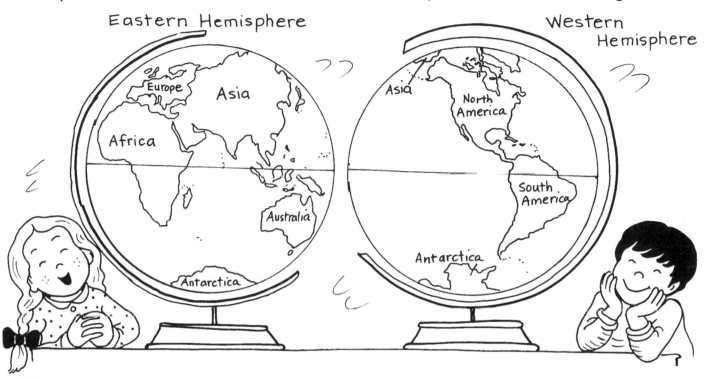

Eastern Hemisphere	Western Hemisphere
Southern Hemisphere	Northern Hemisphere

Name _____

Where Would You Find It?

Detective Bones travels the world to track down amazing things and places.

These are things he is searching for now.

Circle the place where he will probably find each of them.

1. Grand Canyon
   a. under the Atlantic Ocean
   b. in Africa
   c. in Arizona

2. great floating icebergs
   a. in the Arctic Ocean
   b. in every ocean
   c. in Lake Michigan

3. Eiffel Tower
   a. in Texas
   b. in Paris, France
   c. in Tokyo, Japan

4. Panama Canal
   a. in Africa
   b. across Australia
   c. in Central America

5. Mississippi River
   a. in Canada
   b. in the United States
   c. in South America

6. world's tallest mountain
   a. in Alaska
   b. in Turkey
   c. in Antarctica

7. islands of Japan
   a. in the Atlantic Ocean
   b. in the Arctic Ocean
   c. in the Pacific Ocean

8. Statue of Liberty
   a. in Boston
   b. in London
   c. in New York City

9. Sahara Desert
   a. in north Africa
   b. in South America
   c. in Russia

10. Great Wall
    a. in California
    b. in China
    c. in Spain

11. Indian Ocean
    a. near North America
    b. near South America
    c. near Africa

12. great pyramids
    a. in Florida
    b. in Egypt
    c. in France

Name _____

Mix-Up in the Mail Room

Miss Martha works for the post office.
It is her job to sort the mail.

Help her sort the letters.

Find the mail that is addressed to cities and color it green.
Find the mail that is addressed to states and color it blue.
Find the mail that is addressed to countries and color it red.
Find the mail that is addressed to continents
and color it yellow.

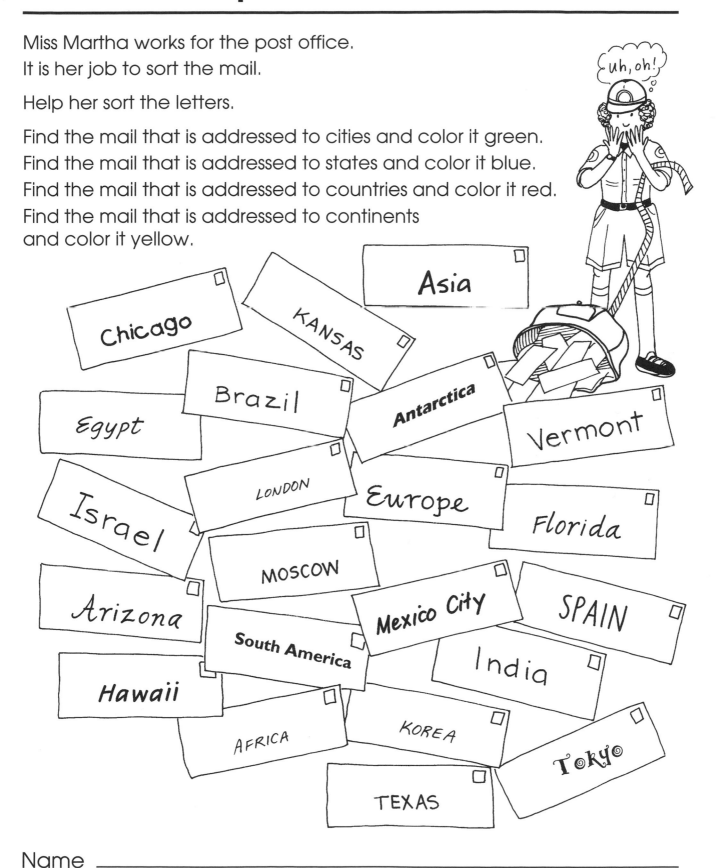

Name _____

The Government Tree

The third graders have discovered that the United States Government is like a tree because it has branches.

They have drawn a tree to show the three branches of government.

Study the tree. Then answer the questions below.

The Three Branches of Government

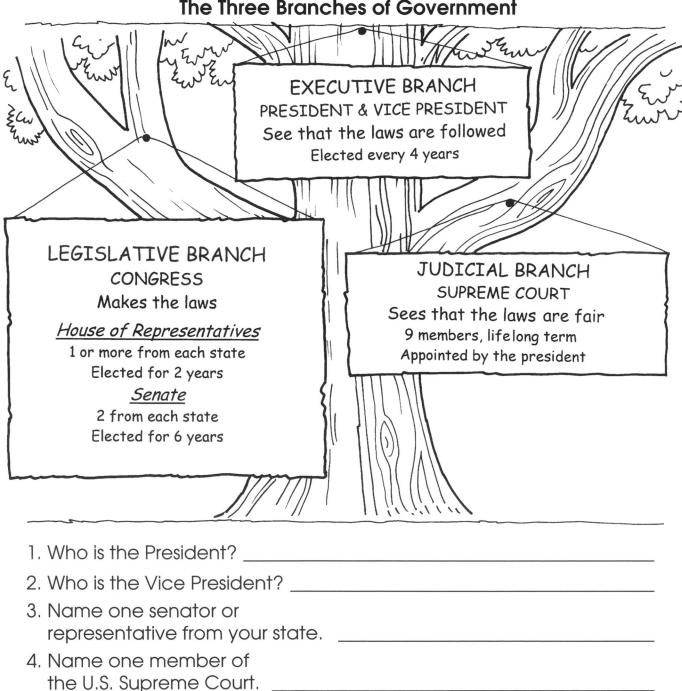

EXECUTIVE BRANCH
PRESIDENT & VICE PRESIDENT
See that the laws are followed
Elected every 4 years

LEGISLATIVE BRANCH
CONGRESS
Makes the laws
House of Representatives
1 or more from each state
Elected for 2 years
Senate
2 from each state
Elected for 6 years

JUDICIAL BRANCH
SUPREME COURT
Sees that the laws are fair
9 members, lifelong term
Appointed by the president

1. Who is the President? _____

2. Who is the Vice President? _____

3. Name one senator or representative from your state. _____

4. Name one member of the U.S. Supreme Court. _____

Name _____

U.S. Government

Eagles, Bells, & Fireworks

Eagles, bells, and fireworks are all part of American tradition.

The eagle is a national symbol. The Liberty Bell is a symbol of freedom.

Fireworks are used to celebrate the day the United States became a nation!

All the squares on the grid show symbols, holidays, places, or things that are important parts of American tradition.

Write the location for each item, showing the square's letter and number.

Color all the blank squares red or blue.

Write the location for each one.

1. Liberty Bell _A, 3_

2. Pilgrim _____

3. Declaration of Independence _____

4. Eagle _____

5. Abe Lincoln _____

6. USA Flag _____

7. Uncle Sam _____

8. Capitol Building _____

9. Washington Monument _____

10. Fireworks _____

11. Statue of Liberty _____

12. George Washington _____

Name _____

Your Fantasy Country

Have you ever wanted to invent your own country?

Well, here's your chance to think about what kind of country you would create.

Who would be the leader?
What laws would there be?

What rights would people have?
How would tax money be used?

Follow the directions to design your fantasy country.

In my country all kids get to vote!

Dogs, too?

Draw your own Country !

Name of Country

_____

Capital City

_____

National Symbol

National Food

National Animal

National Holidays

_____

_____

National Song Title

_____

Name _____

Citizens' Rights

$ TAXES $

Tax money will be used for.....

LAWS

LEADERS

Draw your own flag.

Name _____

Use with page 134.

Old Flag, New Flag

The United States flag we use today is not the same as the first flag!
These kids are painting large pictures of the first flag and the latest flag.
Help them by filling in the color in the right places on both flags.
Look at a picture of these flags to help you find the right colors.
How many stars and stripes are on each flag?

The first U.S. flag was made in 1777.

This flag had:

_____ red stripes

_____ white stripes

_____ stars

The flag has changed 26 times.

This is the flag used since 1959.

This flag has:

_____ red stripes

_____ white stripes

_____ stars

Name _____

Which Happened First?

Look at the giant timeline of U.S. history!
Use the timeline to find out when things happened.

1. Which happened first?
   a. Telephone invented
   b. First airplane ride
   c. Abe Lincoln elected

2. Which happened first?
   a. Women vote
   b. Gold discovered
   c. Kennedy elected

3. Which happened first?
   a. U.S. is born
   b. Pilgrims arrive
   c. Washington elected

4. Which happened first?
   a. Statue of Liberty arrives
   b. Telephone invented
   c. First moon walk

5. Which happened first?
   a. U.S. 200th birthday
   b. First moon walk
   c. Women vote

6. Which happened **last**?
   a. First moon walk
   b. Statue of Liberty arrives
   c. U.S. 200th Birthday

7. Which happened **last**?
   a. Kennedy elected
   b. Lincoln elected
   c. Washington elected

1620	**PILGRIMS ARRIVE**
1776	**THE U.S. IS BORN**
1789	**GEORGE WASHINGTON BECOMES FIRST PRESIDENT**
1848	**GOLD DISCOVERED IN CALIFORNIA**
1860	**ABE LINCOLN BECOMES 16TH U.S. PRESIDENT**
1876	**TELEPHONE INVENTED**
1886	**FRANCE GIVES U.S. THE STATUE OF LIBERTY**
1903	**FIRST AIRPLANE RIDE**
1920	**WOMEN GET THE RIGHT TO VOTE**
1960	**KENNEDY ELECTED PRESIDENT**
1969	**FIRST MOON WALK**
1976	**200TH BIRTHDAY FOR U.S.**

Name _____

Headlines from the Past

Newspaper headlines announce major events in any country. These headlines give news of some events in American history. Read the headlines to help you complete the sentences below.

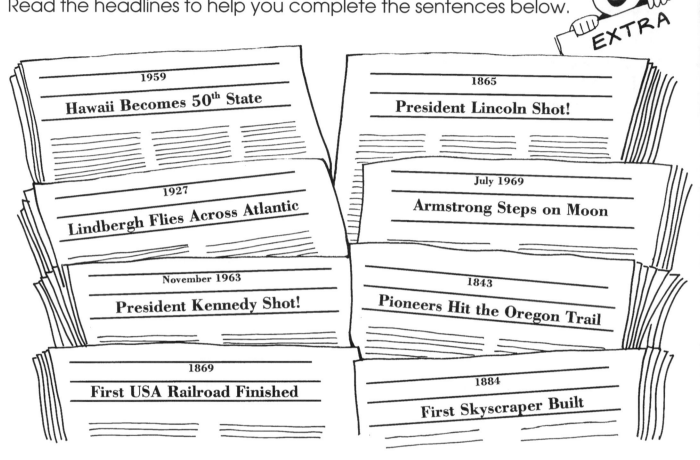

1959
Hawaii Becomes 50th State

1865
President Lincoln Shot!

1927
Lindbergh Flies Across Atlantic

July 1969
Armstrong Steps on Moon

November 1963
President Kennedy Shot!

1843
Pioneers Hit the Oregon Trail

1869
First USA Railroad Finished

1884
First Skyscraper Built

1. President Kennedy was shot about _____ years after President Lincoln.

2. Circle the one that was built first: the first U.S. railroad   the first skyscraper

3. Did Hawaii become a state before the first moon walk? yes   no

4. What year did Charles Lindbergh cross the Atlantic Ocean? _____

5. Was the first skyscraper built before Kennedy was president? yes   no

6. Was the Oregon Trail made before the first cross-country railroad? yes   no

7. What year was the first cross-country railroad finished? _____

8. Who took the first step on the moon? _____

Name _____

Headlines from the Present

Newspaper headlines still announce important events!
Write headlines to tell about things happening
in your school, your town, your state, or your country.
Write the date on the first line of each paper.
Write a short headline on the second line.

Name _____

Some Very Important Americans

It's library day! Abby needs to choose a biography to read.

She is looking for a biography of a famous American, but she is not sure what to choose! Help her find out about these books.

Write the number of each book next to its description.

___ A. the first U.S. president

___ B. explorers who established a route to the West Coast

___ C. nurse who began the American Red Cross

___ D. Indian woman who led explorers to the West Coast

___ E. the 16th U.S. president, who was born in a log cabin

___ F. black leader who gave the famous "I have a dream" speech

___ G. American scientist who did experiments with electricity

___ H. Nez Perce Indian chief who tried to help his tribe escape to Canada

___ I. first woman in the U.S. to become an astronaut

___ J. black woman who would not give up her bus seat to a white person

Name _____

Famous Americans

Citizens on Parade

The kids are showing off their signs about good citizens.
They forgot to finish some of the signs!
Finish the signs for them.
Make each sign tell something about a good citizen.

A good citizen helps others.

Show you care about your city. Keep it clean!

A good citizen does not waste the Earth's valuable resources.

Good citizens remember to vote!

Name _____

Getting Around Washington, D.C.

Do you know how to get to the White House?
Could you find the Washington Monument?
Find your way around the nation's capital with the help of this map!
Use the map on page 143 to locate some of the things in the United
States capital city of Washington, D.C.

1. What street goes to the White House? _____

2. What street goes from the
   White House to the Capitol? _____

3. Circle the monuments that are close to the Potomac River.
   a. Lincoln Memorial
   b. Washington Monument
   c. Jefferson Memorial

4. Circle the two buildings that are east of the Capitol.
   a. Library of Congress
   b. Supreme Court
   c. Lincoln Memorial

5. Circle the buildings that are in the Mall.
   a. The Supreme Court
   b. The Smithsonian Institution
   c. The Museum of Natural History

6. What street borders the Mall on the north?

   _____

7. What street borders the Mall on the south?

   _____

8. Name two places in Washington, D.C. that
   you would like to visit.

   _____

   _____

Name _____

Map of Washington, D.C.

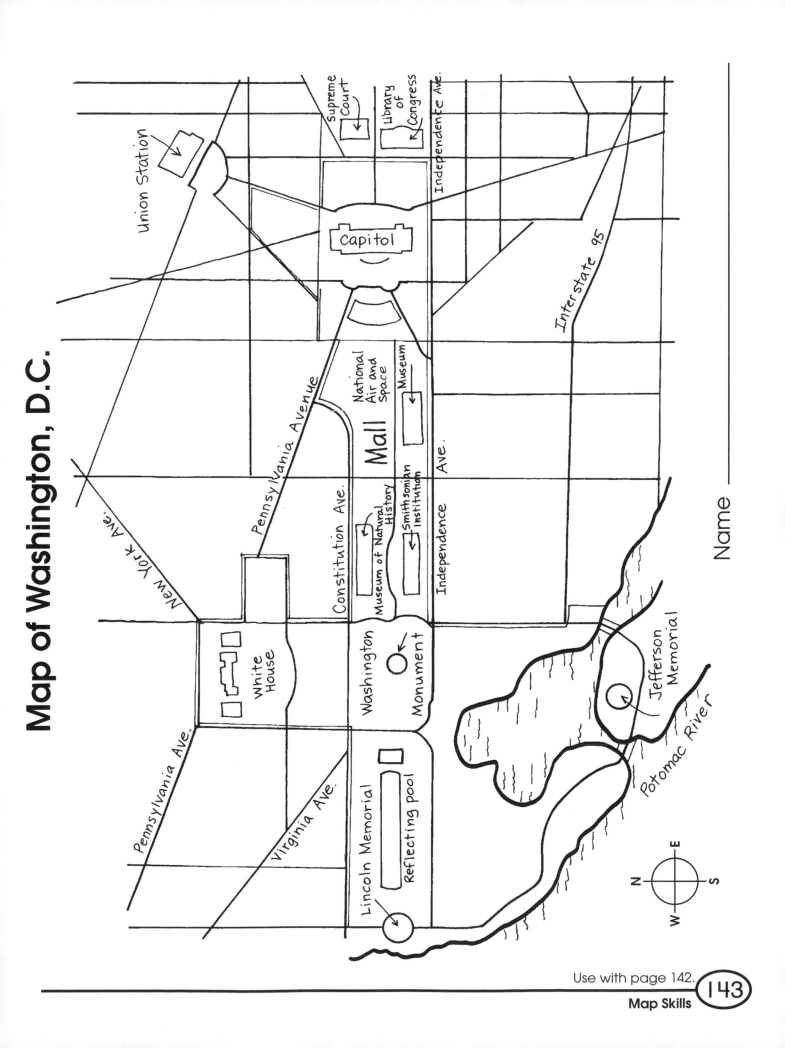

Union Station

Supreme Court

Library of Congress

Independence Ave.

Capitol

Interstate 95

Pennsylvania Avenue

National Air and Space Museum

Mall

New York Ave.

Constitution Ave.

Museum of Natural History

Smithsonian Institution

Independence Ave.

Pennsylvania Ave.

White House

Virginia Ave.

Washington Monument

Lincoln Memorial

Reflecting pool

Potomac River

Jefferson Memorial

N E W S

Name _____

It's a Dog's World!

Abby is wondering where her dog came from!

When she looks in a dog book, she learns that different breeds of dogs come from many countries all over the world!

One map in her book shows some of the dogs that came from Europe.

Draw a line from each dog to the country it matches, and then color the country.

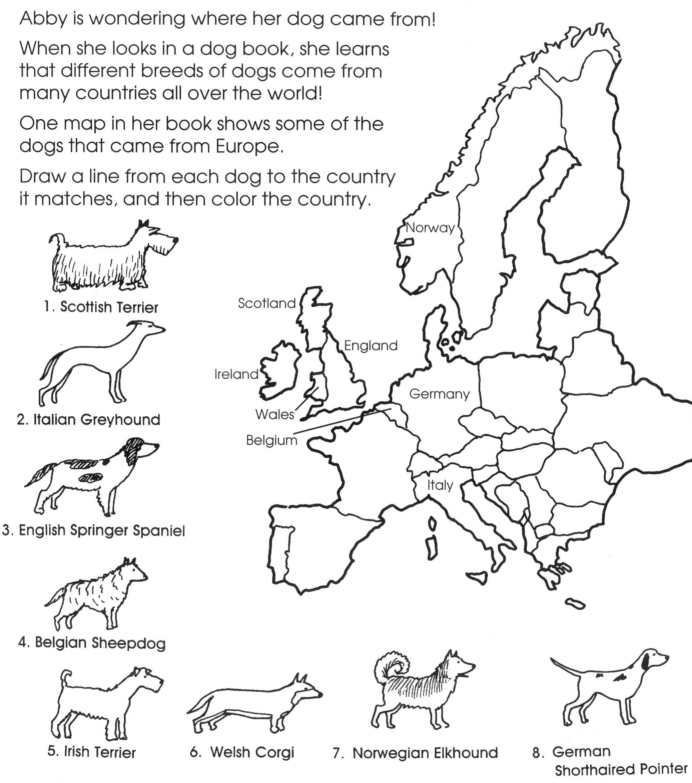

1. Scottish Terrier

2. Italian Greyhound

3. English Springer Spaniel

4. Belgian Sheepdog

5. Irish Terrier

6. Welsh Corgi

7. Norwegian Elkhound

8. German Shorthaired Pointer

If you have a dog, try to find out the country where your dog's breed began.

Name _____

Millions Live in the Top 6

Wow! The top 6 biggest cities in the United States have a lot of people!
If you put them all together, these cities have over 18 million people.
Read the chart to answer the questions about the top 6.

POPULATION in the TOP 6 U.S. Cities	
New York	👤 👤 👤 👤 👤 👤 👤
Los Angeles	👤 👤 👤 👤
Chicago	👤 👤 👤
Houston	👤 👤
Philadelphia	👤 👤
San Diego	👤

👤 = 1 million people

1. Which city has about 3 million people? _____

2. Which city has more people than Los Angeles? _____

3. About how many people live in Philadelphia? _____

4. About how many people live in Los Angeles? _____

5. Which city has about 1 million people? _____

6. Which city has about 2 million people? _____

7. About how many people live in New York City? _____

Find out the population of your town or city. _____

Name _____

Where Are You in the Universe?

You've got mail! This mail delivery creature from outer space has a letter for you.

She needs your address in the universe!

Fill in your universe address, and then help her find you by following the other directions.

From Outer Space

TO:

Name _____

Street _____

City, State, or Province _____

Country _____

Continent _____

Planet _____

Galaxy _____

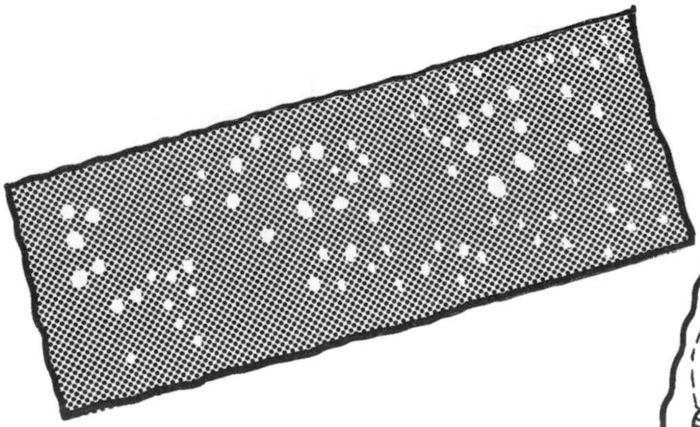

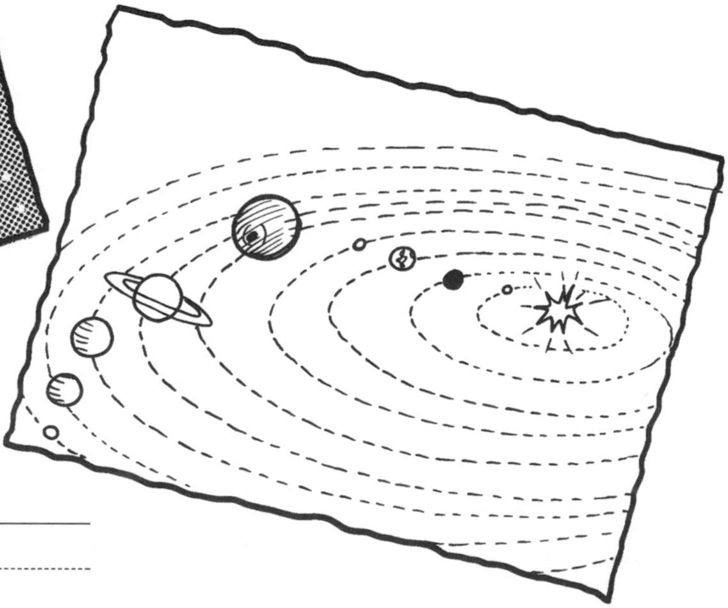

Write the name of your galaxy.

_____

_____

Color in your planet on the solar system.

Name _____

Where Are You in the Universe? cont.

Color your continent. Put a star where you live.

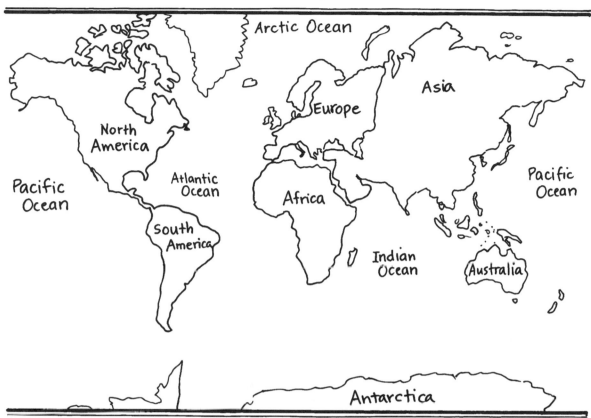

Draw a picture of your home.

Name _____

Mush! Mush! Rush!

Help Natuk make his deliveries—he's in a big hurry!
The map scale shows that 1 inch on the map equals 10 feet.
Use an inch ruler to measure from one dot to the other.

FISH CAKES

Fannie Freeze   The Icebergs   The Shivers

MMMM, Fish cakes!

The Frostbites

Yahoo!   Gabe Goosebump   Hooray!   The Blizzards

1 inch = 10 feet
Scale

Ingrid Icicle

1. How far will Natuk travel from Fannie's to the Frostbites'? _____ feet

2. Whose home is 20 feet northeast of Gabe's? _____

3. How far is it from Ingrid's to the Shivers'? _____ feet

4. How far will he travel from Ingrid's to the Blizzards'? _____ feet

5. How far is it from the Blizzards' to Gabe's home? _____ feet

6. Who lives farther from the Icebergs, the Frostbites or Ingrid? _____

Name _____

The Picnic Under the Picnic

The Bear family does not know that another picnic is being planned right beneath their feet!

The scale shows that every centimeter on the map equals 1 meter in the ant tunnels.

Use a centimeter ruler to connect the dots and measure the distances.

Scale

| 1 cm = 1 meter |

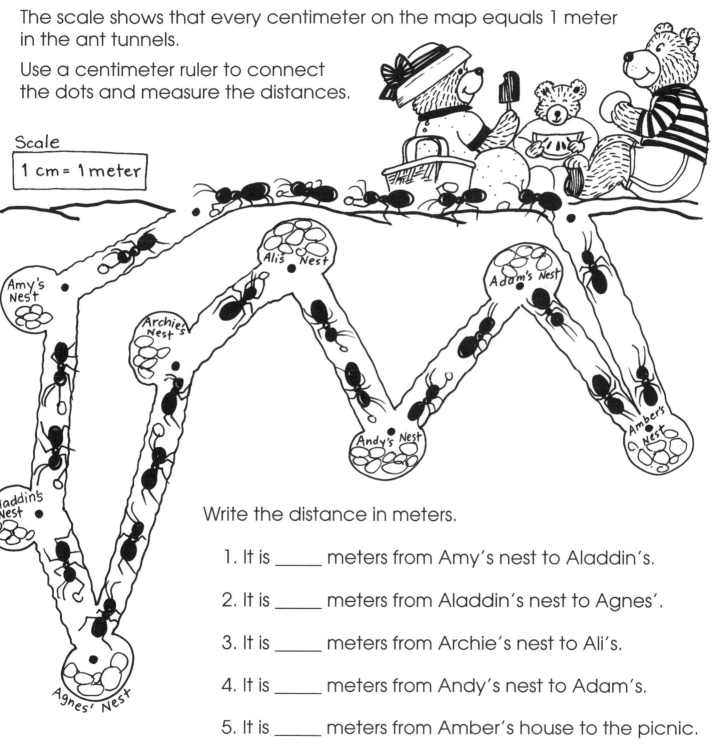

Write the distance in meters.

1. It is _____ meters from Amy's nest to Aladdin's.

2. It is _____ meters from Aladdin's nest to Agnes'.

3. It is _____ meters from Archie's nest to Ali's.

4. It is _____ meters from Andy's nest to Adam's.

5. It is _____ meters from Amber's house to the picnic.

Name _____

Island Hopping

Trader Doug the Sea Dog is always looking for a good trade.
He travels many miles trading things between the islands.
Use the scale on the map to find out how far he will travel today.
Use an inch ruler to measure the distance between the dots.

1. Doug took coconuts from Coconut Grove to Fish Lagoon. How far did he go? _____

2. He took a barrel of fish from Fish Lagoon to Flower Isle, _____ miles away.

3. He traded flowers for bananas on Banana Island, _____ miles from Flower Isle.

4. Next he went to Crab Atoll, _____ miles away, to trade bananas for crab cakes.

5. Then he headed for Home Island, _____ miles away from Crab Atoll, for a dinner of bananas and crab cakes.

Name _____

Use a Map Scale

So Many Boxes!

Everything needed on Eagle Island has to be delivered by boat or helicopter.

Read the labels on the boxes.

Decide where each item needs to go on the map.

Draw a line from each box to the landform where the delivery will be made.

Name _____

Lobsters for the World

Sam's Seafood Company delivers fresh lobsters from Boston to places all over the world. He needs to know a lot about the world in order to find all the right places.

Most maps of the world are flat.

But Sam knows that the Earth is not flat. It is round, like a ball.

So he uses a globe to help him with his travels.

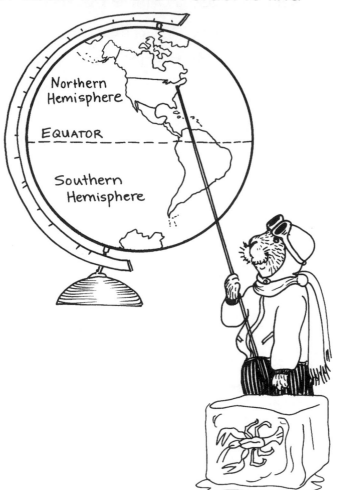

> A globe is a model of the Earth.
>
> The Earth is divided into 2 parts by an imaginary line called the equator.
>
> Each half of the Earth is called a hemisphere. This term means "half a ball."
>
> The equator divides the Earth into the Northern and Southern Hemispheres.

Help Sam get to know the globe!

1. Trace the equator with a red crayon.

2. Color the Northern Hemisphere yellow. Color the Southern Hemisphere blue.

3. Draw a purple flag on the North Pole. Draw a red flag at the South Pole.

4. What continent is entirely in the Northern Hemisphere?

   _____

5. What continent is in both hemispheres?

   _____

6. What continent is totally in the Southern Hemisphere?

   _____

Name _____

Lobsters for the World, cont.

Sam knows that the Earth is also divided into halves from the North Pole to the South Pole.

This makes the Eastern Hemisphere and the Western Hemisphere.

Sam has two maps that show him all four hemispheres.
1. Color the Western Hemisphere pink.
2. Color the Eastern Hemisphere yellow.

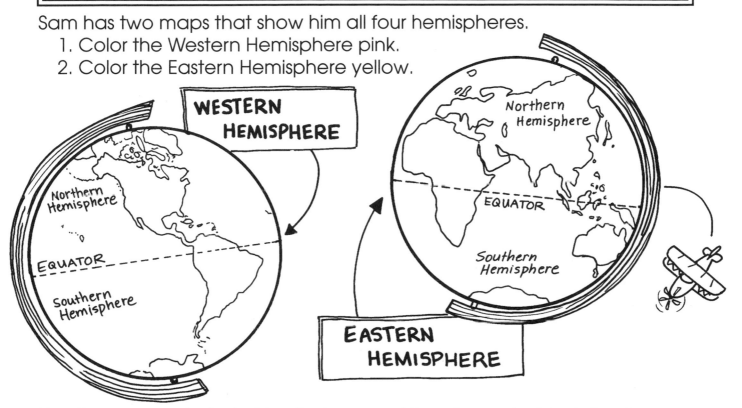

Use these maps to help him find some of the places for his deliveries.

Fill in the blanks to show in what hemisphere each continent is located.

3. North America: Northern and _____ Hemispheres

4. South America: Southern, Western, and _____ Hemispheres

5. Australia: Southern and _____ Hemispheres

6. Africa: Eastern, Northern, and _____ Hemispheres

7. Asia: Northern, Southern, Western, and _____ Hemispheres

8. Europe: Eastern and _____ Hemispheres

9. Antarctica: Southern, _____, and _____ Hemispheres

Name _____

Use with page 152.

Globe • Hemispheres

Delivery Anywhere!

The U-Send-It Delivery Company will deliver to any place in the world.
Here are just a few of the things they've been asked to deliver.
Follow the directions to show the continents and oceans they've visited.

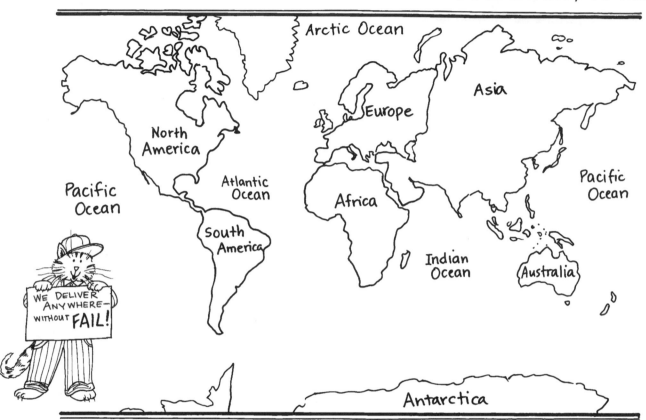

Follow the directions to color each place that receives a delivery.
The name of the place for the delivery is in bold type.

U-Send-It Delivery delivers . . .
1. snowmobiles to **Antarctica**. .... Color it yellow.
2. ice cream to ocean liners in the
   Atlantic Ocean and **Pacific Ocean**. .... Color them green.
3. baby cribs to a day care center in **Europe**. .... Color it blue.
4. food to walruses in the **Arctic Ocean**. .... Color it purple.
5. a gorilla to return to its home in **Africa**. .... Color it red.
6. a wedding cake to a village in **South America**. ...... Color it brown.
7. fresh pineapple from Hawaii to **Asia**. .... Color it orange.
8. baby penguins to a zoo in **North America**. .... Color it black.
9. dinosaur bones to a museum in **Australia**. .... Color it red.
10. 20 scuba divers to the **Indian Ocean**. .... Color it green.

Name _____

Truckloads of Telephones

Tamara Talker has been hired to deliver telephones all over North America. Help her learn about the continent by following these directions.

Greenland

Alaska

Canada

1. Trace the border between Canada and the United States with a red crayon.
2. Trace the border between the United States and Mexico with a green crayon.
3. Color Canada yellow.
4. Color the United States pink.
5. Color Mexico purple.
6. Color Guatemala and Costa Rica blue.
7. Color Belize and Panama green.
8. Color Nicaragua and El Salvador red.
9. Color Honduras brown.
10. Put a ★ on the place where you live.

United States Of America

Mexico

Puerto Rico
Cuba
Jamaica Haiti Dominican Republic
Belize
Honduras
Nicaragua
Costa Rica
Guatemala
Panama
El Salvador

Name _____

Mix-Up at the Post Office

Oops! All the mail fell into a jumble.
Help the mail carriers find the right letters to put into their bags.
Hal Horse only delivers letters to states. Color his mail and bag red.
Gail Snail only delivers letters to cities. Color her mail and bag green.
Gilbert Gull only delivers letters to countries. Color his mail and bag blue.

Name _____

Cities, States, & Countries

Packages Without Names

Charlotte has packages to deliver to different states in the United States.
Each package has a picture of the state but no name.
Can you recognize the states from their shapes?
Write the name of the state on each package. (See some clues below.)

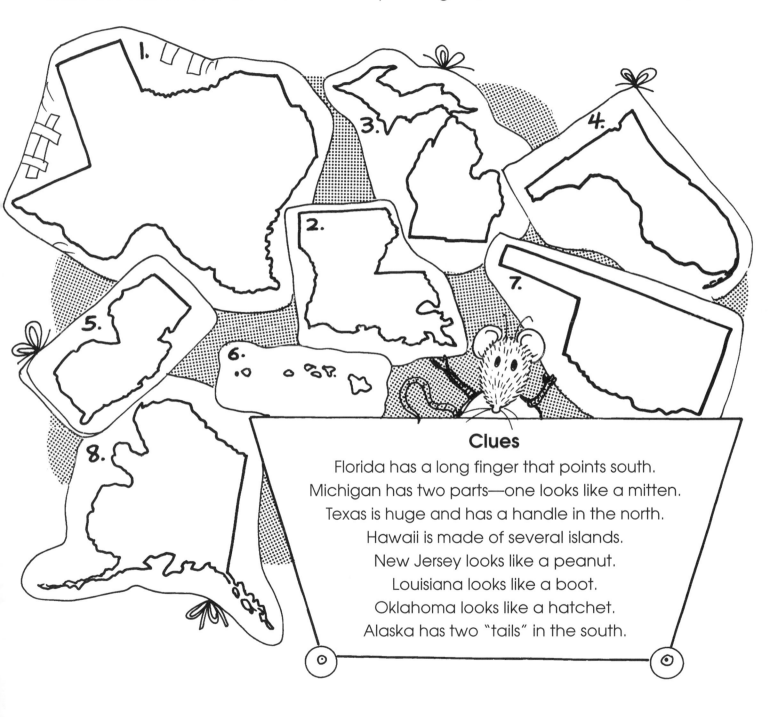

Clues

Florida has a long finger that points south.
Michigan has two parts—one looks like a mitten.
Texas is huge and has a handle in the north.
Hawaii is made of several islands.
New Jersey looks like a peanut.
Louisiana looks like a boot.
Oklahoma looks like a hatchet.
Alaska has two "tails" in the south.

Name _____

State Shapes

Rabbit Relatives

Grandma and Grandpa Rabbit send mail to grandchildren all over the United States.

They have a lot of letters and packages ready for the mailman.

Use the map on the next page to show where their mail will go.

Follow the color code to color each state correctly.

Color Code   **Package**

1. **Red** — a birthday card to little Roberta Floppy in St. Louis

2. **Green** — three boxes of carrot cookies to Phil in Philadelphia, Newt in New Orleans, and Bob in Boston

3. **Orange** — a model spaceship to Billie in the state where rockets are launched at Cape Canaveral

4. **Purple** — toys to triplets Sally, Sammy, and Sandy near the Grand Canyon

5. **Blue** — red sneakers to Ralph, who lives just west of the middle part of Lake Michigan

6. **Yellow** — balloons to Danny in the city of Dallas

7. **Pink** — a box of pretzels to Trina, who lives near the Golden Gate Bridge

8. **Brown** — valentines to Vicki and Val, who live near Great Salt Lake

9. **Red** — a rattle to newborn Willie, who lives near Mt. Rushmore

10. **Green** — skis to Adam in Seattle

11. **Blue** — brownies to little Millie in Niagara Falls

12. **Yellow** — a guitar to Gus in Nashville

13. **Purple** — mittens to Carrie and Connie in Connecticut

14. **Orange** — a kite to Henry in the state that touches Michigan and Lake Erie

Use with page 159.

U.S. Cities, States, & Landmarks

The United States

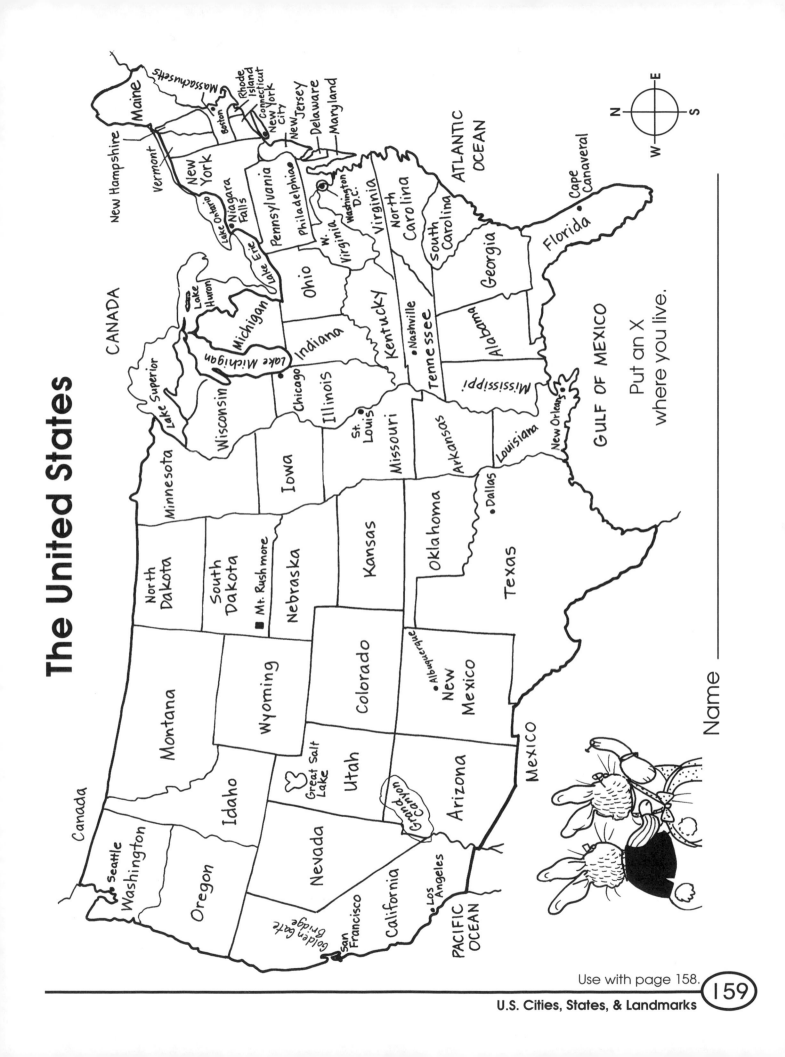

N
W E
S

CANADA

Canada

Washington • Seattle

Oregon

Idaho

Montana

North Dakota

South Dakota

■ Mt. Rushmore

Nebraska

Wyoming

Nevada

Utah

Great Salt Lake

Grand Canyon

Arizona

California

• Los Angeles

San Francisco

Golden Gate Bridge

PACIFIC OCEAN

Colorado

New Mexico
• Albuquerque

Minnesota

Iowa

Kansas

Oklahoma

Texas

Dallas •

MEXICO

Wisconsin

Lake Superior

Lake Michigan

Michigan

Lake Huron

Illinois

Chicago •

Missouri

St. Louis •

Arkansas

Louisiana

New Orleans •

Indiana

Ohio

Kentucky

Tennessee

Nashville •

Mississippi

Alabama

Georgia

Lake Ontario

Niagara Falls •

Lake Erie

Pennsylvania

Philadelphia •

W. Virginia

Virginia

North Carolina

South Carolina

Florida

Cape Canaveral •

Washington D.C.

New Hampshire

Vermont

New York

Maine

Massachusetts

Boston •

Rhode Island

Connecticut

New York City

New Jersey

Delaware

Maryland

ATLANTIC OCEAN

GULF OF MEXICO

Put an X where you live.

Name _____

Use with page 158.

U.S. Cities, States, & Landmarks

Lost Again!

Wrong-Way Walrus is lost again! Every time he goes out on a seaweed delivery, he ends up in the wrong body of water!

This time he popped up in the Gulf of Mexico instead of Boston Harbor.

He needs to check his map and hurry on his way before all the seaweed ice cream melts!

Use the map on the next page (page 161) to help you follow these directions and answer the questions.

1. Draw a sailboat in the ocean that touches the east coast of the U.S.

2. Color the Great Lakes green. How many are there? _____

3. Draw a whale in the Pacific Ocean.

4. Trace the Colorado River in red.

5. Trace the Missouri River in blue.

6. Trace the Mississippi River in green.

7. Trace the St. Lawrence River in yellow.

8. Draw a red arrow to Boston Harbor.

9. The X on the map shows where Wrong-Way Walrus is. What body of water is he in? _____

10. What river flows into the Pacific Ocean? _____

11. What river flows into the Mississippi River from the east? _____

12. Name a city on the Missouri River. _____

13. Name a city on the Rio Grande River. _____

14. Name a city on the Gulf of Mexico. _____

15. What river flows along the border between the U.S. and Mexico? _____

16. Name a city on Lake Michigan. _____

Name _____

United States Bodies of Water

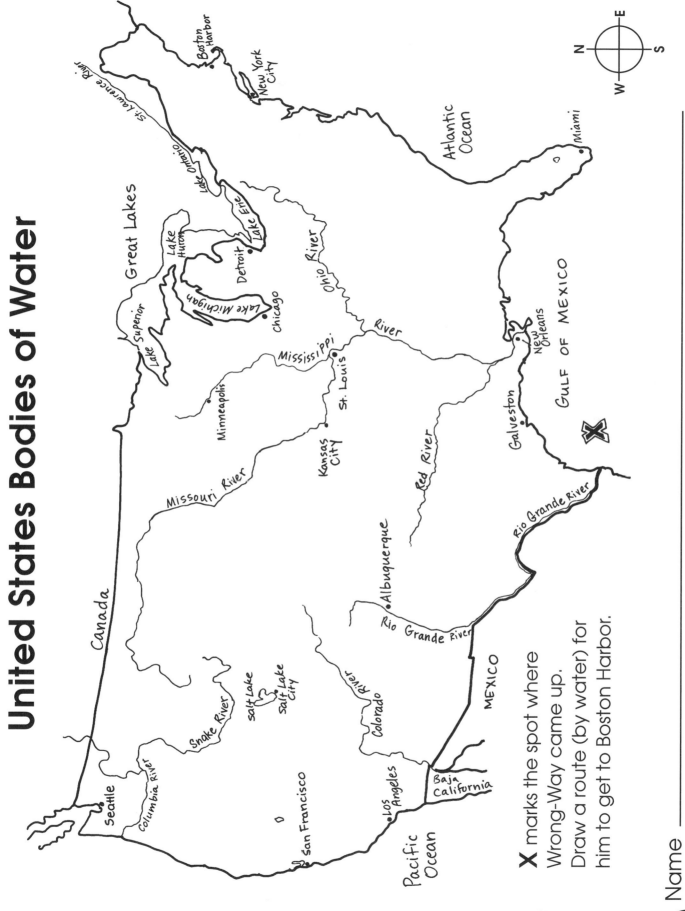

St. Lawrence River
Boston Harbor
New York City
Atlantic Ocean
Miami
Lake Ontario
Great Lakes
Lake Erie
Lake Huron
Detroit
Lake Superior
Lake Michigan
Chicago
Ohio River
River
Gulf of Mexico
New Orleans
Mississippi
Minneapolis
St. Louis
Kansas City
Galveston
Red River
Missouri River
Rio Grande River
Albuquerque
Rio Grande River
Canada
MEXICO
Salt Lake
Salt Lake City
Colorado River
Snake River
Columbia River
Seattle
San Francisco
Los Angeles
Baja California
Pacific Ocean

X marks the spot where Wrong-Way came up. Draw a route (by water) for him to get to Boston Harbor.

Name

Use with page 160.

U.S. Bodies of Water

The Lost Stagecoach

Death Valley Dan, the stagecoach driver, is lost!
He wonders if he will ever find
his way to San Francisco
with his bags of gold.

SOUTHWESTERN STATES

Redwood N.P.

Nevada

Great Salt Lake

Sacramento

Carson City

San Francisco

California

Great Basin

Salt Lake City

Provo

Utah

Boulder

Denver

Colorado

Pike's Peak

Colorado River

Yosemite N.P.

Death Valley N.P.

Las Vegas

Grand Canyon N.P.

Mesa Verde N.P.

Los Angeles

Pacific Ocean

San Diego

Colorado River

Arizona

Rio Grande

Santa Fe

Albuquerque

Baja

Phoenix

New Mexico

Carlsbad

Mexico

Tuscon

U.S. MINT

U.S. MINT

Help Dan read his map.

1. What state touches the
   Pacific Ocean? _____

2. What state is
   south of Utah? _____

3. The Grand
   Canyon is in _____

4. San Francisco
   is in the state of _____

5. What state is east
   of Arizona? _____

6. Is Nevada east or
   west of California? _____

7. Which state is home to
   the Great Salt Lake? _____

8. Where is
   Pike's Peak? _____

9. Dan is now in the state east of
   Utah. Where is he? _____

10. How many national parks
    are shown? (Look for N.P.) _____

Name _____

Skeletons for the Schools

Gabe's job is to deliver science equipment to schools all over the United States.

The mileage chart tells him how far it is between cities.

Use the chart to help him find the distances.

Cities	Chicago	Boston	Denver	Nashville	Washington DC
Chicago	0	1015	1010	930	715
Los Angeles	2030	3025	1020	2030	2690
Miami	1370	1480	2080	900	1040
Seattle	2030	3090	1300	2430	2790
Tucson	1740	2630	890	1615	2280

Deliver To Tucson Grade School

Write the answers in the blanks.

1. Chicago to Seattle _____ miles

2. Tucson to Nashville _____ miles

3. Washington, DC, to Los Angeles _____ miles

4. Boston to Miami _____ miles

5. Miami to Washington, DC _____ miles

6. Denver to Tucson _____ miles

7. Which 2 cities are farthest apart? _____ and _____

8. Which 2 cities are closest together? _____ and _____

Name _____

Fresh Air for Floats

Wanda has an unusual job! She pumps air into the floats at water parks. She gets to try out the floats at every park, too!

Use the information chart to answer some questions about the parks she visits.

PARKS	Number of Water Slides	River	Open Year-Round	Overnight Camping	Snack Bar	Adults Allowed	Floats for Rent
Water Wonderworld	12	X	X		X	yes	X
Wild West Waterworks	7	X		X	X	yes	X
Dino-Land Park	0	X	X	X	X	no	
Water Thrills & Chills	10	X	X		X	yes	
Wet & Wild	14	X	X			no	X

Write the answers.

1. Can Wanda camp overnight at Wet & Wild?_____

2. Will Wanda have floats to fill at Dino-Land Park?_____

3. Can Wanda get a snack at Wild West Waterworks? _____

4. How many water slides are there at Water Thrills & Chills? _____

5. How many water slides are there at Water Wonderworld? _____

6. Is there a river at Wet & Wild? _____

7. Are adults allowed at Dino-Land? _____

8. Are adults allowed at Wild West? _____

9. Can Wanda camp overnight at Dino-Land? _____

10. Which park is not open year-round? _____

Name _____

Read a Chart

Underwater Invitations

The Sea Bottom Ball is the biggest event of the year in the underwater world.
Oliver is delivering the invitations today.
Help Oliver get them to the right places.
Find the square on the grid that holds each undersea object.

For example: The starfish is in the square where row F and row 2 meet.
It is located at F, 2 on the grid.

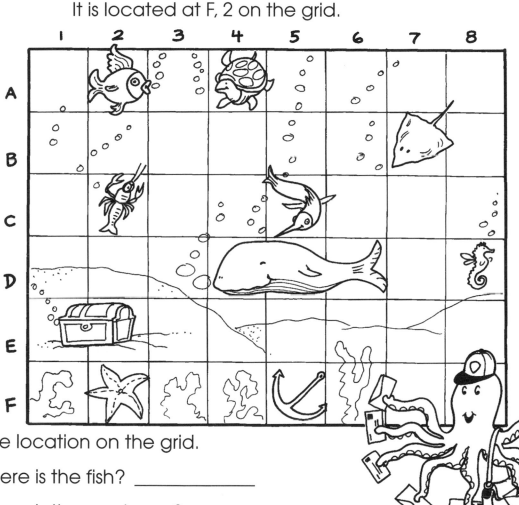

Write the location on the grid.

1. Where is the fish? _____

2. Where is the sea horse? _____

3. Where is the anchor? _____   7. What is in E, 1 and E, 2?

4. Where is the lobster? _____   _____

5. Where is the stingray? _____   8. What is in D, 4; D, 5; and D, 6?

6. Where is the swordfish? _____   _____

Color the picture.

Name _____

Worms for the Garden

Gardener Gus is getting some nice, fat worms for his garden.
The worms make the soil good for growing healthy plants.
Help the worms find their way to the right spots in the garden.

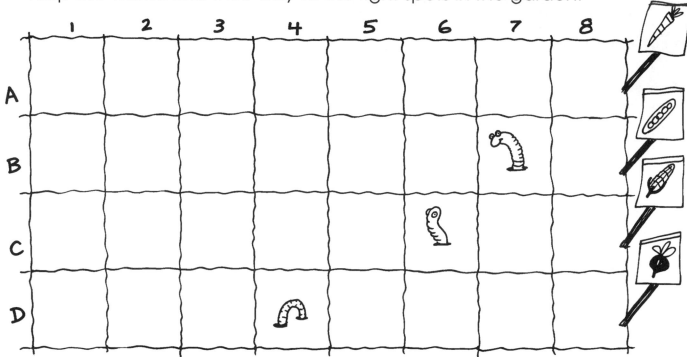

1. Some worms are already in the garden. Where are they?

   _____ , _____ , and _____

2. Draw a worm in A, 5.

3. Draw two worms in D, 7.

4. Draw a worm in B, 3.

5. Draw a worm in C, 2.

6. Draw a worm in B, 1.

7. Draw a worm in A, 4.

8. Draw a worm in D, 6.

9. Draw a worm whose head comes up in C, 6 and tail comes up in B, 8.

10. Draw two worms in the same hole in D, 2.

Name _____

Delivery to Happy Camp

Bernie the Mail Bear has bug spray for the campers at Happy Camp. Finish the map that shows his trail through the campground.

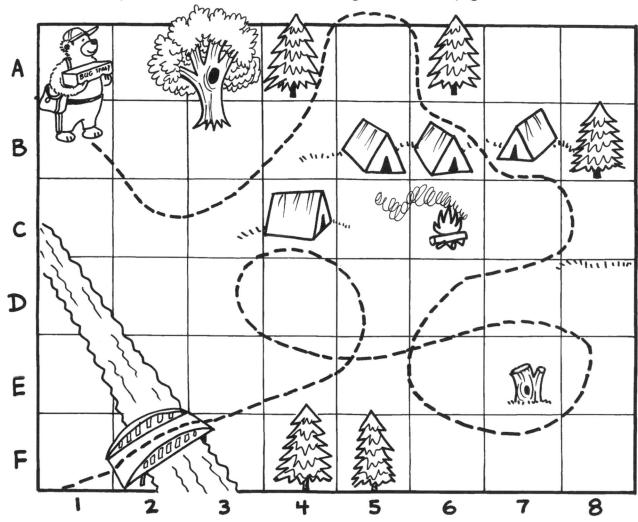

Draw these things on the map in the correct places.

1. Bernie hopped over a puddle ⟨⋅⟩ at B, 2.
2. He went around a big tree 🌲 at A, 5.
3. Bernie put a package inside a tent ⛺ at C, 8.
4. Then he tripped over a rock ⬭ in E, 6.
5. He bumped into a trash can 🗑 in E, 5.
6. He stopped to rest on a stump 🪵 in D, 4.
7. He crossed over a _____ in F, 2.

Name _____

Search for the Missing Flowers

The delivery bees are trying to gather honey to deliver to the beehive, but all the flowers are missing!

Follow the directions, and draw the flowers for the bees to find.

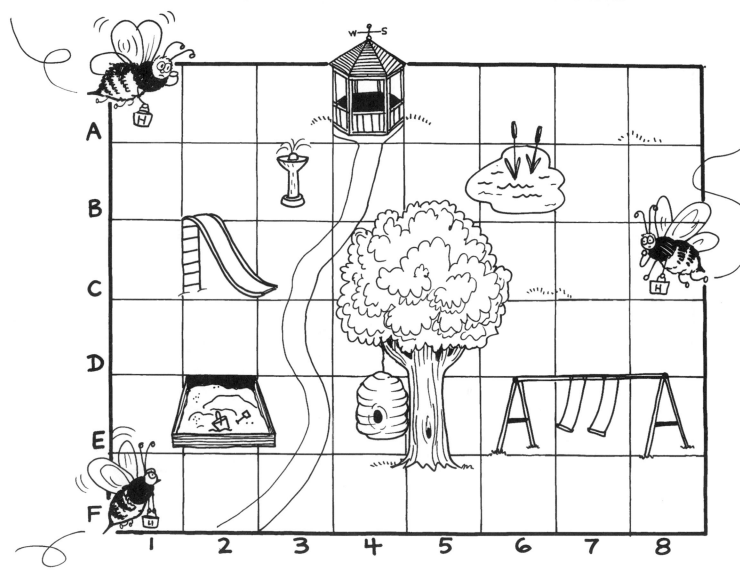

1. Draw 2 ✿ in D, 2.

2. Draw a ✿ in A, 2 and A, 7.

3. Draw a ✿ in C, 1 and F, 7.

4. Draw a ✿ in D, 7 and F, 4.

5. Where is the fountain? _____

6. Where is the beehive? _____

7. Where is the sandbox? _____

8. Where is the slide? _____

Name _____

Read a Grid

Flowers for the Queen

Beatrice's Flower Shop has a delivery of flowers for the queen bee.
Beatrice needs a grid to find the queen's chamber in the hive.
Use the grid and the map key to help Beatrice find her way around the hive.

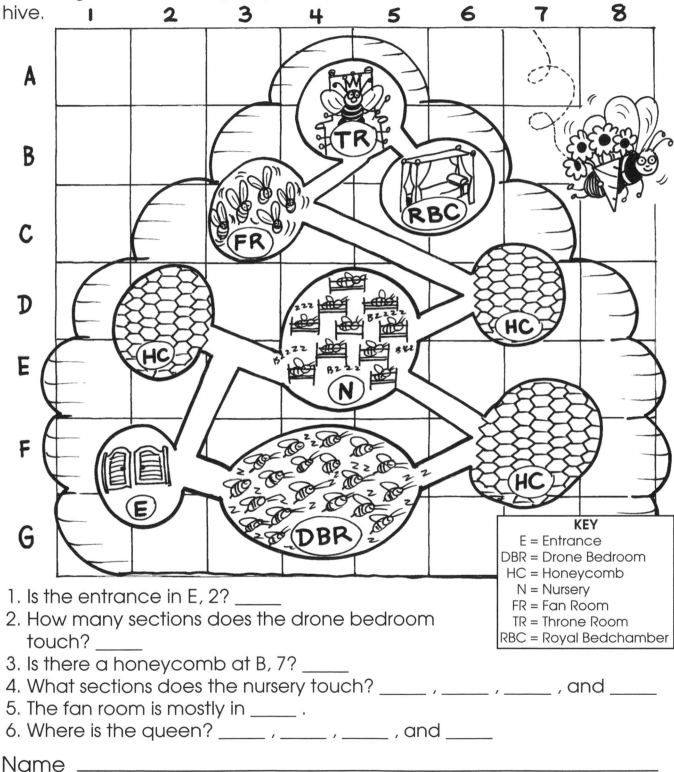

KEY
E = Entrance
DBR = Drone Bedroom
HC = Honeycomb
N = Nursery
FR = Fan Room
TR = Throne Room
RBC = Royal Bedchamber

1. Is the entrance in E, 2? _____
2. How many sections does the drone bedroom touch? _____
3. Is there a honeycomb at B, 7? _____
4. What sections does the nursery touch? _____ , _____ , _____ , and _____
5. The fan room is mostly in _____ .
6. Where is the queen? _____ , _____ , _____ , and _____

Name _____

The Whereabouts of Bears

The hungry bears in Jellyshine Park are eating the campers' food. Camper food is not good for bears, so the ranger has ordered tons of berries.

The truck driver has a map of the bear population in Jellyshine Park. Use the map to help her figure out where all the bears are.

1. Which section of the park will need the most berries? _____

2. What is the bear population in the Winter Caves Area? _____

3. Which has more bears: the campground or the Green Lakes District?

_____

4. What is the bear population in the Canyon Cliffs Area? _____

5. Which area has the smallest bear population? _____

6. What is the bear population in the campground? _____

Name _____

No Shooting Allowed

In Africa, dozens of photographers track endangered animals.
They only shoot these animals with cameras!

Frannie Photog's map of Africa's endangered species helps her get to the right places.

AFRICA'S ENDANGERED SPECIES

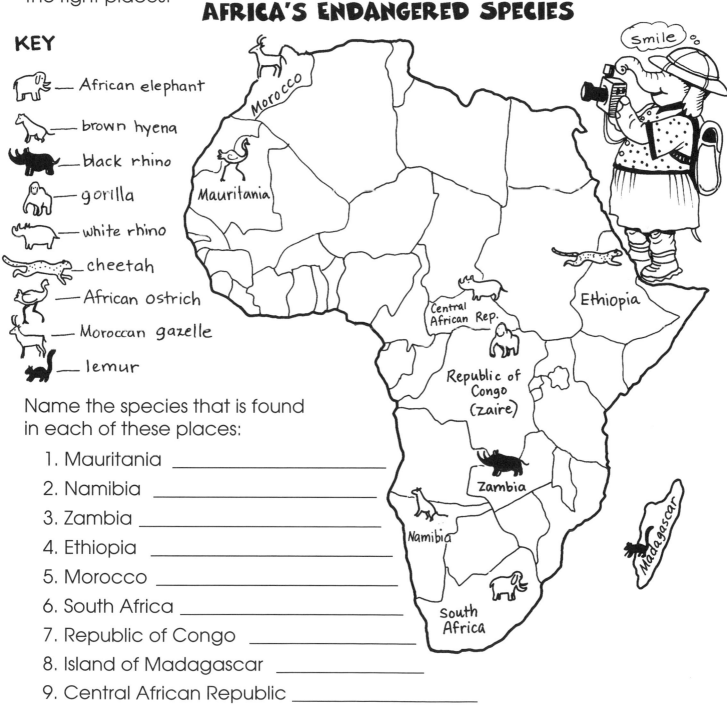

KEY

— African elephant

— brown hyena

— black rhino

— gorilla

— white rhino

— cheetah

— African ostrich

— Moroccan gazelle

— lemur

Name the species that is found in each of these places:

1. Mauritania _____

2. Namibia _____

3. Zambia _____

4. Ethiopia _____

5. Morocco _____

6. South Africa _____

7. Republic of Congo _____

8. Island of Madagascar _____

9. Central African Republic _____

Name _____

Bananas for the Neighbors

Juan grows bananas to be delivered all over South America!
His map shows some products produced in the countries he visits.

Write the name of a country that
shows these products on the map.

PRODUCTS OF SOUTH AMERICA

1. cattle and sheep

_____

2. coffee, fish,
   and oil

_____

3. cattle, oil,
   and coffee

_____

4. fish

_____

5. grain

_____

6. diamonds

_____

Write the answers.

7. Name a product
   produced in Columbia.

_____

8. Name a product
   produced in Bolivia. _____

9. Where is the most
   timber grown? _____

10. In what country does
    Juan grow bananas? _____

VENEZUELA
GUYANA
SURINAM
FRENCH GUIANA
COLUMBIA
ECUADOR
PERU
BRAZIL
BOLIVIA
PARAGUAY
CHILE
ARGENTINA
URUGUAY

KEY

= oil
= trees
= coffee
= fruit
= cattle
= sheep
= bananas
= grains
= diamonds
= fish

Name _____

In All Kinds of Weather

Bouncing Barb the mail carrier never fails to deliver the mail on time!
She carries a weather map so she will be prepared for all kinds of weather.
Use her weather map to answer the questions about Australia's weather.

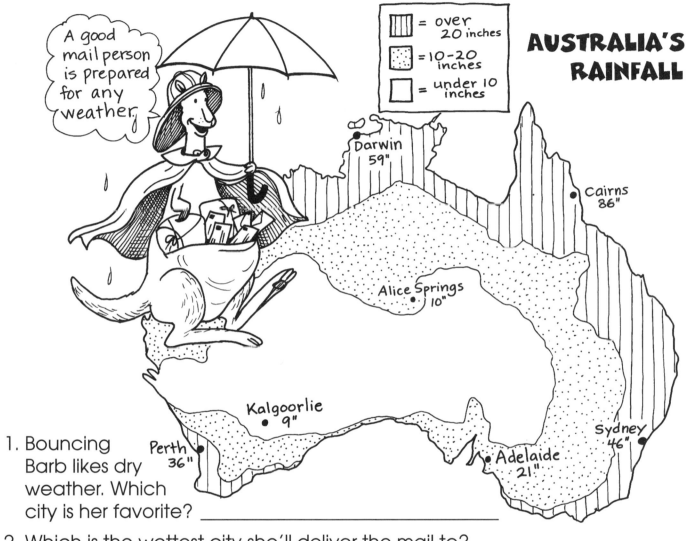

1. Bouncing Barb likes dry weather. Which city is her favorite? _____

2. Which is the wettest city she'll deliver the mail to? _____

3. Which gets more rain, southern or eastern Australia? _____

4. Which part of the country is the driest, the middle or the coastline? _____

5. Can they expect more rain in Kalgoorlie or Perth? _____

6. What is the rainfall each year in Sydney? _____

7. What rainfall is expected each year in Darwin? _____

Name _____

On the Road Again

Freddy Fox has to drive from Cocoaville to Sweet Town to deliver chocolate chips to the Crispy Cookies Company.

It's a long way, but Freddy has a good road map.

Read his map to find the answers to the questions.

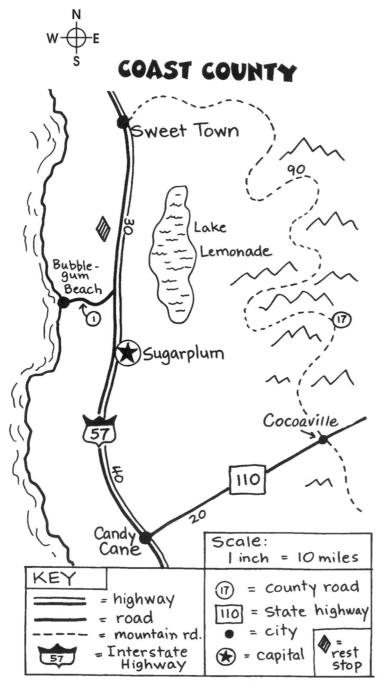

COAST COUNTY

Sweet Town

90

Lake Lemonade

Bubble-gum Beach

Sugarplum

Cocoaville

57

110

Candy Cane

20

17

1

30

40

Scale:
1 inch = 10 miles

KEY

= highway

= road

= mountain rd.

= Interstate Highway

(17) = county road

[110] = State highway

• = city

⊛ = capital

= rest stop

1. What capital city is shown?

   _____

2. On the scale,
   1 inch = _____ miles.

3. Candy Cane is on
   Interstate Number _____ .

4. Does Route 110 go
   through Cocoaville? _____

5. Is Lake Lemonade
   east of Interstate 57? _____

6. The county road goes
   from Cocoaville to

   _____ .

7. How far is it from Cocoaville
   to Candy Cane?

   _____ miles

8. What route goes
   from Interstate 57 to
   Bubblegum Beach?

   _____

Chips-R-US

Name _____

A Puzzling Delivery

Miss Cross, the puzzle champion, has waited all day for the newspaper with the new crossword puzzle in it. Finally it has arrived!

Today's puzzle uses map words.

Help her solve it with the words in the **Word Box.**

WORD BOX

poles	key
equator	bay
continent	road
west	states
peninsula	ocean
scale	sea
hemisphere	island

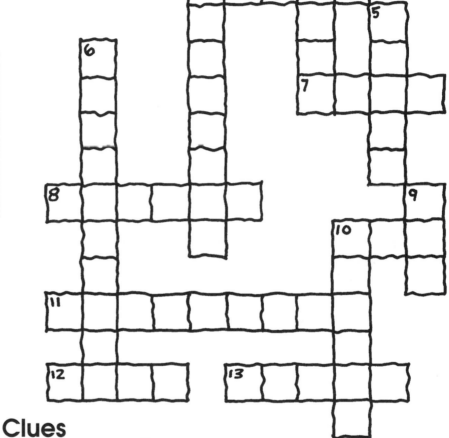

Clues

Across

1. part of a map that shows symbols
4. largest body of water in the world
7. way to travel between cities
8. land surrounded by water
10. another name for ocean
11. land surrounded on 3 sides by water
12. the opposite of east
13. The _____ are at the top and bottom of Earth.

Down

2. imaginary line around center of Earth
3. large body of land
5. tells distances on a map
6. half of the Earth
9. area of water sheltered by land
10. The United States has 50 of these.

Name _____

Where Are the Elephants?

Homer has a load of hay for the circus elephants.
Complete the directions on the next page to help Homer find the elephant compound.

Use the map on page 176 and the compass to complete the directions below.

Homer travels _____ until the road turns _____ . When the road splits at Circus Circle, he turns right and travels _____ . At Cotton Candy Lane, he turns right again and travels _____ . Oops! There is a big curve in the road. Homer turns _____ and then _____ .

Whew! He finally reaches the elephant compound.

Delivery for Elmo.

Pant

Good! Just in time for lunch!

Follow the directions and answer the questions.

1. Color the ride that is northeast from the Big Top Tent.

2. Color the tent that is southeast from the Big Top Tent.

3. Color the booth that is in the northwest corner.

4. What is southwest of the Big Top? _____

5. Will Homer find elephants west of the Big Top? _____

6. Is the Roller Coaster north of the Big Top? _____

7. Is the Ring Toss west of the Big Top? _____

8. Is the Food Tent north of the Roller Coaster? _____

9. Is the Clown Tent farther east than the hay truck? _____

10. Can you buy cotton candy to the southeast of the Food Tent? _____

Name _____

Where Are the Stamps?

Edward, the mail bear, is waiting at the door for Gilda's letter. Gilda is madly searching her room for a stamp to put on the letter. Where are the stamps?

Make a map of Gilda's room.

Include these things on the map:

a title
a scale
symbols
a key
a place for the stamps

Title:

Scale:

Key

Name _____

Make a Map

Make a Map

Now that Gilda is a map maker, she is ready for you to draw a map of your favorite place. Is it your town? Is it your tree house, the amusement park, or another place?

Choose your favorite place and make a map of it. Don't forget to give the map a title, a compass rose, a key, a map maker's signature, and date.

Title:

Made by:

KEY:

SCALE:

Name _____

SCIENCE

Skills Exercises
Grade Three

SKILLS CHECKLIST
SCIENCE

✔	SKILL	PAGE(S)
	Describe characteristics and needs of living things	183
	Describe characteristics of different body systems	184, 185
	Define some diseases and ailments of the human body	186
	Define and use vocabulary related to the human body	187
	Identify and describe some ways to take care of your health	188
	Identify some safety behaviors and skills	189
	Identify nutritious foods	190
	Describe the relationship of bodies in the solar system	191, 192
	Identify and compare objects in space	191, 192
	Identify some changes to the Earth's surface	193
	Identify some landforms on the Earth's surface	194, 195
	Describe Earth changes caused by internal processes	196
	Identify some features of the ocean and the ocean bottom	197, 198
	Identify properties and states of matter	199, 200
	Describe and define some changes in matter	200
	Identify some properties of air and the Earth's atmosphere	201, 202
	Recognize some types of clouds	202, 203
	Describe different kinds of precipitation and weather conditions	204
	Recognize the results of force; identify some forces	205
	Identify some simple machines	206
	Identify some characteristics and properties of sound	207
	Identify some characteristics and properties of heat	208
	Define and use science vocabulary terms	209

Alive and Well

All living things have something in common. They all grow and change. They all need air, light, and water. They all respond to environmental conditions.

Some living things are plants, some are animals.

Most plants have roots, stem, leaves, and flowers or fruit.

Finish the picture; label the parts.

Human beings are living things. If you could turn yourself inside out, you would see a skeleton comparable to this.

Draw the missing parts. Label the parts.

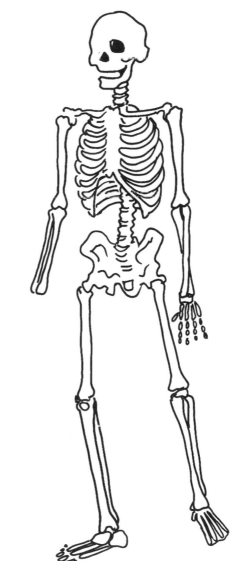

Name _____

Plenty of Bones

You are loaded with bones! If you didn't have them, your body would be all floppy like jelly. Bones are stiff. They support and hold all the softer body parts in place. It's a good thing bones are strong, because they protect important organs like the heart, lungs, brain, liver, and kidneys.

Draw a line from each bone to the correct term in the box below.

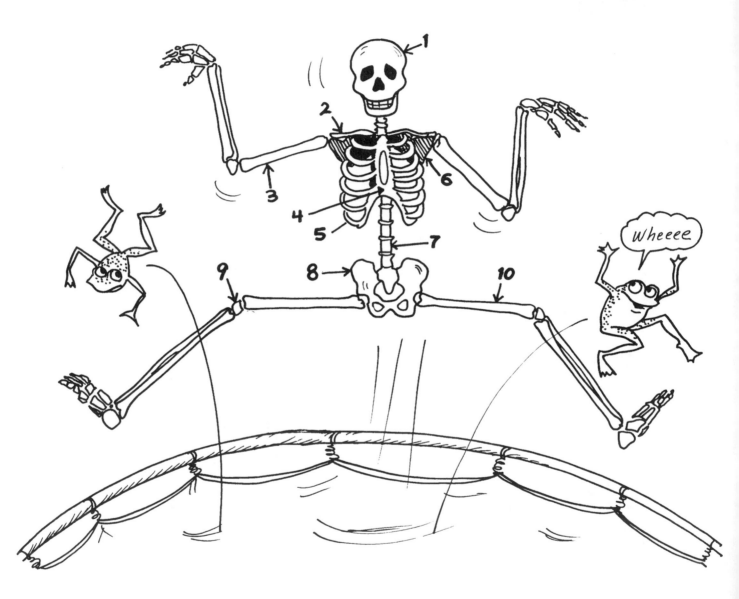

skull	collarbone	shoulder blade	humerus	kneecap
ribs	pelvis	backbone	breastbone	femur

Name _____

Body Parts in Hiding

Each word in the puzzle belongs to one of these body systems.
Color the puzzle pieces these colors:

Circulatory System—blue   **Respiratory System**—green
Skeleton-Muscle System—yellow   **Nervous System**—purple
Digestive System—red   **Senses**—black

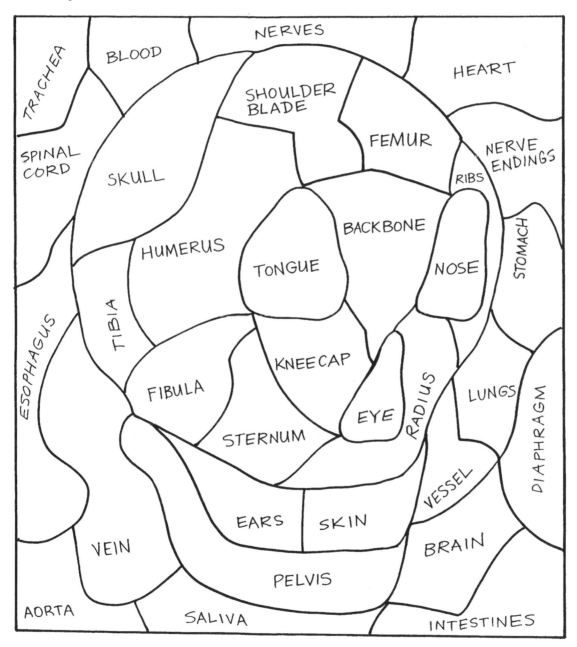

Which body part does the picture show? _____

Name _____

Aches & Pains

Chester is a mess! He has all kinds of aches and pains. Read each complaint he has. Decide which word matches his complaint. Write the number of the complaint beside the word.

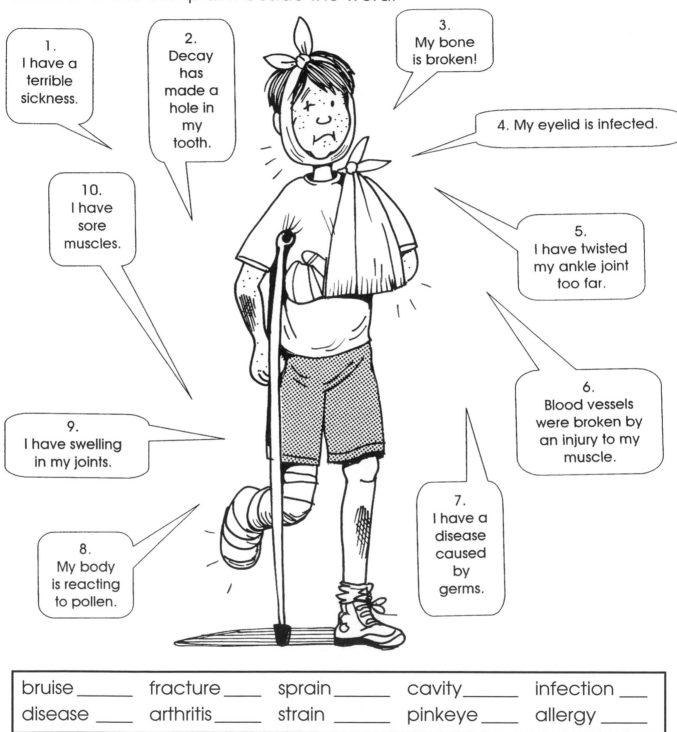

1. I have a terrible sickness.

2. Decay has made a hole in my tooth.

3. My bone is broken!

4. My eyelid is infected.

5. I have twisted my ankle joint too far.

6. Blood vessels were broken by an injury to my muscle.

7. I have a disease caused by germs.

8. My body is reacting to pollen.

9. I have swelling in my joints.

10. I have sore muscles.

bruise _____	fracture _____	sprain _____	cavity _____	infection ___
disease ___	arthritis _____	strain _____	pinkeye ___	allergy _____

Name _____

Body Talk

There are special words to use when you talk about the human body. Some of these words are pictured here.

Write the body word in the space with the same number as the matching picture.

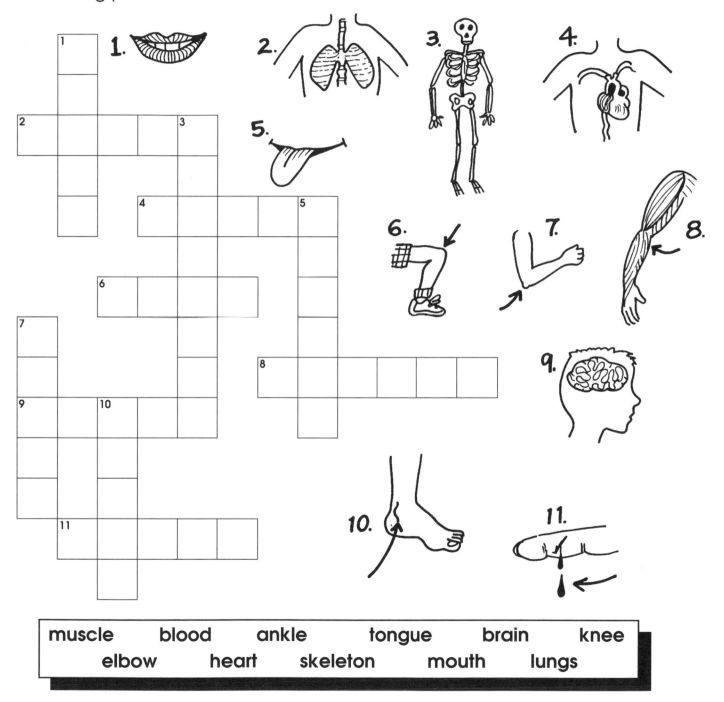

muscle	blood	ankle	tongue	brain	knee
elbow	heart	skeleton	mouth	lungs	

Name _____

Vocabulary

Health Opposites

There are 6 pairs of opposites shown here. In each pair, one twin is practicing a healthy behavior. The other twin is practicing something unhealthy or unsafe. Match the pairs of opposites by connecting them with a line.

Name _____

Health Behaviors

Safety First

Sam is excited about meeting his friends for a picnic in the park. In his rush to get there, he is overlooking some important safety precautions.

Look at the picture carefully. Then use the picture clues to select words from the word box to complete each sentence below.

Circle the unsafe situation.

WORD BOX

crossing	hands	signs
animals		lines

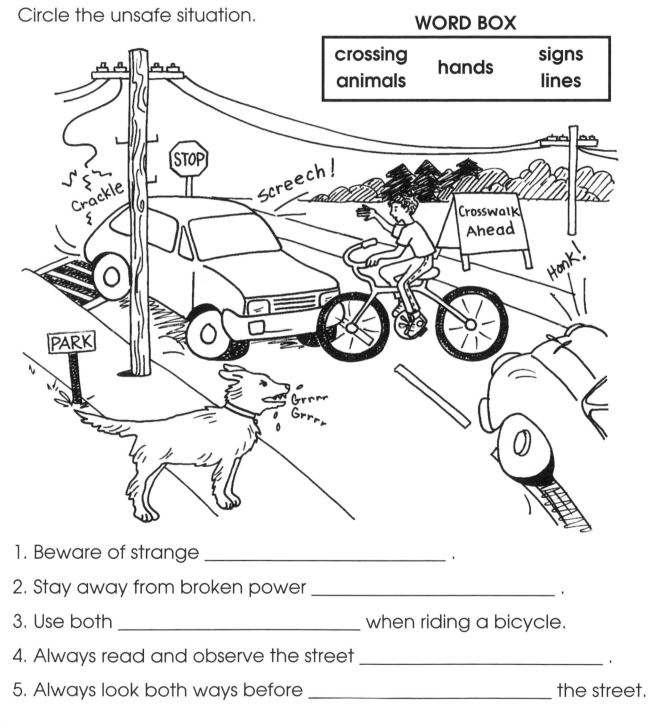

1. Beware of strange _____ .

2. Stay away from broken power _____ .

3. Use both _____ when riding a bicycle.

4. Always read and observe the street _____ .

5. Always look both ways before _____ the street.

Name _____

Refrigerator Inspection

Sam's refrigerator is crammed with all kinds of foods. Some of them will help him have a healthy diet.

Color the foods that are healthy for Sam to eat. Do not color foods that he should eat only in small amounts.

Name _____

Bodies in Space

There are things out in space called bodies. They don't look anything like our bodies. But they are out there, and many of them are moving.

Sue and Sam think they know a lot about the bodies in our solar system.

They have written down some things they think they know. Are they right?

Put **T** next to the correct statements.
Put **F** next to the ones that are not right.

_____ 1. The sun is a star.

_____ 2. The Earth turns every day.

_____ 3. The sun travels around the Earth.

_____ 4. The Earth travels around the sun.

_____ 5. The Earth travels around the moon.

_____ 6. The sun is the only star we can see.

_____ 7. The Earth is the closest planet to the sun.

_____ 8. The Earth is the largest planet in its solar system.

Name _____

Space Maze

5 astronauts are on trips through space. Color each path with the color given below to help them get to the right place.

Blue — Bob is on his way to the planet we live on.
Red — Bill is headed for the body that revolves around the Earth.
Green — Bo needs to get to the largest planet in the solar system.
Yellow — Bev is on her way to a planet that is next to Earth.
Purple — Barb wants to visit the star closest to Earth.

Name _____

Solar System

Cracks & Rumbles

Earth may look pretty solid on the surface, but lots of moving and rumbling takes place on the inside. Some of these inside changes cause big changes on the surface.

Solve this puzzle about some changes that start inside the Earth.

1. sudden movement of Earth's rock

2. melted rock that pours out of a volcano

3. dust-like matter that shoots out of a volcano

4. During an earthquake, Earth _____ .

5. a crack in Earth's surface

6. an earthquake vibration

7. A fault is a _____ in the Earth.

8. A volcano explodes, or _____ .

9. a mountain formed by material that has been forced out of the inside of the Earth

10. the top layer of Earth

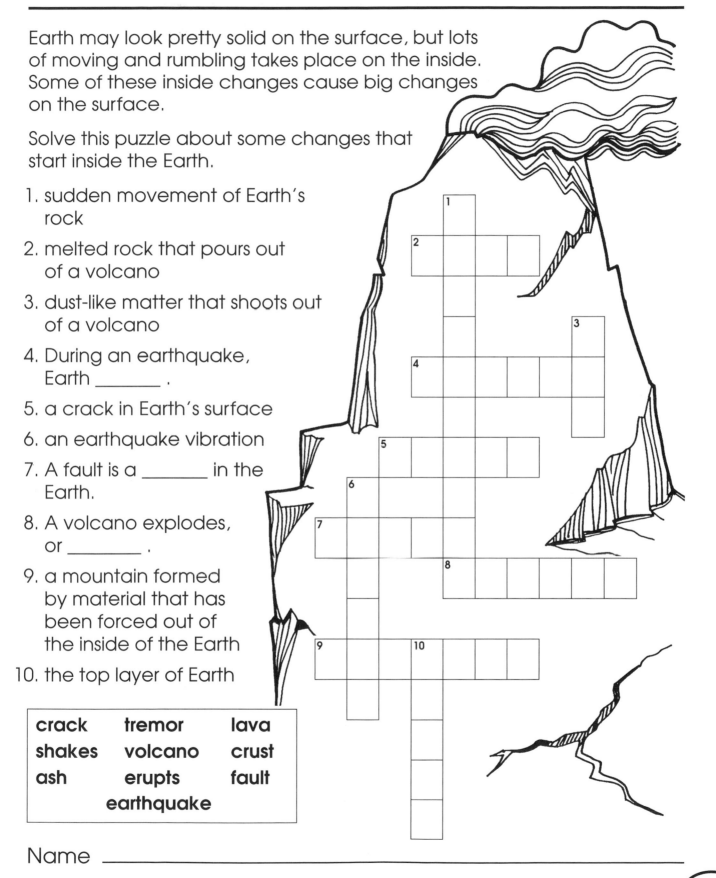

crack	tremor	lava
shakes	volcano	crust
ash	erupts	fault
	earthquake	

Name _____

Surface Search

The Earth's surface is covered with many different bumps, lumps, holes, and ditches. Most of these are called **landforms** or **bodies of water.**

Look at some of these landforms and bodies of water on the map on the next page (page 195). Do you know what they are?

Follow the directions below to show what you know.

1. Draw a ![man] standing on the plateau.

2. Draw two ![penguins] on the iceberg.

3. Draw a ![flag] flag on the mountain peak.

4. Put an ![X] on the source of the river.

5. Draw some ![trees] on the hill.

6. Draw a ![shark] in the ocean.

7. Draw a  in the lake.

8. Draw a ![palm tree] on the island.

9. Draw ![lighthouse] on the peninsula.

10. Draw a ![fish] in the waterfall.

11. Draw a ![raft] going down the river.

12. Draw a ![life ring] in the bay.

13. Write ![Help!] coming out of the canyon.

Name _____

Surface Search, continued . . .

Name _____

Use with page 194.

Earth Surface Features

Slow? Or Sudden?

The Earth is always changing. Sometimes it happens very slowly. Sometimes it happens fast—all of a sudden! It is wearing away and moving.

Clyde has gotten himself in the middle of many Earth changes. What is happening around Clyde? Draw a line from each picture to a word in the box that describes the change. Then tell whether the change is fast or slow by circling the right word.

1. fast?   slow?

2. fast?   slow?

3. fast?   slow?

4. fast?   slow?

DUNES

5. fast?   slow?

6. fast?   slow?

7. fast?   slow?

GRAND CANYON

| earthquake | volcano | moving water | fire |
| lightning | wind | people & machines | |

Name _____

Underwater Treasure Hunt

Help Dianna the diver find her way through the ocean to the treasure. Use a crayon to follow the path of words that name things found in the ocean. Don't let her wander into any wrong corners of the ocean bottom.

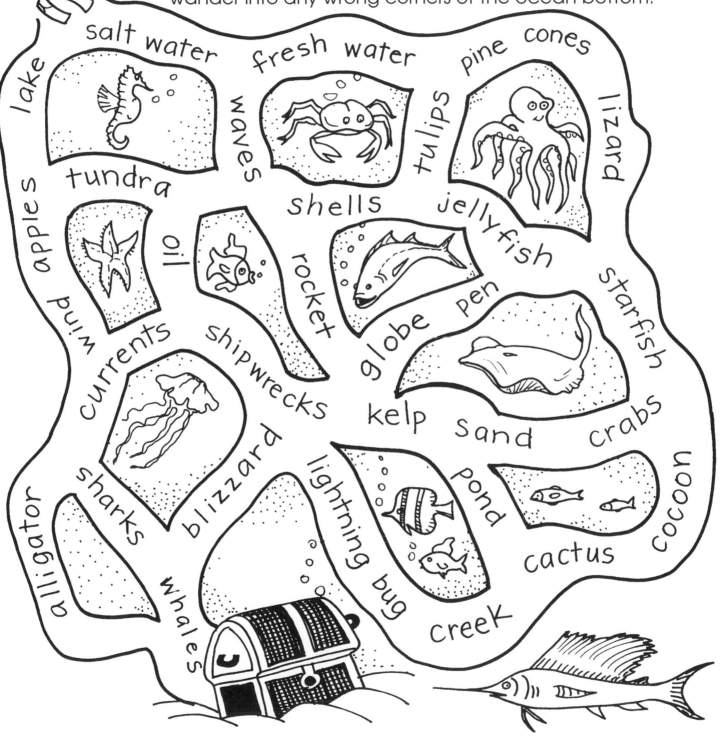

Name _____

Deep-Sea Facts

Where is the surfer? Where is the diver? Where is the lobster? If you know some facts about the ocean, you can answer these questions! Use the picture to find the answers. Write the answer to each question.

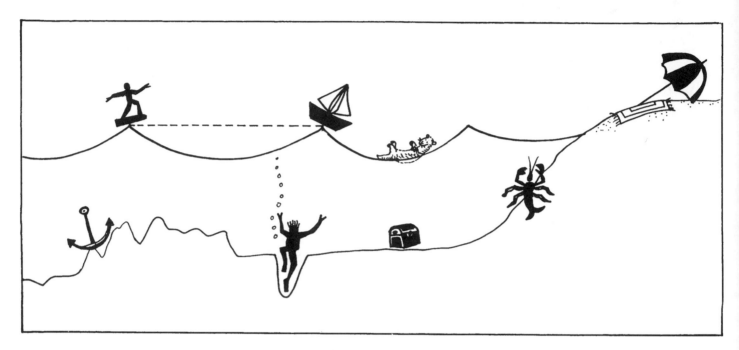

1. What are on the crests of the waves? _____ and _____

2. What is in the wave trough?_____

3. What is on the beach?_____

4. The wavelength is the distance
   between the surfer and the _____ .

5. What is on the ocean plane? _____

6. What is on the continental shelf? _____

7. What is on the underwater mountain range?_____

8. What is in the ocean trench?_____

Name _____

What's the Matter?

Matter is anything that takes up space and has weight.
There are 3 kinds of matter: solid, liquid, and gas.

Find 5 squares that have to do with solids. Color them red.
Find 6 squares that have to do with liquid. Color them blue.
Find 5 squares that have to do with gases.
Color them yellow.

solid		has a definite shape	
has a definite size			**liquid**
has no definite shape		has no definite shape	has no definite size
gas	can be poured		has a definite size

Name _____

A Matter of Change

Things are changing! Jonah's ice cubes disappeared when he left his lemonade in the sun. His wet hair dried, too! Matter comes in three forms (or states): solid, liquid, and gas. Each of these can change to other states. These changes have names.

For each name, tell what change is happening.

1.   **MELT** = a change from _____ to _____

2.   **FREEZE** = a change from _____ to _____

3. **EVAPORATE** = a change from _____ to _____

4. **CONDENSE** = a change from _____ to _____

Tell which kind of change is happening in each picture. Write one of the words above.

5. _____

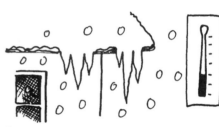

6. _____

7. _____

8. _____

9. _____

10. _____

Name _____

The Air Up There

The kites describe some things about the air around the Earth. Who is flying these kites? Draw a string from each kite to the word that matches it. Use a different color of string for each kite.

1. Water evaporates where it meets _____ .

2. the air that surrounds the Earth

3. when water turns into water vapor (a gas)

4. when water vapor turns into water

5. Clouds are made of tiny drops of _____ .

6. Water evaporates from lakes, rivers, & _____ .

EVAPORATE

OCEANS

WATER

CONDENSE

AIR

ATMOSPHERE

Name _____

Lost in the Clouds

This traveling bird is lost in the clouds. But what kind of cloud is he on?

A **cloud** forms when air cools. The cooling air causes water vapor (a gas) to condense into tiny drops of water. Sometimes these drops freeze. These tiny drops of water are clouds.

This page describes different kinds of clouds. Read about them.
Then look at the pictures on the next page.
Write the name of the cloud where each bird is flying or resting.

cumulus—large, thick, puffy clouds with a flat bottom
Cumulus clouds usually come with good weather.

cirrus—thin, wispy, white clouds that are high above the ground
They tell us the weather will change.

stratus—low, gray blanket of clouds that covers the sky
Stratus clouds often produce rain.

cumulonimbus—tall, towering clouds
They often produce rain, snow, or hail.

fog—stratus clouds that are very close to the ground

Name _____

Use with page 203.

Lost in the Clouds, continued . . .

Color the pictures on both pages.

Name _____

Use with page 202.

Ready for Anything

Tara is going on vacation. She doesn't know what kind of weather to expect, so she's decided to be ready for anything!

Read each weather report she might hear. Find the word that names that kind of weather condition. Write the word under the report.

1. "Watch out for a powerful, whirling funnel of air."

2. "There will be no clouds today."

3. "Droplets of water in the clouds will join together and pour down."

4. "Temperatures will rise to uncomfortable levels today."

5. "The air will move at very fast speeds tonight."

6. "Be prepared for heavy snow along with high winds."

7. "Be ready for a storm with flashes of electricity."

8. "There will be no precipitation this week."

blizzard dry hot
lightning
sunny
tornado
rain windy

Name _____

Pushing & Pulling

What's missing in this picture?

Draw what's missing in the picture.
What would make these things move?

A **force** is a push or
pull on something.

Name _____

Hidden Machines

There are 6 kinds of simple machines. Find 1 or more of each of these in the picture. Color it or outline it in color.

Machines do work.

A **machine** is used to change the amount or direction of a force.

lever

inclined plane

wedge

screw

wheel & axle

pulley

Name _____

The Sound of the Drum

When Todd hits his drum, a sound is made.
The sound travels through the air to his ears.

Each drum has a word about sound.
Each pair of drumsticks has a description to match one word.
Find the sticks to match each drum. Draw a line to connect them.

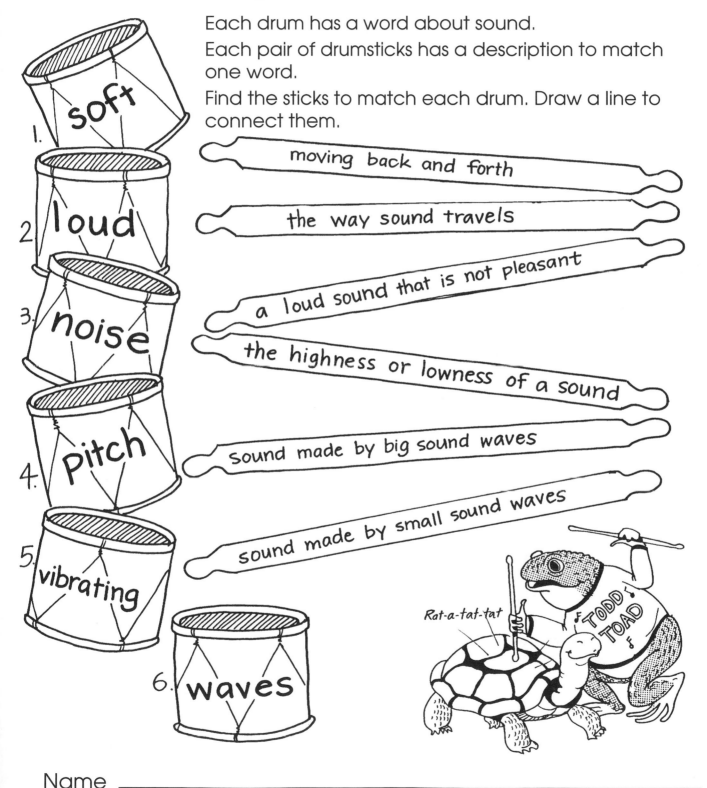

1. soft
2. loud
3. noise
4. pitch
5. vibrating
6. waves

moving back and forth

the way sound travels

a loud sound that is not pleasant

the highness or lowness of a sound

sound made by big sound waves

sound made by small sound waves

Rat-a-tat-tat

TODD TOAD

Name _____

Hot Words

Hiding in this puzzle are some words that have something to do with heat. Read the clues. Then find the word. The clues tell you what color to color each puzzle piece. Look out for hot words!

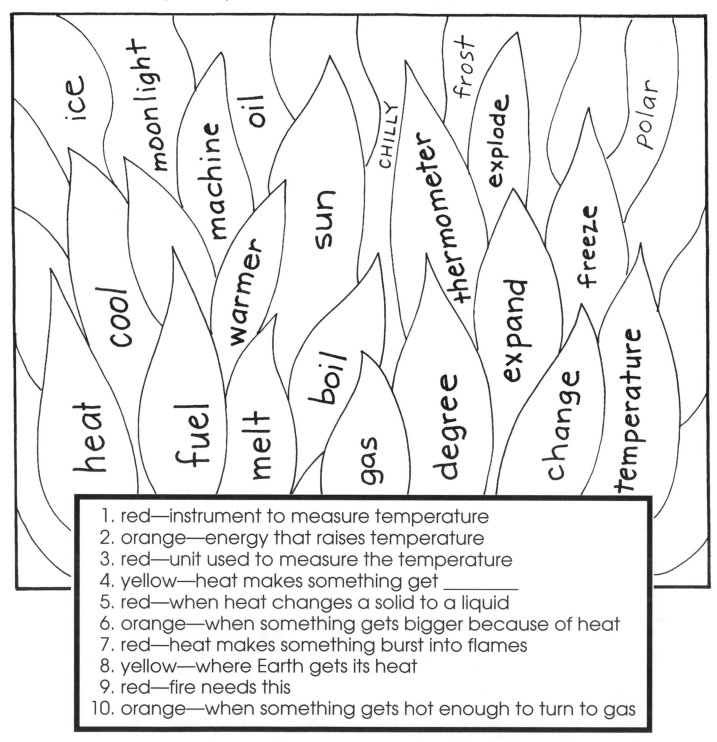

Words hidden in the puzzle: ice, moonlight, oil, machine, frost, explode, polar, warmer, sun, CHILLY, thermometer, cool, freeze, heat, expand, change, temperature, fuel, melt, boil, gas, degree

1. red—instrument to measure temperature
2. orange—energy that raises temperature
3. red—unit used to measure the temperature
4. yellow—heat makes something get _____
5. red—when heat changes a solid to a liquid
6. orange—when something gets bigger because of heat
7. red—heat makes something burst into flames
8. yellow—where Earth gets its heat
9. red—fire needs this
10. orange—when something gets hot enough to turn to gas

Name _____

Where Would You Find It?

Would you find a **patella** in your fruit salad?

Would you find a **vitamin** in the solar system?

Would you find a **pulley** in your blood?

Look at each science word.
Tell where you would find it.
Circle the correct answer.

Where would you find . . .

1. a patella?
   a. in your skeleton
   b. in a fruit salad
   c. inside a plant leaf

2. a planet?
   a. going around the Earth
   b. going around the sun
   c. floating in your blood

3. a stomata?
   a. on a plant's leaf
   b. in your stomach
   c. on a glacier

4. a cloud?
   a. on an amphibian
   b. in the atmosphere
   c. in a sound wave

5. a predator?
   a. in a plant seed
   b. circling Mars
   c. eating an animal

6. a casting?
   a. in a worm's burrow
   b. in your ear
   c. in a storm cloud

7. an inclined plane?
   a. in a flower
   b. in your digestive system
   c. in a machine

8. a conifer?
   a. orbiting the sun
   b. growing in a forest
   c. hibernating underground

Name _____

MATH

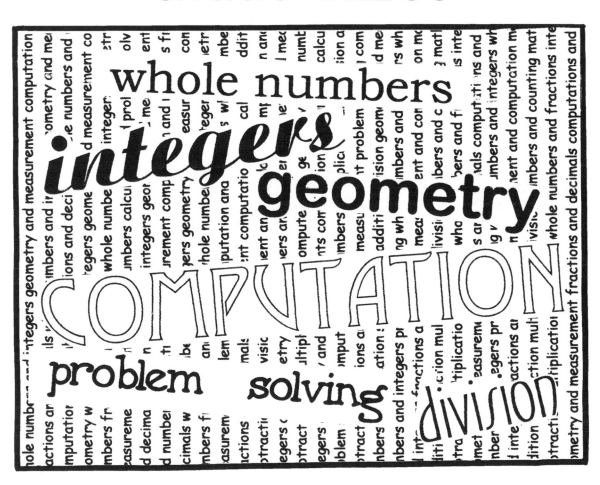

Skills Exercises
Grade Three

SKILLS CHECKLIST
NUMBER CONCEPTS & RELATIONSHIPS

✔	SKILL	PAGE(S)
	Read and compare whole numbers on number lines	215
	Match numerals to whole number word names	216
	Read and write whole numerals	216
	Identify odd and even numbers	217
	Explore big numbers	218
	Compare whole numbers using <, >, and = signs	219
	Compare number amounts using words (larger, smaller, greater, less, etc.)	220
	Use whole number concepts in problem-solving situations	221
	Identify place value through thousands	222, 223
	Read and write whole numbers in expanded notation	224, 225
	Recognize and extend number patterns and sequences	226
	Read and write fractions to match models	227–230
	Read and write mixed fractional numerals; match mixed numerals to models	227, 230, 231
	Match fractional numbers to match word names	227, 231
	Compare fractions using <, >, and = signs	232
	Compare fractions using words (larger, smaller, greater, less, etc.)	232
	Use fractions in problem-solving situations	233
	Count money	234, 235
	Identify values of coins	234, 235
	Estimate and compare amounts of money	236
	Show number sense	237
	Read decimals; recognize decimals on a number line	238
	Describe relationships between numbers	239–241
	Use number sentences to show relationships between numbers	240, 241
	Show understanding of simple probability concepts	242, 243

SKILLS CHECKLIST
GEOMETRY, MEASUREMENT, & GRAPHING

✔	SKILL	PAGE(S)
	Compare geometric figures	244
	Identify and draw different kinds of angles	244
	Identify and draw plane geometric figures	244
	Identify and draw points and lines	244
	Identify and use units for measuring length	246, 247
	Compare measurements and units of measure	246, 247, 253–255
	Identify and find length	246–249
	Do a variety of measurement tasks	246–258
	Find perimeter of plane figures	248, 249
	Estimate area of plane figures	250
	Find and compare area of plane figures	250, 251
	Explore volume concepts	252
	Identify and use units for measuring weight	253, 254
	Identify and find units for measuring liquid capacity	255
	Perform a variety of time-telling tasks	256, 257
	Solve problems with time	257
	Solve problems with measurements	257–259
	Answer questions from data on graphs and charts	260–269
	Read a variety of graphs	261–269
	Make simple graphs	263
	Locate items on a grid	264, 265
	Place items on a grid	266–269
	Use math vocabulary correctly	270

SKILLS CHECKLIST
MATH COMPUTATION & PROBLEM SOLVING

✔	SKILL	PAGE(S)
	Identify place value to 6 places	273
	Read and write whole numbers	273, 278, 279, 284
	Identify odd and even numbers	275
	Work with ordinals	276
	Identify patterns in groups of numbers	279
	Compare and order whole numbers	279–281, 274, 277
	Solve problems using illustrations	280, 292–295, 297–299
	Compare measurements	282, 283
	Round numbers to the nearest place	284
	Use addition facts to 20; identify fact families	285
	Use subtraction facts to 20; identify fact families	285
	Check accuracy of answers	286
	Add whole numbers with and without renaming	286, 287, 291, 294
	Subtract whole numbers with and without renaming	286, 287, 291, 294
	Use multiplication/division facts for 1–10; identify fact families	288, 289
	Skip count	289
	Do simple division computations	290, 291
	Use multiplication for computations	291
	Use estimation and mental math to make computations	291, 294
	Find missing numbers in simple equations	292
	Choose the correct operation for a problem	293, 304, 305
	Read and write fractions	295–298
	Add and subtract fractions with like denominators	296
	Identify some equivalent fractions	297
	Write fractions (with tenths) as decimals	298
	Read, write, and order decimals	298, 299
	Complete a variety of time-telling tasks; work with dates	300–302
	Solve problems using maps, charts, and tables	300–302
	Solve word problems, including multi-step problems	300, 305
	Count money	303
	Solve problems with money	303, 304
	Write, compare, and estimate amounts of money	303, 304

The Swamptown Races

The Swamptown Derby Race is one of the biggest events of the year.

Follow the directions to figure out who is where on the 400-meter race track.

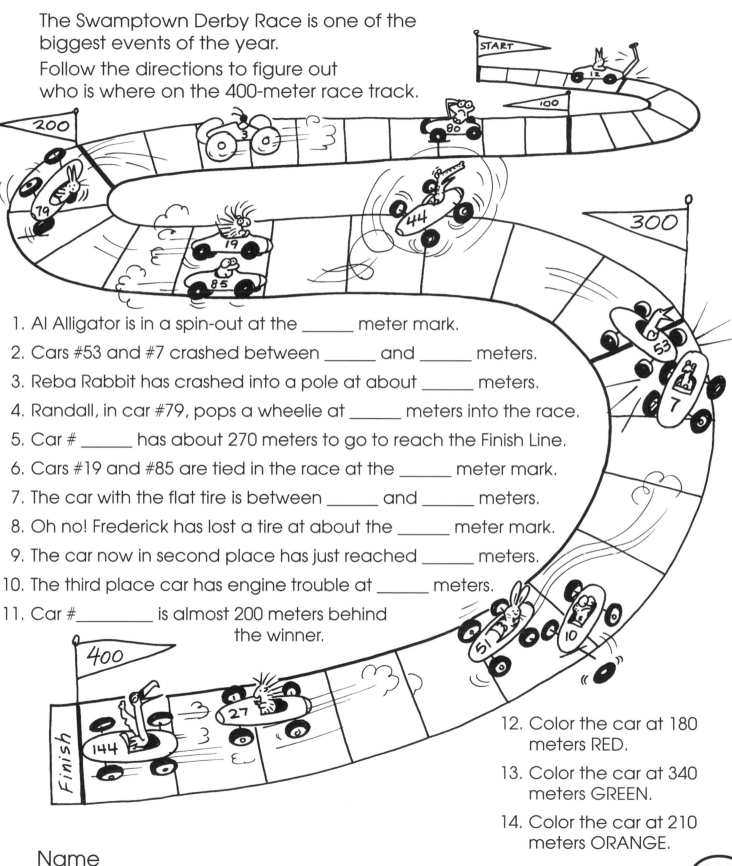

1. Al Alligator is in a spin-out at the _____ meter mark.

2. Cars #53 and #7 crashed between _____ and _____ meters.

3. Reba Rabbit has crashed into a pole at about _____ meters.

4. Randall, in car #79, pops a wheelie at _____ meters into the race.

5. Car # _____ has about 270 meters to go to reach the Finish Line.

6. Cars #19 and #85 are tied in the race at the _____ meter mark.

7. The car with the flat tire is between _____ and _____ meters.

8. Oh no! Frederick has lost a tire at about the _____ meter mark.

9. The car now in second place has just reached _____ meters.

10. The third place car has engine trouble at _____ meters.

11. Car #_____ is almost 200 meters behind the winner.

12. Color the car at 180 meters RED.

13. Color the car at 340 meters GREEN.

14. Color the car at 210 meters ORANGE.

Name _____

Bayou Bouncers

The baby alligators are bouncing on the boggy trampoline in the bayou.
Listen to them bragging about their bounces!
Write the whole number word names to go with each number.

A.
I bounced 4,900 times!

B.
My sister bounced 620 times!

C.
Can you bounce 2,000 times?

D.
I am on bounce number 77!

E.
Yesterday, I bounced 990!

F.
I am going to bounce to 10,000!

G.
I just got up to 333!

Write the words.

A. _____

B. _____

C. _____

D. _____

E. _____

F. _____

G. _____

Name _____

Read & Write Whole Numbers;
Match Numerals to Word Names

Soaring Over the Swamp

Soaring over the swamp in parachutes can be tricky!

Ouch! Watch out for that tree!

If a part of the parachute has an ODD number, color it green, purple, or blue.

If a part of the parachute has an EVEN number, color it red, orange, or yellow.

1. Write an **ODD** number. Use these:

   4 3 0 _____

2. Write an **EVEN** number. Use these:

   2 7 9 _____

3. Write an **ODD** number. Use these:

   1 0 8 0 _____

4. Write an **EVEN** number. Use these:

   5 6 7 _____

Name _____

Dragonfly Dive-Bombers

Three billion bugs are buzzing in the bog!
Some of them are bugging Mr. Muskrat on his morning jog.
Every dragonfly has a number.
Draw a line from the question to the matching dragonfly.

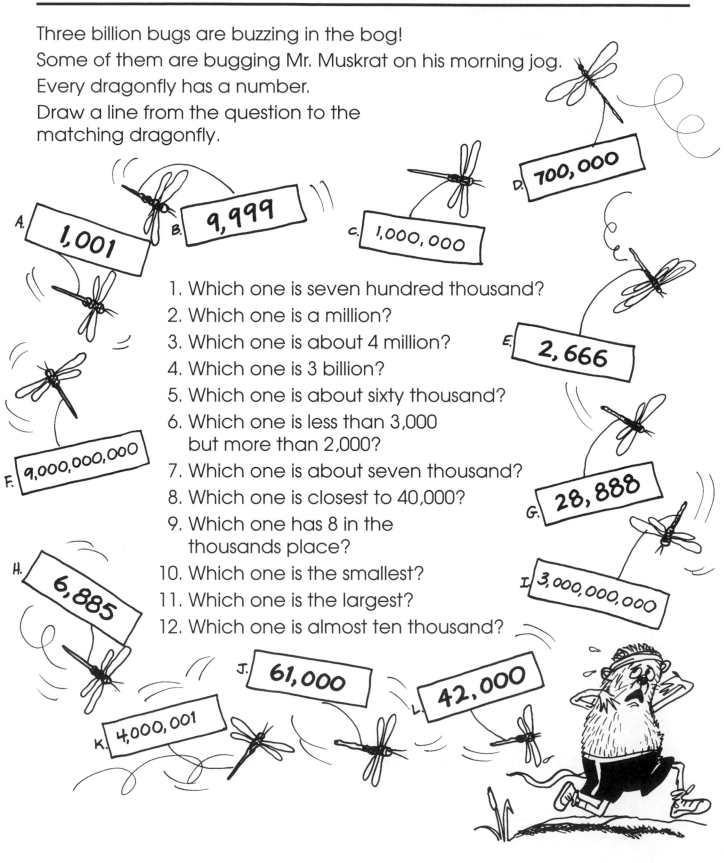

D. **700,000**

C. **1,000,000**

A. **1,001**

B. **9,999**

E. **2,666**

F. **9,000,000,000**

G. **28,888**

I. **3,000,000,000**

H. **6,885**

1. Which one is seven hundred thousand?
2. Which one is a million?
3. Which one is about 4 million?
4. Which one is 3 billion?
5. Which one is about sixty thousand?
6. Which one is less than 3,000 but more than 2,000?
7. Which one is about seven thousand?
8. Which one is closest to 40,000?
9. Which one has 8 in the thousands place?
10. Which one is the smallest?
11. Which one is the largest?
12. Which one is almost ten thousand?

J. **61,000**

L. **42,000**

K. **4,000,001**

Name
Explore Big Numbers

Some Fishy Problems

Pokey Porcupine and Finn Frog are fishing for "problems" today.
Who will catch the most?
Write the symbol that is missing from each number sentence. (<, >, or =)

Finn is fishing for "greater than" problems.
How many of these are in the water?

Pokey is fishing for "less than" problems.
How many of these are in the water?

A. 440 ☐ 540

H. 67,321 ☐ 67,231

B. 1,001 ☐ 1,100

C. 40 + 50 ☐ 90

I. 779 ☐ 797

D. 10,000 ☐ 11,000

E. 5,005 ☐ 5,500

J. 50 + 10 ☐ 70 – 10

F. 222 ☐ 202

K. 10 x 10 ☐ 200

L. 999 ☐ 899

G. 20,000 ☐ 19,009

M. 200,000 ☐ 20,000

Name

Use Symbols to Compare Whole Numbers

Swampy Olympics

The Hokee Penokee Swamp has the world's tiniest underwater Olympics.
The athletes are SO small that they are measured in MICRONS.
You would have to line up 25,000 MICRONS to make one inch.
Study the chart to answer the questions about the tiny Olympic athletes.

Animal	Size
Water Flea	1,520 microns
Stento	1,200 microns
Coiled Vorticella	801 microns
Wheel Animal	2,160 microns
Water Bear	1,305 microns
Cyclops Water Hopper	4,432 microns
Walking Bean	986 microns
Water Mite	8,333 microns

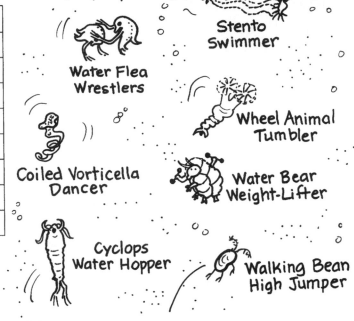

Water Flea Wrestlers

Stento Swimmer

Coiled Vorticella Dancer

Wheel Animal Tumbler

Water Bear Weight-Lifter

Cyclops Water Hopper

Walking Bean High Jumper

Water Mite Diver

1. Which athlete is the longest?
_____

2. Which athlete is the smallest?
_____

3. Which is between the walking bean and the water bear in size?
_____

4. Which is smaller than the stento but larger than the vorticella?
_____

5. Which is bigger, the wheel animal or the cyclops water hopper? *(Circle one.)*

6. Which is shorter, the water flea or the water mite? *(Circle one.)*

7. Which is longer, the coiled vorticella or the stento? *(Circle one.)*

8. Circle the greatest in size:
water flea, cyclops water hopper, wheel animal

9. Circle the least in size:
stento, walking bean, water mite

10. Circle the one larger than the wheel animal: water mite, stento, water flea

11. Circle the smallest of these:
walking bean, coiled vorticella, water bear

12. Which animal is about 1,000 microns larger than the stento?
_____

Muggy Work-Outs

The swamp can be a hot and muggy place, especially when you are exercising.

Read about the swamp critters and their workouts. Then solve their problems.

1. Finn Frog jumped rope so many times! He rounded the number to the nearest ten and got 2,230. Circle the number of times he jumped.

   a. 2,238   b. 2,130   c. 2,227

2. Slicky Snake did 27 push-ups on Monday. Sammy did 14 more than Slicky. About how many did Sammy do? (Circle the answer.)

   About: 40 35 60 15 50

3. Pokey Porcupine did a whole lot of jumping Jacks. The number he did is an odd number larger than 500. It has these digits: 8, 3, 4. What is the number? _____

4. Catfish workouts include flying leaps in the air.
   Big Daddy did 4,020.
   Big Mama did 4,420.
   Big Baby did 4,002.
   Big Sissy did 4,040.
   Who did four thousand forty?

   _____

5. Cranky Crocodile swam 170 laps. Charlie swam 50 laps less. How many did Charlie swim?

   _____

6. Six friends jogged for these lengths of time:
   Allie: 27 minutes
   Abby: 92 minutes
   Alfy: 64 minutes
   Andy: 51 minutes
   Angie: 38 minutes
   Aggie: 19 minutes
   Who jogged the 2nd longest time?

   _____

7. Molly Muskrat did 3,033 tail lifts. How many is this? (Circle the answer.)
   a. three thousand and three
   b. three thousand three hundred thirty
   c. three thousand thirty three
   d. three thousand thirty

8. Darla Dragonfly did the number of stretches that is about 30 more than 200. How many did she do? (Circle the answer.)
   228 218 280 170 152

Name _____

Snorkeling with Sam

Tootsie Turtle was invited to go snorkeling with Snorkel Sam.
See what they discover underwater in the Hokee Penokee Swamp!
Find the numbers of things they saw by using
the clues below.

1. Sam saw this many spoonbill catfish:

   ☐ ☐ ☐ ☐ *Clues:*

   - The 5 is in the ones place.
   - The 6 is in the tens place.
   - The 2 is in the hundreds place.
   - The 3 is in the thousands place.

2. Tootsie saw this many tiny snails:
   (Use 1, 2, 6, & 6.)

   ☐ ☐ ☐ ☐ *Clues:*

   - The greatest numbers are in
     the tens and thousands places.
   - The ones place has the
     smallest number.

3. Sam and Tootsie gawked at this many
   purple sunfish: (Use 3, 2, 5, & 9.)

   ☐ ☐ ☐ ☐ *Clues:*

   - The smallest number is in the
     thousands place.
   - The greatest number is in
     the ones place.
   - The 5 is in the tens place.

4. They blew this many air bubbles:
   (Use 5, 8, 0, & 4.)

   ☐ ☐ ☐ ☐ *Clues:*

   - The biggest number is in the
     thousands place.
   - An ODD number is in the ones place.
   - A 0 is in the hundreds place.

5. Sam and Tootsie gazed at this many
   yellow-bellied carp: (Use 7, 3, 6, & 2)

   ☐ ☐ ☐ ☐ *Clues:*

   - The 7 is in the tens place.
   - The number in the thousands place is
     TWICE the number in the hundreds
     place.

6. They saw this many tadpoles:
   (Use 2, 4, 1, & 6)

   ☐ ☐ ☐ ☐ *Clues:*

   - The largest number is in the thousands
     place.
   - The smallest number is in the ones place
   - The number in the tens place is < the
     number in the hundreds place.

7. They saw this many crayfish:
   (Use 1, 0, 0, and 7)

   ☐ ☐ ☐ ☐ *Clues:*

   - The numbers in the hundreds and ones
     places are even numbers.
   - The largest number is in the tens place.

Name

Place Value

Staying Cool

Staying cool on a hot, muggy swamp day is simply heavenly!
Flossy is not only cool. She is also feeling lazy.

Help her solve the number puzzle.
Read the clues.

Then write the correct numerals in
the right puzzle spaces.

CLUES

ACROSS
  A. 9 ones and 8 tens
  B. 7 hundreds, 4 tens, 6 ones
  E. 5 hundreds, 5 tens, 5 ones,
       3 thousands
  G. 2 ones and 4 thousands
  H. 5 thousands, 7 hundreds,
       3 tens, 6 ones
  J. 9 ones, 1 hundred, 2 thousands
  L. 8 hundreds, 9 thousands, 7 tens
  N. 3 tens, 5 ones, 1 hundred

DOWN
  A. 8 thousands, 6 hundreds,
       6 tens, 5 ones
  C. 3 tens, 2 ones, 6 thousands
  D. 90 thousands, 7 ones
  F. 5 thousands, 7 hundreds,
       2 ones
  I. 2 tens, 6 hundreds
  J. 2 thousands, 4 hundreds,
       8 tens, 3 ones
  K. 9 ones, 9 tens
  M. 7 tens, 7 thousands, 1 hundred
  N. 6 ones, 1 ten

Name

Place Value

Turtle Hurdles

The crickets need some hurdles for their track race.

They have decided to use the turtles for hurdles!

Help them finish the race by finishing the problems.

Below each turtle is a number written to show the place value of each digit.

Write a BIG numeral on the turtle to match the expanded number.

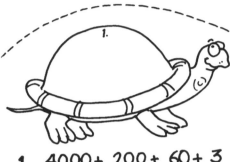

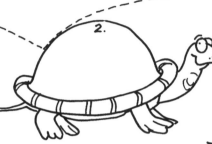

1. 4,000 + 200 + 60 + 3

2. 1,000 + 800 + 10

3. 9,000 + 200 + 40 + 6

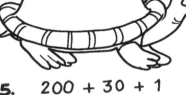

4. 7,000 + 200 + 20 + 1

5. 200 + 30 + 1

6. 5,000 + 200 + 2

How far did the crickets leap today?

Write the expanded number on the line.

Sample: 6,294 feet = <u>6000 + 200 + 90 + 4</u>

7. Cissy Cricket hopped 329 feet = _____

8. Crusty Cricket hopped 678 feet = _____

9. Crabby Cricket hopped 590 feet = _____

10. Creaky Cricket hopped 1,572 feet = _____

11. Charlie Cricket hopped 4,477 feet = _____

12. Chirpy Cricket hopped 2,831 feet = _____

Name _____

Expanded Notation

Bubble-Blowing Bats

The Bat twins are blowing bubbles while they relax after flying practice.
Oops! Some of the answers in the bubbles are WRONG.

Find the correct bubbles. Color them different colors.

Do NOT color bubbles with wrong answers.

Take your pencil and "pop" the wrong ones. Write the correct number inside!

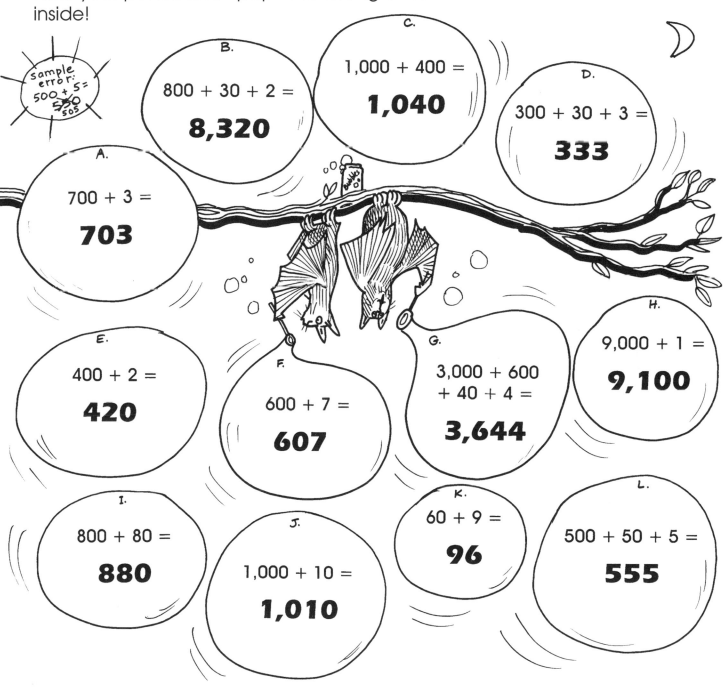

sample error:
$500 + 5 =$
~~550~~
505

B.
$800 + 30 + 2 =$
8,320

C.
$1,000 + 400 =$
1,040

D.
$300 + 30 + 3 =$
333

A.
$700 + 3 =$
703

E.
$400 + 2 =$
420

F.
$600 + 7 =$
607

G.
$3,000 + 600 + 40 + 4 =$
3,644

H.
$9,000 + 1 =$
9,100

I.
$800 + 80 =$
880

J.
$1,000 + 10 =$
1,010

K.
$60 + 9 =$
96

L.
$500 + 50 + 5 =$
555

Name _____

Expanded Notation

Butterfly Show-Offs

The flying of Team Butterfly is one of the best parts of the Swamptown Air Show.

They always fly in difficult and beautiful patterns.

Notice the pattern of decoration on the butterflies.

Finish the pattern by drawing the designs on the last butterfly.

Figure out each pattern. Draw or write the missing parts to finish the pattern.

1.

2.

3.

4. **10, 11, 20, 21, 30, 31, ___, ___**

5.

6. **bit, bite, rat, rate, cut, _____, mat, mate, kit, _____**

Obstacles in the Swamp

Arthur loves to jet ski around the swamp.

He must use all his skill, because the swamp is full of obstacles.

Look at the obstacles in the swamp. Read the fractional numerals on them.

Look in the picture to find the fractional number that matches each set of words.

Write the number next to the correct words.

1. two thirds _____

2. ten and four fifths _____

3. five and three fourths _____

4. one quarter _____

5. three quarters _____

6. two fourths _____

7. five and six tenths _____

8. eight thirds _____

9. ten halves _____

10. two and two fourths _____

11. two and three halves _____

12. three and one fourth _____

Name

Match Fractional Numerals to Word Names

Dance Till You Drop

At the Swampville Line Dancing Contest, the last one left dancing is the winner. These dancers are still going strong!

There are 6 dancers. 1 of them is singing. So, $\frac{1}{6}$ of the dancers are singing.

There are 12 feet. On 2 of the feet there are work boots. So, $\frac{2}{12}$ of the feet have on work boots.

Write a fraction to answer each question about the dancers at the top of the page.

1. What fraction of the dancers are wearing skirts? _____

2. What fraction of the dancers are wearing hats? _____

3. What fraction of the dancers have on vests? _____

4. What fraction of the dancers are prickly? _____

5. What fraction of the dancers have a hair flower? _____

6. What fraction of the feet are wearing cowboy boots? _____

7. What fraction of the feet are bare feet? _____

8. What fraction of the feet are bear feet? _____

9. What fraction of the bandannas are black? _____

10. What fraction of the vests have fringe? _____

11. What fraction of the girls have hair bows? _____

12. What fraction of the skirts have flowers? _____

13. What fraction of the skirts have fringe? _____

14. What fraction of the hats are white? _____

Name

Eyes in the Night

The soccer game was not over until after dark.
As Finn Frog was on his way home, he lost his way in the thick, dark forest.
He feels as if someone is watching him in the night. Is he right?

Write a fraction to answer
each question about the eyes.

Sample: How many pairs of eyes are
shaped like triangles? $\frac{1}{14}$

1. How many pairs are open? _____

2. How many pairs are asleep? _____

3. How many pairs have eyelids? _____

4. How many pairs have eyebrows? _____

5. How many pairs are round or oval? _____

6. How many pairs are cross-eyed? _____

7. How many pairs belong to tiny creatures? _____

8. How many pairs look mad? _____

9. How many pairs are shaped like diamonds? _____

10. How many pairs are shaped like squares? _____

Name _____

Write Fractions; Match Fractions to Models

Dinner at Dino's Diner

Dino makes the most delicious pizzas for all the Swamp Little League teams.
Take a look at how much pizza these players are eating!
Read the fraction and color the pizzas to show how much
each team has eaten.

1. The Frog Legs ate $2\frac{2}{3}$ pizzas.

2. The Possum Pistols ate $3\frac{1}{5}$ pizzas.

3. The Alligator Alleycats ate $3\frac{5}{6}$ pizzas.

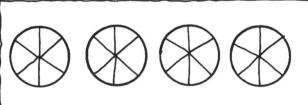

4. The Ladybugs ate $1\frac{7}{8}$ pizzas.

6. The Turtle Terrors ate _____?

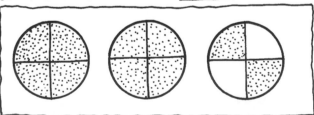

5. The Pelican Pitchers ate $2\frac{2}{5}$ pizzas.

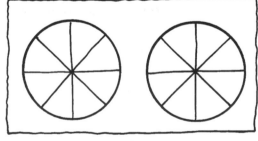

7. The Slippery Snakes ate _____

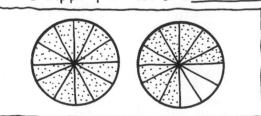

Name

Write Mixed Numerals to Match Models

Daring Dives

The judges at the diving contest were dazzled by Flossie!
She performed her famous jackknife dive very well.

The judges each gave Flossie a score of $9 \frac{7}{10}$ points.
Which words tell her score? Circle the answer.

    a. ninety-seven and seven tenths
    b. nine tenths
    c. nine and seven tenths
    d. nine and seven hundredths.

Write the mixed fraction numerals to match these.

1. sixteen and five ninths _____

2. ten and two thirds _____

3. forty-five and one half _____

4. twenty-two and five sixths _____

5. twelve and two fifths _____

6. eighteen and eight ninths _____

7. eight and one seventh _____

8. twenty-five and two thirds _____

9. five and sixteen twentieths _____

10. twelve and three fourths _____

11. fifteen and six eighths _____

12. ten and one sixth _____

Write the words to match these.

13. $20 \frac{4}{5}$ _____

14. $10 \frac{1}{6}$ _____

15. $9 \frac{3}{4}$ _____

16. $2 \frac{1}{3}$ _____

Name _____

Match Fractional Numerals to Word Names

The Great Shell Race

Hurrah! The Swampville Hardshells have finally pulled ahead in the big race!

The Bogtown Racers were ahead for $\frac{1}{4}$ of the race.

Now the Hardshells have been ahead for $\frac{2}{4}$ of the race.

How much of the race is left? _____

Circle the answer to each question about comparing fractions.

1. Which fraction is greater? $\frac{6}{8}$ $\frac{1}{4}$

2. Which shows a smaller amount? $2\frac{1}{2}$ $1\frac{9}{10}$

3. Which is less than $1\frac{3}{4}$? $3\frac{3}{4}$ $1\frac{1}{2}$ $2\frac{1}{4}$ $2\frac{3}{4}$

4. Which shows a greater amount than $10\frac{1}{3}$? $9\frac{2}{3}$ $10\frac{1}{9}$ $9\frac{1}{3}$ $10\frac{1}{2}$ $9\frac{1}{2}$

5. Which fraction shows the largest amount? $\frac{1}{2}$ $\frac{1}{10}$ $\frac{1}{4}$ $\frac{1}{5}$

Write <, >, or = in each space.

6. $6\frac{1}{2}$ ☐ $\frac{3}{4}$ 11. $4\frac{9}{10}$ ☐ $4\frac{1}{10}$

7. $\frac{9}{10}$ ☐ $\frac{1}{4}$ 12. $\frac{1}{3}$ ☐ $\frac{2}{3}$

8. $\frac{2}{5}$ ☐ $\frac{4}{5}$ 13. $100\frac{1}{2}$ ☐ $100\frac{8}{10}$

9. $\frac{5}{6}$ ☐ $\frac{1}{2}$ 14. $5\frac{3}{10}$ ☐ $4\frac{9}{10}$

10. $\frac{1}{2}$ ☐ $\frac{2}{4}$ 15. $\frac{1}{5}$ ☐ $\frac{1}{10}$

Name _____

Compare Fractions

Picnic Problems

Oh, oh! Some things have gone wrong at the Hokee Penokee Picnic.

Read about the problems. Then find the answers.

A. $\frac{4}{5}$ of the boiled bumblebee nests were spoiled by the rain. Write this number in words.

_____

B. $\frac{2}{3}$ pounds of the barbecue bark chips washed away into the swamp. Write this number in words. _____

C. Tootsie Turtle and Freddy Frog ate too much. Freddy ate $42\frac{4}{5}$ swamp moss pancakes. Tootsie ate $42\frac{1}{2}$ swamp moss pancakes. Who ate more?

_____

D. $\frac{5}{9}$ of the frozen chocolate slush mud servings melted. Another $\frac{2}{9}$ were sat on by Grandma Crocodile. How much was ruined in all? _____

E. The baby frogs found the candied bugs before the feast. Baby Fran ate $6\frac{1}{2}$. Baby Frankie ate $2\frac{1}{2}$ bugs. All together, did they eat more than 10 bugs?

_____

F. Cook ordered $222\frac{3}{4}$ pounds of swamp cookies for the feast. The order was 200 pounds short. How many pounds of cookies came?

_____

G. Only $\frac{3}{7}$ of the stuffed moss ball appetizers were ready on time. Write this number in words.

_____

H. The Floppy Mud Puppy Band arrived $3\frac{1}{4}$ hours late because their boat got tangled in tree roots. The singers arrived $3\frac{9}{10}$ hours late. Who was the latest, the band or the singers?

_____

Name _____

Problem Solving with Fractional Numbers

Pocket Change

The skunk sisters, Suzi and Samantha, are off to the Hokee Penokee basketball game with their pockets full of coins!

They plan to buy lots of popcorn and candy.

Help them count their money by answering these questions.

1. Suzi uses 3 coins on a milkshake that costs 60¢.
   What are the coins? _____

2. Samantha brings 4 coins out of her pocket that total 22¢.
   What are the coins? _____

3. Suzi uses 5 coins that total 25¢.
   What are the coins? _____

4. Samantha says, "All my 4 coins are different, and I have 41¢."
   What are the coins? _____

5. Suzi says, "I have 26¢ and I have only 2 coins."
   What are the coins? _____

6. Samantha says, "I have 7 coins that make a dollar."
   What are the coins? _____

7. Samantha buys popcorn for 45¢. Can she do this with exactly 9 coins? _____

8. Suzi has 4 coins in her pocket. What 4 coins would give her enough money to buy an 80¢ drink ? _____
   _____ Will she get any change? _____

9. At the end of the game, Suzi has 3 dimes and 2 quarters. How much does she have? _____

10. At the end of the game, Samantha has 6 nickels and 4 pennies. How much does she have? _____

Name
Identify Coin Values; Count Money

River Bottom Surprises

Ollie and Ara Otter are so excited!
They have spotted a whole pile of coins on the
bottom of the river.
Tell how much money they find each time they dive.

1. Ollie found 2 quarters, and 3 dimes. How much? _____

2. Ara found 1 quarter, 5 nickels, and 2 dimes. How much? _____

3. Ara found 3 quarters, 2 dimes, and 4 pennies. How much? _____

4. Ollie dived for 2 pennies, 1 dime, and 2 nickels. How much? _____

5. Ara got 2 nickels, 6 dimes, and 8 pennies. How much? _____

6. Ollie dived for 7 dimes, 3 nickels, and 1quarter. How much? _____

7. Ollie found 4 dimes. Ara found 2 quarters and 1 nickel.
   Who found more? _____

8. Ara found 9 coins equaling 45¢. What are the coins? _____
   _____

9. Ollie found 4 coins that totaled 85¢. What coins did he find?
   _____

10. Ara found 6 coins totaling 42¢. What coins did she find?
    _____

11. Ara found 5 quarters. Ollie found 15 dimes. Who found
    more money? _____

12. Ollie found 10 nickels. Ara found 6 dimes and 3 nickels.
    Who found more money? _____

Name

Swamp Meet Ticket Sale

Today is the day that tickets go on sale for the Spring Swamp Meet. Help the Rabbit family solve their money questions before they buy their tickets.

Two adults and 27 children, please.

SPRING SWAMP MEET
Get Your Tickets Here

EVENT	PRICE
Swamp Soccer Game	$ 4.85
Alligator Wrestling Match	$ 12.20
Bayou Basketball Game	$ 7.15
Swampy River Swim Meet	$ 3.80
Trampoline Tournament	$ 6.90
Frog Leap Finals	$ 8.25
Dance Contest	$ 7.90
Water Ski Races	$ 17.00
High Dive Show	$ 9.90

1. Which tickets are about $5.00? _____

2. Which tickets are close to $8.00? _____

3. Which tickets are about $10 more than those for the basketball game? _____

4. Would $20 be enough to buy a ticket to the Alligator Wrestling Match and the Swim Meet? _____

5. Which tickets cost about $3.00 more than the Swim Meet tickets?
   _____

6. Which cost the least? _____

7. Which tickets are closest in price to the Frog Leap Finals?
   _____

8. About how much would it cost for four Rabbit family members to watch the Trampoline Tournament? _____

9. Which ticket is about $10.00? _____

10. Which ticket is closest to $20.00? _____

11. Could someone buy 2 tickets to the Dance Contest for $15? _____

12. Will it cost the Rabbit Family about $280 to all see the High Dive Show? _____

Name _____
Estimate & Compare Amounts of Money

Number Sense or Nonsense?

When he sleeps on his tree limb in the swamp, Ollie Owl dreams of numbers.
Some of his dreams are pretty outrageous! Could they be true?
If the numbers in one of his dreams make sense, color it BLUE.
If the numbers in one of his dreams do
NOT make sense, color it ORANGE.

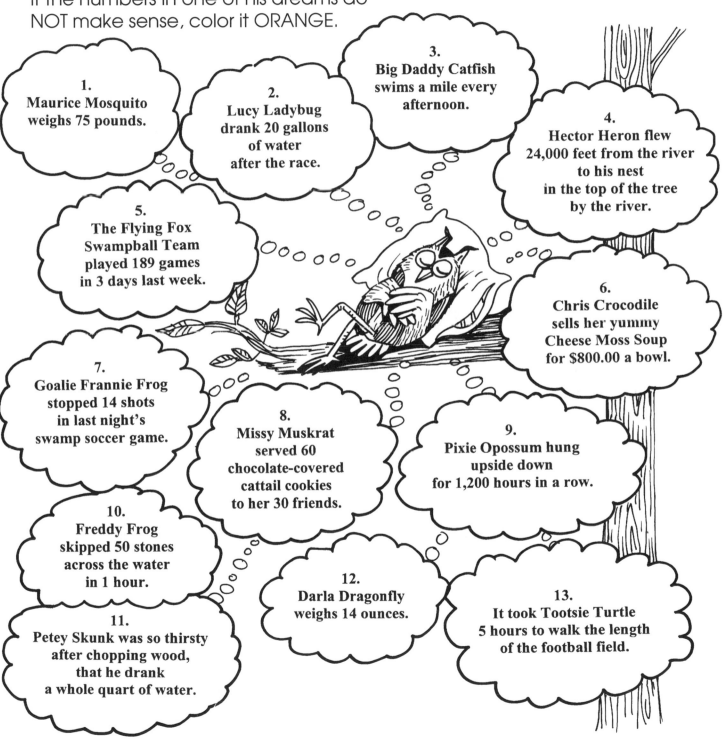

1.
Maurice Mosquito
weighs 75 pounds.

2.
Lucy Ladybug
drank 20 gallons
of water
after the race.

3.
Big Daddy Catfish
swims a mile every
afternoon.

4.
Hector Heron flew
24,000 feet from the river
to his nest
in the top of the tree
by the river.

5.
The Flying Fox
Swampball Team
played 189 games
in 3 days last week.

6.
Chris Crocodile
sells her yummy
Cheese Moss Soup
for $800.00 a bowl.

7.
Goalie Frannie Frog
stopped 14 shots
in last night's
swamp soccer game.

8.
Missy Muskrat
served 60
chocolate-covered
cattail cookies
to her 30 friends.

9.
Pixie Opossum hung
upside down
for 1,200 hours in a row.

10.
Freddy Frog
skipped 50 stones
across the water
in 1 hour.

11.
Petey Skunk was so thirsty
after chopping wood,
that he drank
a whole quart of water.

12.
Darla Dragonfly
weighs 14 ounces.

13.
It took Tootsie Turtle
5 hours to walk the length
of the football field.

Name

So Many Feet!

Cherie is a prize-winning Cha Cha dancer. She has so many feet!
It takes her a long time to get dressed for the Swamp Dance Contest.
Look closely at Cherie's feet to see what things she's putting on them.

Write a decimal numeral to tell the location of each thing:

1. feet with high boots ____
2. feet with running shoes ____
3. legs with striped socks ____
4. feet with ice skates ____
5. shoes with bows _____
6. bow on her tail at ____
7. a pair of bare feet ____

_____

8. bows on
   Cherie

_____

Draw these things.

9. red shoes on the feet
   at 8.5

10. blue shoes on the feet
    at 13.8

11. tall boots on the legs at 4.2

12. purple socks on the legs
    at 10.3

13. pink slippers on the feet at 12.6

14. green shoes on the feet at 2.4

15. small red hearts on Cheri's back
    at about 0.2, 2.5, 4.7, 8.3,
    10.5, and 13.4

Name

Read & Write Decimals

A Daring Balancing Act

Frederick Frog is last year's champion in the Log-Balancing Race.
If he can stay on the log all the way down the rushing river, he will win again.
He is counting as the log rolls, but his numbers are all mixed up.
Use his numbers to solve these problems.

...76...431...
29....610...398...
502...100...50...
2...

...25...5,003...
298...2,300...40...
12,000...4,321...
300...

1. Which number is about the same as 400? _____ Circle it in PINK.

2. Which number is about half of 1,000? _____ Circle it in PURPLE.

3. Which number is much larger than 5,000? _____ Circle it in GREEN.

4. Which number is much smaller than 30? _____ Circle it in ORANGE.

5. Which number is about half of 60? _____ Circle it in BLUE.

6. Which number is about 3/4 of 100? _____ Circle it in YELLOW.

7. Which number is 10 > 600? _____ Draw a PURPLE box around it.

8. Which number is 100 < 531? _____ Draw a RED box around it.

9. Which number is close to 300? _____ Draw a BLUE box around it.

10. Which shows the same amount as five dimes? _____ Circle it in RED.

11. Which number is 3 > 5,000? _____ Draw a GREEN box around it.

12. Which number is > 30 and < 50? _____ Draw a BLACK box around it.

Name _____

The Swamp's Strongest Lifters

It's time for this year's weight lifting contest in the Hokee Penokee Swamp. The swamp critters lift the biggest rocks they can find.

Lucy Ladybug weighs $\frac{1}{4}$ pound. Allie Alligator weighs 150 pounds more.

This number sentence shows how their own weights compare:

$$A \text{ (for Allie)} = \frac{1}{4} + 150$$

1. Tootsie Turtle is lifting 88 pounds. Freddy Frog is lifting 50 pounds more. Which number sentence is true?

   F = 88 + 50   T = 50 + 88
   F = 88 − 50   T = 88 − 50

2. Rodney River Rat is lifting 200 pounds today. Betsy Beaver lifts 150 pounds less. Which number sentence is true?

   200 − 150 = R   200 + 150 = B
   200 + 150 = B   200 − 150 = B

3. Al Alligator lifts 17 pounds less than Lucy Ladybug. Lucy lifts 320 pounds. Which number sentence is true?

   A = 320 + 17   A = 320 − 17
   L = 320 x 17   L = 320 − 17

4. Together, Al Alligator and Freddy Frog can lift 441 pounds. Which number sentence shows this?

   F = 441 x 2   A = 441 − 2
   F − A = 441   F + A = 441

5. Yesterday, Tootsie lifted 4 times as much weight as Betsy. Betsy lifted 250 pounds. What number sentence is true?

   T = 4 x 250   T = 4 + 250
   B = 4 x 250   T = 250 − B

A Prize Fly-Catcher

Grandpappy Bullfrog is a prize-winning fly-catcher. He wins all the contests.

Look at the chart of Grandpappy's scores from the latest contest.

Which number sentences about Grandpappy's scores are true?

Write T (for True) on the lines for the true sentences.

_____ 1. M (Monday) < SN (Sunday)

_____ 2. T > TH

_____ 3. TH + ST = 9,000

_____ 4. TH + 250 = M

_____ 5. SN − TH = 2,000

_____ 6. F < W

_____ 7. SN > F

_____ 8. T + ST = 10,000

_____ 9. T < SN

_____ 10. TH + ST = 10,000

_____ 11. W > F

_____ 12. M < SN

_____ 13. T − TH = 1,000

_____ 14. F + 100 = 4,000

_____ 15. M + W > 10,000

_____ 16. T + TH + ST = 14,000

_____ 17. F + T < 10,000

_____ 18. 4,000 = F + 10

_____ 19. SN + M + T = 15,000

_____ 20. W − 4 = 3,900

Grandpappy's Scores
Swamptown Fly-Catching Contest, 1999

	Day	Number of Flies Caught
SN	Sunday	4,520
M	Monday	4,250
T	Tuesday	5,000
W	Wednesday	3,904
TH	Thursday	4,000
F	Friday	3,990
ST	Saturday	5,000

Name _____

Sentences to Show Number Relationships

Take a Chance on Golf

Between golf games, Chester searches for lost golf balls.

First, he comes to an area with 6 green balls, 2 red balls and 1 blue ball hiding under a clump of moss. He reaches down to grab a ball.

What is the chance that the ball is RED?
There are a total of 9 balls. 2 are red. So the chance is $\frac{2}{9}$ that he'll grab a red ball.

There is a $\frac{1}{9}$ chance it will be BLUE, and a $\frac{6}{9}$ (or $\frac{2}{3}$) chance that it will be GREEN.
Write fractions to show these chances.

1. Chester's next stop is a spot with 10 balls: 4 white, 3 yellow and 3 red.
   a. What is the chance Chester will pick up a yellow ball first? _____
   b. What is the chance Chester will pick up a white ball first? _____
   c. What is the chance he will pickup a red ball first? _____

2. Chester finds a deep hole with 25 balls in it: 10 are orange, 5 are red, 7 are white, and 3 are yellow.
   a. What is the chance Chester will pick up a red ball first? _____
   b. What is the chance he will pick up a yellow ball first? _____
   c. What is the chance he will pick up an orange ball first? _____
   d. What is the chance he will pick up a white ball first? _____

3. Chester finds 24 balls in the blackberry bushes at the edge of the golf course: 10 of these are white, 3 are red, 5 are yellow and 6 are blue.
   a. What is the chance Chester will pick up a white ball first? _____
   b. What is the chance he will see a red ball first? _____
   c. What is the chance he will see a blue ball first? _____

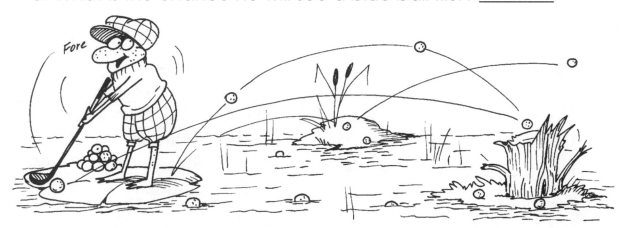

Sylvia's Sock Search

It's time for the Kickball Play-offs and Sylvia is late!
She is trying to find socks to match her uniform, so she will look her best.
She is grabbing socks out of her drawers in a big hurry, WITHOUT LOOKING.
The labels on the drawers tell the color of the socks inside.

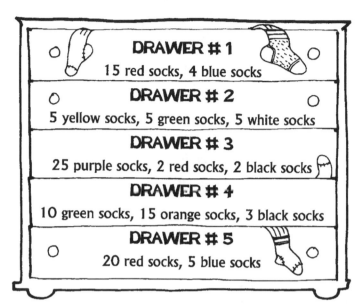

DRAWER # 1
15 red socks, 4 blue socks

DRAWER # 2
5 yellow socks, 5 green socks, 5 white socks

DRAWER # 3
25 purple socks, 2 red socks, 2 black socks

DRAWER # 4
10 green socks, 15 orange socks, 3 black socks

DRAWER # 5
20 red socks, 5 blue socks

Help Sylvia find the right socks. (Circle the correct answer to each question.)

1. She grabs 2 socks from Drawer # 1. Which is she MOST likely to grab?
   2 blue socks   1 blue sock and 1 red sock   2 red socks

2. She grabs 3 socks from Drawer # 2. Which is she MOST likely to grab?
   3 yellow socks   3 green socks
   3 white socks   1 yellow, 1 green, and 1 white sock

3. She grabs 3 socks from Drawer #3. Which is she MOST likely to grab?
   2 red and 1 black   1 red, 1 black, 1 purple   3 purple

4. She grabs 2 socks from Drawer #4. Which is she MOST likely to grab?
   2 black   1 green and 1 orange   2 orange

5. She grabs 5 socks from Drawer #5. Which is she LEAST likely to grab?
   5 red   5 blue   4 red and 1 blue

6. She grabs 3 socks from Drawer #1. Which is she LEAST likely to grab?
   1 red and 2 blue   3 blue   3 red

7. She grabs 4 socks from Drawer #3. Which is she LEAST likely to grab?
   2 black and 2 red   1 red and 3 purple   4 purple

Name

Setting Up Camp

The Turner Triplets are off on a long hike.
They set up their campsite by a river.
See the picture on page 245.
Their campsite is full of things
that have to do with geometry.
Follow the directions to find all kinds of
points, lines, angles, and figures.

1. Find a point. ●
    Make it green.
	6. Here is a circle.
	    Find a circle.
	    Color it orange.

2. Here is a cone. Color 2 cones green.	7. Rectangles have 4 sides. Find a rectangle. Color it pink.

3. These drawings are
    angles. Find 3 angles.
    Trace them in red.
	8. A square has 4 equal sides.
	
	 Find a square. Color it purple.

4. Parallel lines do not
    touch each other.
    Find a set. Trace
    them in blue.
	9. Line segments are
	    pieces of straight
	    line. Find 5. Trace
	    them in yellow.

5. Here are some curved
    lines. Find 2 in the
    picture. Trace
    them in brown.
	10. Triangles have
	    3 sides. Find 2
	    triangles. Color
	    them gray.

Name _____

Use with page 245.
Lines, Points, Angles, & Figures

Setting Up Camp, continued . . .

Measurements at the Ball Field

Do you usually take a ruler to a baseball game? Probably not! But, how would you measure a hot dog or a baseball cap if you needed to?

Think about the units of measurement you would need. Tell what unit you would use to measure the real length of each of these.

1. around the diamond _____

2. how far the team traveled to get to the game _____

3. the bat _____

4. the pitcher's nose _____

5. your hot dog _____

6. the height of the grandstand _____

7. around the catcher's waist _____

8. a baseball mitt _____

9. around a baseball cap _____

10. around the scoreboard _____

11. from the pitcher's mound to home plate _____

12. length of the team's bus _____

Write in. for inches, ft for feet, and mi for miles.

SCORE BOARD

Color the picture.

Name _____

Choosing Units of Length: U.S.

Motorcycle Measurements

Remember:
cm = centimeter
m = meter (=100 cm)
km = kilometer (=1000 cm)

How would you measure a motorcycle?
Choose the best unit to measure Marty's
cycle and the other things at his
motorcycle race.

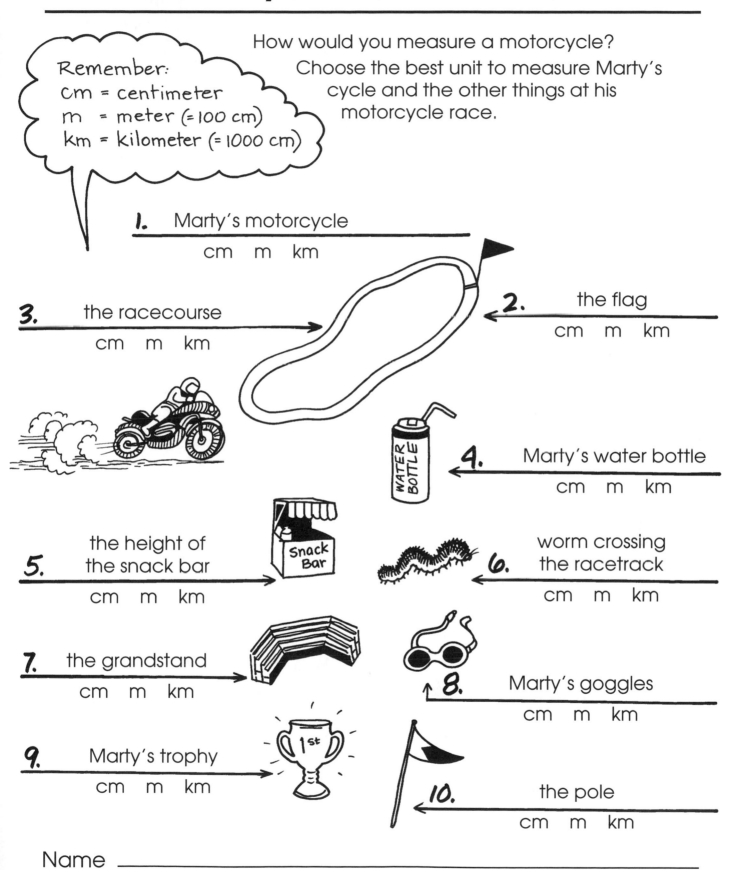

1. Marty's motorcycle
cm   m   km

2. the flag
cm   m   km

3. the racecourse
cm   m   km

4. Marty's water bottle
cm   m   km

5. the height of the snack bar
cm   m   km

6. worm crossing the racetrack
cm   m   km

7. the grandstand
cm   m   km

8. Marty's goggles
cm   m   km

9. Marty's trophy
cm   m   km

10. the pole
cm   m   km

Name _____

Choosing Units of Length: Metric

Good Exercise

Gary's pet grasshopper, Garfus, is getting his exercise by hopping around the neighbors' gardens.

To find out how far he hopped, you will need to find the perimeter of each garden.

Write the number of feet Garfus hopped around each garden. You can add in your head or use a separate piece of paper.

Remember: Perimeter is the distance around the outside of a shape!

A. ___ ft   D. ___ ft   F. ___ ft

B. ___ ft   E. ___ ft

C. ___ ft

A.
10
10
10
10

B.
20   30
30   20
30   20

C.
5
5
5
10
5
10

D.
8   8
8

E.
5
40   40
5

F.
50
10   10
50

Color Garfus.

Name _____

At the Sports Store

The sports store is one of Joe's favorite spots.

The shelves are full of great stuff for all kinds of sports.

Find the perimeter of each of the items on the shelves.

You can add in your head or work the problems on another piece of paper.

BIG SALE TODAY!

1. JETS T-SHIRT — 20", 5", 5", 5", 5", 10", 10", 10"

2. PENNANT — 5", 10", 10" ½ OFF

3. SKI BOOT — 5", 15", 10", 10"

4. SURFBOARD — 50", 20", 30", 50", 20"

5. BEACH TOWEL — 30", 40", 40", 30"

Remember: Perimeter is the distance around the outside of a shape!

1. _____ inches

2. _____ inches

3. _____ inches

4. _____ inches

5. _____ inches

Color the clothing and equipment.

Name _____

Space on the Beach Blanket

Josie has left a lot of her beach stuff on her blanket.
About how much area does each thing cover?
Write the number that tells about how many
squares each one covers.

Area is the amount of space covered by something.

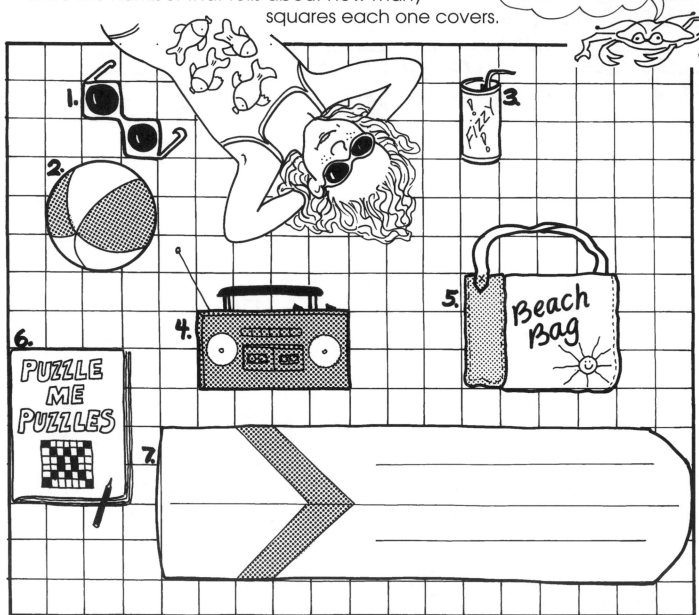

1. _____ square units   4. _____ square units   7. _____ square units

2. _____ square units   5. _____ square units   * Josie covers about

3. _____ square units   6. _____ square units   _____ square units.

Name _____

Cover Up!

Someone left a lot of sports equipment lying around the gym floor. Tell how much space each piece covers.

> Area is the measure of how much space is covered by something. It is measured in square units.

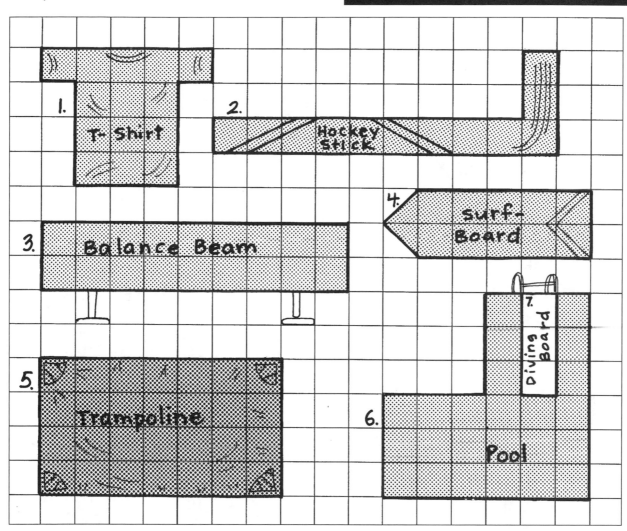

1. _____ square units
2. _____ square units
3. _____ square units
4. _____ square units
5. _____ square units
6. _____ square units

7. _____ square units

8. Which has the greatest area? _____

9. Which has the smallest area? _____

10. Which area is greater: the area of the T-shirt or the area of the hockey stick? _____

11. Do the beam and hockey stick have the same area? _____

Name _____

The Climber

Samantha Spider climbs everything she sees!
Look at every stack of blocks she is climbing.
Write the number of cubes in each stack
to find the volume of each stack.

Volume is the amount of space that something takes up. It is measured in cubic units.

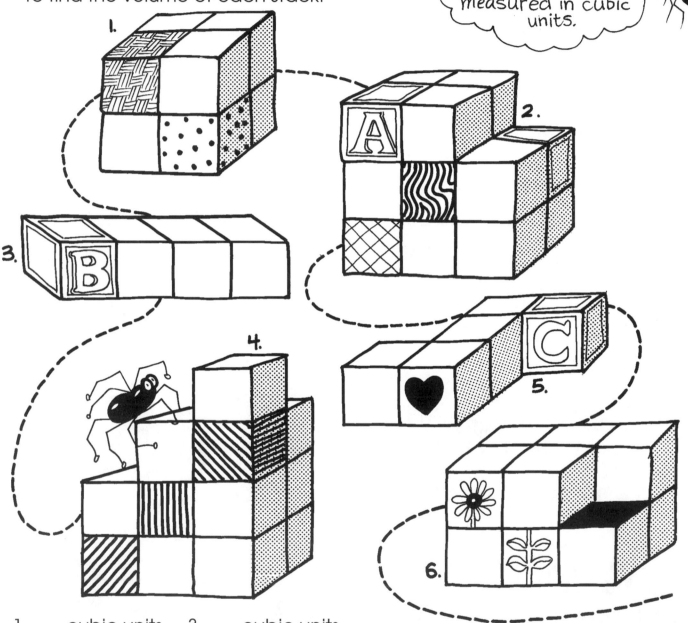

1. ___ cubic units   3. ___ cubic units

2. ___ cubic units   4. ___ cubic units   5. ___ cubic units   6. ___ cubic units

Color the blocks.

Name _____

Weighty Questions

How would you measure a horse?
If you wanted to measure its weight, which unit of weight would you use?
Choose the best unit of measurement to weigh each of these things
at a horse show.

oz—ounce
lb—pound (1 lb = 16 ounces)
t—ton (1 t = 2000 pounds)

1. Hannah's horse _____

2. Hannah _____

3. Hannah's blue ribbon _____

4. Hannah's boots _____

5. Hannah's gloves _____

6. the horse's blanket _____

7. the apple _____

8. the truck that
   carries 10 horses _____

9. Hannah's shirt _____

10. the horse's shoes _____

Color Hannah and her horse.

Name _____

More Weighty Questions

A beach ball is too light for bowling.

A bowling ball wouldn't float very well in the ocean.

Their weights are very different.

What would you use to measure their weights?

Write **g** or **kg** as the best unit for measuring each of the things below.

table tennis ball

A table tennis ball weighs about a gram (g).

shoe

A pair of shoes weighs about a kilogram (kg).

1. nose plugs _____

2. badminton birdie _____

3. baseball cap _____

4. ice skates _____

5. baseball mitt _____

6. tennis ball _____

7. flying disk _____

8. bicycle _____

9. surfboard _____

10. swim goggles _____

11. bowling ball _____

12. weights _____

13. beach ball _____

14. kite _____

Name _____

Choosing Units of Weight: Metric

Could You Swim in a Cup?

Could the Ladybug Swim Team swim in a cup of water? Probably not, unless they are really bugs!

A cup does not hold much water.

A cup holds 16 tablespoons of water.

A pint holds 2 cups.

A quart holds 4 cups (or 2 pints).

A gallon holds 4 quarts (or 8 pints or 16 cups).

cup   pint   quart   gallon

Which unit would you use to measure each of these amounts? Circle the best unit.

1. water in a pool
   cups   gallons

2. water in a bathtub
   quarts   gallons

3. water in a water bed
   pints   gallons

4. water in a river
   quarts   gallons

5. sports drink in a glass
   cups   gallons

6. milk for a team of 20 players
   cups   gallons

Name _____

Choosing Units of Liquid Capacity: U.S.

A Very Silly Field Day

Some very silly events are taking place at the Laugh-a-Lot School Field Day.

Help the timekeeper with some time problems.

The first clock shows when an event starts.
The words tell how long each event takes.
Show what time the event ends.
Draw hands on the clocks, or write in the time.

1. Running Egg Dodge
took
15 min.

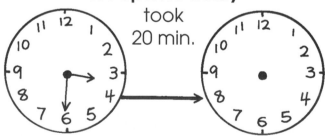

2. Ear Wiggling Marathon
took
½ hour

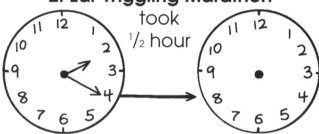

3. Popsicle Relay
took
20 min.

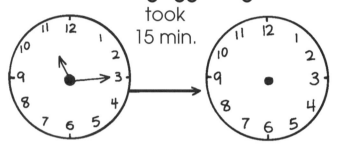

4. Lunch
took
1 hour

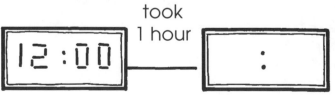

5. Headstand in Water
took
40 min.

6. Baby Buggy Races
took
30 min.

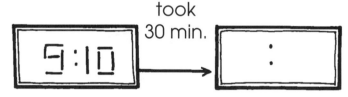

7. Banana Peel Slide
took
45 min.

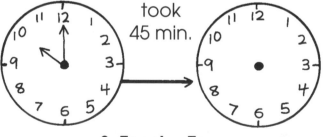

8. Toaster Toss
took
20 min.

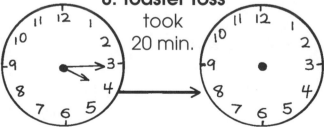

Name _____

A Wild Bull Ride

These brave cowgirls are riding wild bulls in a contest to see who can stay on the longest.

Answer all the questions and fill in the chart to find out who won the contest.

1. Wanda stayed on 10 seconds longer than Trixie. Fill in her time.

2. Barb stayed on 45 seconds longer than Wanda. Fill in her time.

3. Annie O. stayed on 30 seconds more than Barb. Fill in her time.

4. Cactus Cath stayed on 2 minutes less than Annie O. Fill in her time.

5. Who won the bull riding contest? _____

6. Did any 2 of the cowgirls stay on the same amount of time? _____

7. Barb's record time is 5 minutes. How much longer is that than her time in this contest? _____

RODEO RECORDS

NAME:	TIME:
Trixie	2 min. 5 sec.
Cactus Cath	
Wild Wanda	
Annie O.	
Barb	

Name _____

Bear Gymnastics

Belinda dreamed that all of her teddy bears went to a gymnastics meet.

Lots of measuring went on at the meet.

Solve the measurement problems for the bears.

1. Elizabear is balancing on the beam. She stayed on for 75 seconds without falling. Her second try was 1 minute less. How long did she stay on the second time?

_____

2. Fuzzy Bear weighs 45 pounds. Buzzy Bear weighs 73 pounds.

How much more does Buzzy weigh?

_____

When Maybear does her exercises, she likes the temperature to be 65°F. Today it is 80°F. How many degrees difference is this?

_____ °

Is this cooler or warmer than she likes it to be?

_____

Name _____

4. Shakesbear drank 4 quarts of bear juice before the competition. How many cups is that?

_____

5. When Tuffy stands on his head, his body is 5 feet, 7 inches from his toes to his hands. Scruffy's body is 4 feet, 3 inches from his toes to his hands. How much taller is Tuffy?

_____

6. Flip clears the vault by 7 inches. Flop clears it by 1 foot. How many inches higher does Flop jump?

_____

7. Beau Bear is doing tumbling on the mat. How many square units does the mat cover?

_____

Name _____

Champion Jumpers

Read the chart to find out what happened at the Frog Jumping Contest.
Then answer the questions.

Number Of Feet Jumped Each Day	Jumping Jake	Barney Bouncer	Harvey Hopper	Tilly Toad	Larry Leaper
Monday	4	8	2	4	6
Tuesday	6	8	4	6	2
Wednesday	8	4	2	6	8
Thursday	10	6	8	4	8
Friday	8	4	6	6	4

1. Who jumped farthest on Thursday? _____

2. What was Larry's worst day? _____

3. How many feet did Jake jump all week? _____

4. How far had Tilly jumped by the end of the day on Wednesday? _____

5. What was Harvey's best day? _____

6. Which days did Jake jump the same distance? _____

7. Which frogs jumped the same distance on Tuesday? _____

8. Who had the longest jump? _____

9. What was Larry's worst day? _____

Name _____

The Silly Olympics

The kids in the neighborhood are having fun at the Silly Olympics.
They are doing some silly sports.
Look at the sports on the circle graph.
See how many kids did each event.
Then answer the questions.
Color each slice of the graph
a different color.

Circle graph slices:
- cabbage throw 5
- banana peel hop, skip & jump 20
- lawn chair obstacle course 15
- nose wiggling 20
- gelatin juggling 10
- broom balance 30

1. How many kids were in the broom balance? _____

2. How many juggled gelatin? _____

3. Which event had the least entries? _____

4. Which event had the most entries? _____

5. Which events had the same number of entries?
   _____ and _____

6. How many more nose wigglers were there than cabbage throwers?___

7. How many kids entered the contest all together? _____

Name _____

Reading a Circle Graph

Bumps & Lumps

aches and breaks

pains and sprains

These skiers are in trouble!
The graph tells about the
injuries and sicknesses
the ski team had this year.
Read the graph.
Answer the questions.

1. How many skiers
got sunburned? _____

2. Which injury did skiers
get the most? _____

3. How many broken bones were there? _____

4. How many sprains were there? _____

5. Which injury happened 4 times? _____

6. Which injury happened 8 times? _____

7. How many more sprains than black eyes were there? _____

8. How many frostbites and sunburns were there all together? _____

9. Which injury happened the least? _____

10. How many more headaches than tummy aches were there? _____

Ski Team Aches & Pains

	2	4	6	8	10	12	14	16	18	20
sunburn	▮	▮	▮	▮	▮	▮				
broken bones	▮									
sprains	▮	▮	▮	▮	▮	▮	▮			
frostbite	▮	▮	▮	▮						
black eyes	▮	▮	▮							
tummy aches	▮	▮	▮	▮						
headaches	▮	▮	▮	▮	▮	▮	▮	▮		
bruises	▮	▮	▮	▮	▮	▮	▮	▮	▮	

Number of Injuries:

Name _____

Talented Feet

The Jetsville Junior Jumping Jacks are having fun at the jump rope jamboree.

Look at this table.

It tells how many times each jumper jumped without missing.

Judy	10
Jane	50
Jackie	80
Joey	90
Jenny	40
Jay	70
Jacob	100

Color in the bar graph to show the number of jumps for each jumper.

Use a different color marker for each bar.

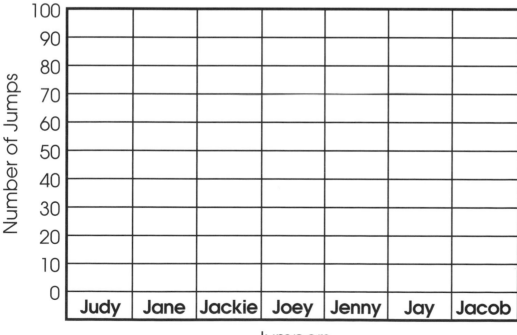

Name _____

The Messy Room

Elijah's room is a mess. Help him locate the things thrown around his rug.

Answer the questions beside the grid.

Write number pairs like this: (5, 6).

Remember: To locate things on a grid, you need two numbers. The first number counts over. The second number counts up.

What a mess!

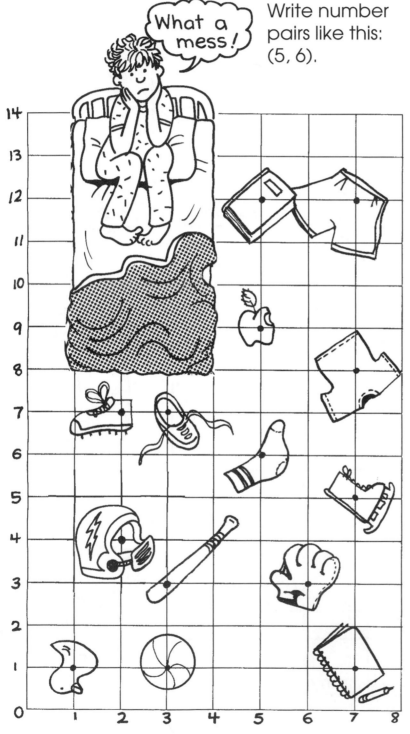

1. What is at (7, 5)?

_____

2. What is at (5, 9)?

_____

3. What is at (3, 3)?

_____

4. Is the T-shirt at (6, 0)? _____

5. Where is the helmet?
(_____)

6. Where is the ball? (_____)

7. What is at (1, 1)?

_____

8. What is at (7, 1)?

_____

9. Is the baseball mitt at (3, 6)? _____

10. What is at (2, 7)?

_____

11. Where are the shorts?
(_____)

12. Where is the sock?
(_____)

Name _____

Oh! Can She Jump!

Leaping Liz is a great high jumper.

Use the number pairs below to connect the points on the grid to find out what Liz is jumping over now.

Work each column of number pairs from top to bottom. Then move to the next column.

Number Pairs

(9, 3)	(13, 2)	(9, 9)	(0, 11)	(2, 8)	(3, 6)	(3, 4)	(2, 1)	(8, 1)
(12, 0)	(12, 4)	(6, 11)	(0, 9)	(3, 9)	(4, 6)	(3, 3)	(2, 0)	(8, 2)
(14, 0)	(12, 6)	(5, 13)	(4, 11)	(4, 8)	(5, 7)	(4, 2)	(6, 0)	(6, 3)
(14, 1)	(11, 8)	(3, 13)	(1, 8)	(3, 7)	(6, 6)	(4, 1)	(6, 1)	(6, 4)

Name _____

Visitors at a Picnic

Remember: The pair of numbers tells you to go over...then up.

Matt and Mandy are getting ready for a picnic. You'll see their picnic blanket on the next page (page 267). They have lots of good food—and some unexpected visitors, too.

Follow the directions to help them find things at their picnic.

1. What is at (1, 2)? _____

2. What is at (3, 2)? _____

3. Is the soda at (4, 1)? _____

4. What is at (3, 8)? _____

5. Is the burger at (7, 3)? _____

6. Is the radio at (7, 9)? _____

7. What is at (5, 10)? _____

8. What is at (2, 3)? _____

9. What is at (6, 5)? _____

10. Is the sandwich at (2, 6)? _____

11. What is at (5, 6)? _____

12. Is the pitcher at (4, 4)? _____

13. What is at (3, 10)? _____

14. Where are the grapes? _____

15. What is at (6, 4)? _____

16. What is at (4, 9)? _____

17. What is at (1, 4)? _____

18. Draw ants at (5, 0) and (0, 8).

19. Draw ants at (2, 7) and (4, 7).

20. Draw a cupcake at (1, 1).

21. Which piece of food has attracted the most ants?

_____

I smell a picnic...

Name _____

Use with page 267.
266
Placing Items on a Grid

Name _____

Follow the Trail

Chris is starting off on a cross-country bike path.

He doesn't know the way. Help him find it by plotting points on the grid.

Plot each point where the number pairs tell you to put it.

Connect the points in the first column from top to bottom. Then connect the points in the next column, and so on.

(1, 12)	(5, 10)	(11, 9)	(14, 6)	(11, 3)	(3, 5)
(2, 11)	(7, 11)	(12, 8)	(10, 6)	(8, 3)	(3, 3)
(3, 10)	(10, 10)	(14, 8)	(11, 4)	(6, 5)	(1, 1)

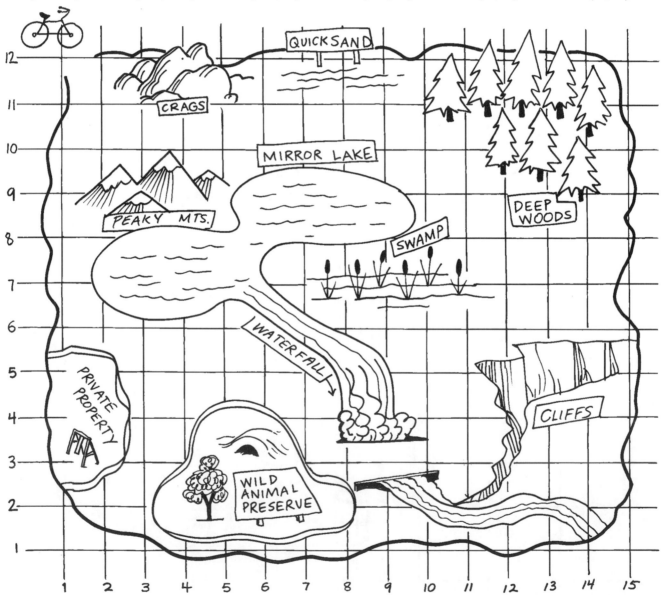

Name _____

Plotting Points on a Grid

Scared or Excited?

What sport is Buck doing? Is he scared or excited?
Plot each point on the grid. Write the letter next to it.
Then connect the points in A-B-C order.
You'll find out what Buck is doing!

Remember: Read number pairs on a grid this way.
First go over. Then go up. (2, 5) means 2 over and 5 up.

Number Pairs

A (1, 3)   C (6, 2)   E (12, 7)   G (10, 8)   I (7, 10)   K (6, 11)   M (1, 6)
B (2, 2)   D (9, 4)   F (13, 9)   H (12, 12) J (10, 12) L (3, 9)   N (1, 3)

Do you think Buck is scared or excited? _____

Name _____

Speaking of Math

Chad knows all the words in this puzzle, because he's good at math.
Do you know these math words, too?
Read the clues. Write the words in the right spaces.
Use the words in the word box.

Clues

Across

4. having exactly the same shape
6. unit for measuring temperature
7. unit of time = 60 seconds
9. figure with 4 equal sides

Down

1. part of a line with a starting point and an end
2. unit of time = 60 minutes
3. unit for measuring liquid = 4 cups
5. figure with 3 sides
8. number of square units that something covers

Word Box

triangle   degree
square   congruent   segment
hour   area   minute   quart

Name _____

Math Vocabulary

Geometry, Measurement, & Graphing
Words to Know

area—the number of square units that will fit inside a figure.
The area of this figure is 4.

bar graph—a picture that uses bars to show information.

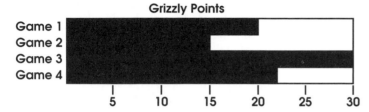

Grizzly Points

centimeter (cm)—a standard metric unit for measuring length. 100 cm = 1 meter (m)

circle—a flat, round figure.

cone—a space figure that looks like this:

congruent—having exactly the same size and shape. These 2 figures are congruent.

cube—a space figure with six faces, all of which are the same size.

cubic unit—a unit used for measuring volume.

cup (c)—a U.S. Customary unit of capacity. 2 c = 1 pt

cylinder—a space figure that looks like this:

degree (°)—a standard unit for measuring temperature.

foot (ft)—a U.S. Customary unit for measuring length. 1 ft = 12 in.

gallon (gal)—a U.S. Customary unit for measuring capacity. 1 gal = 4 qt

gram (g)—a standard metric unit used to measure the mass of light objects. 1000 g = 1 kg

hour—a unit of time equal to 60 minutes.

inch (in.)—a U.S. Customary unit for measuring length. 12 in. = 1 ft

kilogram (kg)—a standard metric unit for measuring mass. 1 kg = 1000 g

kilometer—a standard metric unit for measuring length. 1 km = 1000 m

line graph—a picture that uses line segments to show changes in information.

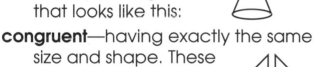

Joe's Miles Run

liter (L)—a standard metric unit for measuring capacity.

meter (m)—a standard metric unit for measuring length. 1 m = 100 cm

mile (mi)—a U.S. Customary unit for measuring long distances. 1 mi = 1760 yds or 5280 ft

minute—a unit of time. There are 60 minutes in an hour.

number pair—two numbers whose order shows a location on a grid. The B is at (3, 2)— 3 over and 2 up.

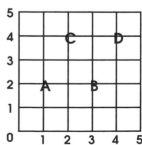

ounce (oz)—a U.S. Customary unit for measuring weight. 16 oz = 1 lb

perimeter—the distance around a figure. The perimeter of this figure is 7 ½.

pictograph—a graph in which pictures stand for objects.

pint (pt)—a U.S. Customary unit of capacity. 1 pt = 2 c

polygon—a figure formed by joining 3 or more segments.

pound (lb)—a U.S. Customary unit measuring weight. 1 lb = 16 oz

pyramid—a space figure that looks like this:

quart (qt)—a U.S. Customary unit for measuring capacity. 1 qt = 2 pt

rectangle—a figure with 4 sides.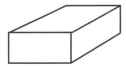

rectangular prism—a space figure with 6 sides, all of which are rectangles.

segment—part of a line with a starting point and an ending point.

sides—the segments that make a polygon.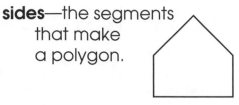

This polygon has 5 sides.

sphere—a round space figure.

square—a figure with 4 sides, all the same length.

square unit—a unit used for measuring area.

This figure has an area of 6 square units.

temperature—the measure in degrees (°) of how hot or cold something is.

triangle—a figure with three sides.

volume—the amount of space a figure takes up.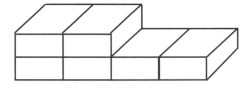

This figure has a volume of 6 cubic units.

yard (yd)—a U.S. Customary unit for measuring length. 1 yd = 3 ft or 36 in.

Which Number Am I?

Athletes wear many different kinds of footwear.
Each of these pieces of footwear has a question for you.
The answer is the number described by the clues. Write each number.

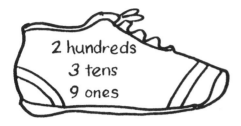

2 hundreds
3 tens
9 ones

1 hundred
0 tens
6 ones

0 hundreds
9 tens
9 ones

1. How many miles
have I run ?

_____ miles

2. How many jumps
have I landed?

_____ jumps

3. How many goals
have I scored?

_____ goals

4 hundreds
2 tens
2 ones

3 hundreds
4 tens
0 ones

2 hundreds
0 tens
0 ones

4. How many points
have I scored?

_____ points

5. How many miles
have I swum?

_____ miles

6. How many lifts
have I ridden?

_____ lifts

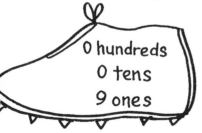

0 hundreds
0 tens
9 ones

1 hundred
1 ten
0 ones

9 hundreds
0 tens
8 ones

7. How many bases
have I stolen?

_____ bases

8. How many games
have I bowled?

_____ games

9. How many dances
have I performed?

_____ dances

Name _____

The Big Race

These rowers are in a big race. Who is racing against them?
Follow the dots to find out.

Start with number 67. Connect the dots from the smallest to the largest number shown.

Color the picture!

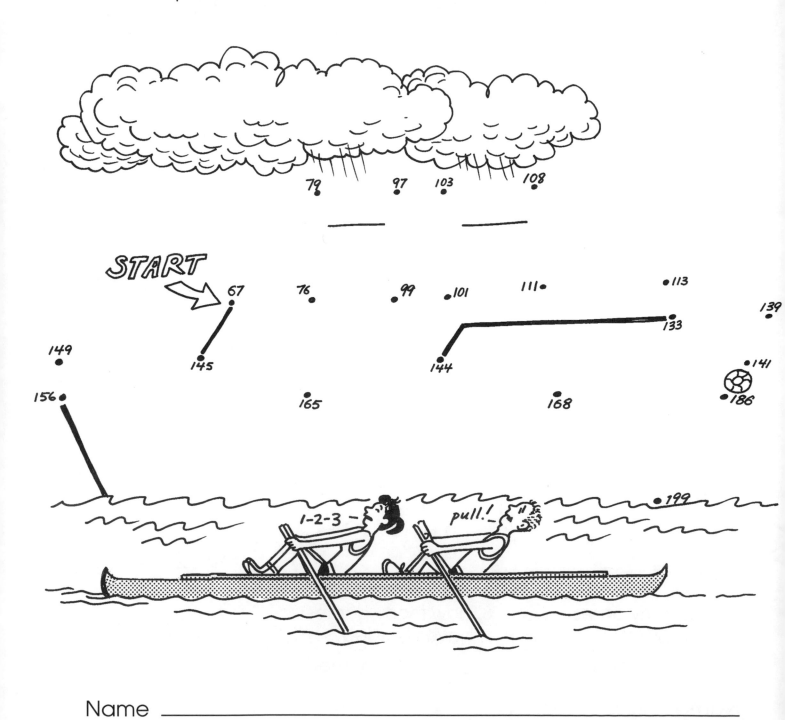

Number Search

Numbers are everywhere in this picture!
Some are odd. Some are even.
Color all the **even** numbers in red.
How many did you find? _____
Color all the **odd** numbers in green.
How many did you find? _____

An **even** number is a number with
0, 2, 4, 6, or 8 in the one's place.
An **odd** number is a number with
1, 3, 5, 7, or 9 in the one's place.

33
75
13
2947
103
86
12
50
72
9
100
66
22
27
444
999
39

Name _____

Meet the Athletes

Here are some of the athletes in Benjy's neighborhood. Read the name, age, and sport of each one. Then answer the questions about the order they are in from left to right.

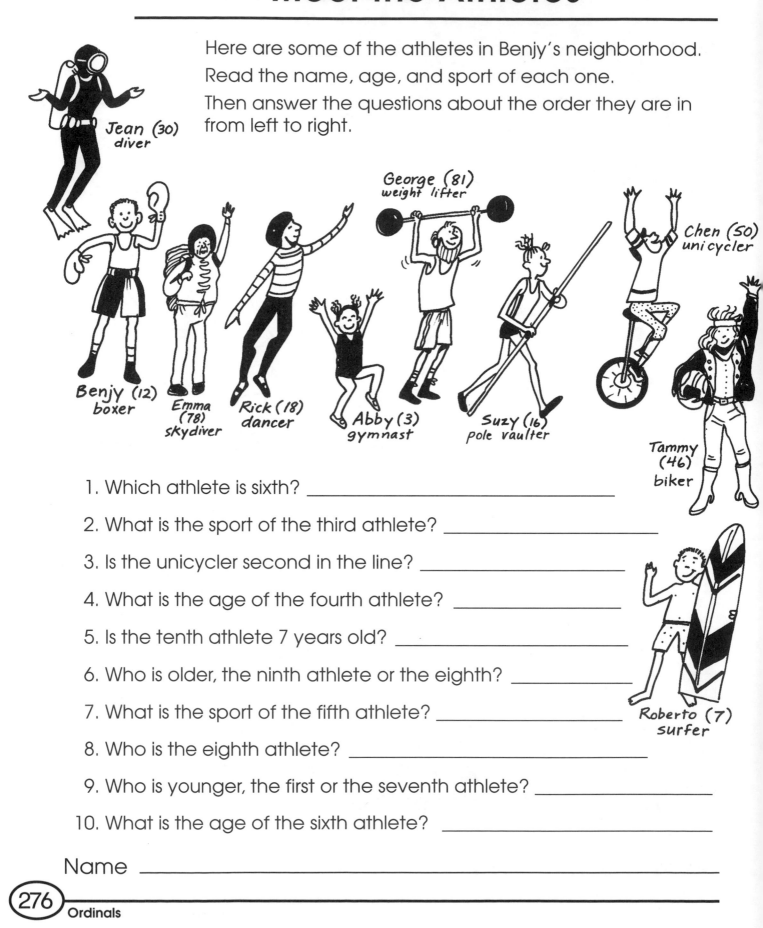

Jean (30) diver

George (81) weight lifter

Chen (50) unicycler

Benjy (12) boxer

Emma (78) skydiver

Rick (18) dancer

Abby (3) gymnast

Suzy (16) pole vaulter

Tammy (46) biker

Roberto (7) surfer

1. Which athlete is sixth? _____

2. What is the sport of the third athlete? _____

3. Is the unicycler second in the line? _____

4. What is the age of the fourth athlete? _____

5. Is the tenth athlete 7 years old? _____

6. Who is older, the ninth athlete or the eighth? _____

7. What is the sport of the fifth athlete? _____

8. Who is the eighth athlete? _____

9. Who is younger, the first or the seventh athlete? _____

10. What is the age of the sixth athlete? _____

Name _____

Numbers Dropping From the Sky

The sky is filled with numbers! Each parachute has one.
Find the numbers to match the number words written below.
Color each parachute as the chart shows.

497

19,058

12.67

763,002

414

24,263

9100

4907

	Number	Color
1	seven hundred sixty-three thousand, two	blue
2	four hundred ninety-seven	pink spots
3	nineteen thousand, fifty-eight	green stripes
4	four hundred fourteen	red stripes
5	twenty-four thousand, two hundred sixty-three	black & purple
6	nine thousand, one hundred	yellow
7	four thousand, nine hundred, seven	orange
8	one thousand, two hundred, sixty-seven	blue & green

Name _____

A Whole Lot of Bouncing Going On!

22 kids have taken turns on Jana's trampoline.
The numbers in the puzzle tell how many
times each one has bounced.
Read the clues that give the number words.
Write the numbers into the puzzle.

CLUES

Down

1. two hundred sixty-two
2. one thousand
3. nine thousand, one hundred, thirty
4. seven hundred sixteen
6. nineteen
9. three hundred twelve
10. four hundred twenty-one
11. two hundred ninety-five
12. nine hundred three
13. two hundred eighty-six
15. seventeen

Across

1. twenty-nine
4. seven thousand
5. two hundred eleven
7. thirty
8. ninety-six
9. three hundred four
11. twenty
13. twenty-two
14. fifty-one
16. eighty-eight
17. thirty-nine

Name _____

Reading & Writing Whole Numbers

Patterns on the Bench

Some members of the softball team are waiting on the bench.
The numbers on their shirts follow a pattern.

The pattern is +3 to each shirt. The next number will be 24.

Fill in the missing numbers for each row of shirts.

1. 2 4 8 ___ 32 64

2. 3 7 ___ 15 ___

3. 15 11 ___ 3

4. 2 3 5 8 ___

5. 9 ___ 7 6 ___

Name _____

Underwater Search

Snorkeler Sam is counting things under the sea.
Follow the directions at the bottom of the page for coloring the picture.
Use the picture to solve the problems on the next page (page 281).

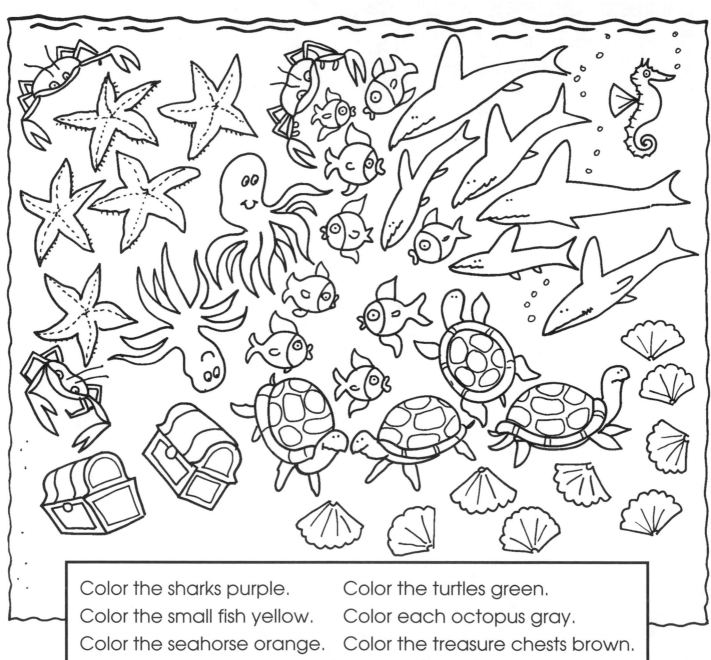

Color the sharks purple.   Color the turtles green.
Color the small fish yellow. Color each octopus gray.
Color the seahorse orange.   Color the treasure chests brown.
Color the crabs red.   Color the shells pink.

Name _____

Underwater Search, continued . . .

Compare the numbers of things
in the picture on page 280.
Put >, <, or = in each box below.

> **means greater than**
< **means less than**
= **means equal to**

1.  ☐ 🐟

2. 🧰 ☐ 🐙

3. 🐟 ☐ 🦈

4. 🧰 ☐ 🦀

5. 🦈 ☐ ⭐

6. 🐢 ☐ 🐚

7. 🦀 ☐ 🐢

8. 🐙 ☐ 🦈

9. ⭐ ☐ 🐢

10. 🐚 ☐ 🦈

11. ⭐ ☐ 🧰

12. 🐚 ☐ 🐟

13. 🐴 ☐ 🐢

14. 🐟 ☐ 🐚

15. 🦈 + 🐟 ☐ 🧰 + 🐢

16. 🐙 + 🐢 ☐ 🦀 + 🦈

Name _____

The Long and Short of It

The athletes keep all their sports stuff in their lockers.

When they open their lockers, many things fall out!

Look at all the equipment!

Compare the sizes and weights.

Circle the best answers.

1. The 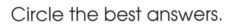 is **longer** **shorter** than the .

2. The is **longer** **shorter** than the .

3. The is **longer** **shorter** than the .

4. The is **longer** **shorter** than the .

5. The is **longer** **shorter** than the .

6. The is **longer** **shorter** than the .

Name _____

Comparing Measurements

The Long and Short of It, continued

7. The weighs **more** **less** than the .

8. The weighs **more** **less** than the .

9. The weighs **more** **less** than the .

10. The weighs **more** **less** than the .

11. The weighs **more** **less** than the .

12. The weighs **more** **less** than the  .

13. The holds **more** **less** than the .

14. The holds **more** **less** than the .

15. The holds **more** **less** than the .

Color the pictures.

Name _____

Use with page 282.

Comparing Measurements

Join the Round-up!

If a digit is less than 5, round down.
If a digit is 5 or greater, round up!

This cowgirl is rounding up some numbers so you can do some rounding.

Follow the directions for each row of lassos.

Round these numbers to the nearest ten.

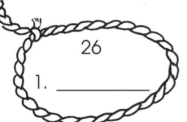

26

1. _____

74

2. _____

688

3. _____

Round these numbers to the nearest hundred.

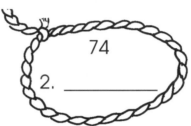

562

4. _____

1,848

5. _____

860

6. _____

Round these numbers to the nearest thousand.

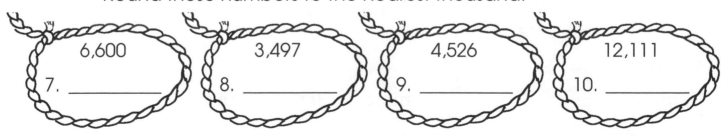

6,600

7. _____

3,497

8. _____

4,526

9. _____

12,111

10. _____

Name _____

Sports Runs in the Family

READY... AIM..., SMILE !

The Morris family is a family of sports lovers.
The problems below each show
a fact family.

Addition and subtraction facts
come in families.

8, 7, and 15 are all in
a family because

$8 + 7 = 15$ $7 + 8 = 15$
$15 - 7 = 8$ $15 - 8 = 7$

Fill in the missing fact in each of these families.

1) $12 - 6 = \boxed{}$

$\boxed{} + 6 = 12$

2) $2 + \boxed{} = 9$

$9 - \boxed{} = 2$

3) $3 + \boxed{} = 7$

$7 - 3 = \boxed{}$

4) $6 + \boxed{} = 10$

$10 - 6 = \boxed{}$

5) $\boxed{} + 2 = 10$

$10 - 2 = \boxed{}$

6) $9 - \boxed{} = 5$

$5 + \boxed{} = 9$

7) $7 - 5 = \boxed{}$

$7 - \boxed{} = 5$

8) $9 - 6 = \boxed{}$

$6 + \boxed{} = 9$

9) $9 + \boxed{} = 17$

$17 - 9 = \boxed{}$

Name _____

+ and − Facts

Homework at the Gym

GYMNASTIC PRACTICE

We did our homework at the gym. Did we do a good job?

Check all their answers.
Circle any wrong answers. Fix them.
Who has the most right answers?

Terry

A. 17
  +97
  117

B. 56
  -23
  33

C. 106
  +14
  110

D. 234
  -214
  20

Kerry

E. 372
  +419
  781

F. 64
  +56
  120

G. 487
  + 74
  561

H. 312
  +486
  798

Mary

I. 42
   89
  +15
  146

J. 5
   3
  +8
  17

K. 34
   44
  +54
  132

L. 642
  -161
  803

Barry

M. 112
  -56
  56

N. 328
  +67
  387

O. 550
  -275
  285

P. 300
  -179
  121

Name _____

Addition & Subtraction • Accuracy

Surprising Sports Facts

When you solve these problems, you will get answers to some interesting sports facts. You might already know some of these facts. Others might surprise you!

1. 71
    − 49

    feet on a starting soccer team

2. 48
    − 39

    Olympic gold medals held by U.S. swimmer Mark Spitz

3. 99
    − 74

    age of the youngest world champion race-car driver

4. 1340
   +1151

    points scored by Michael Jordan in 1995-1996 season

5. 123
    −109

    age of the youngest women's world champion figure skater

6.   11
    + 15

    miles in a marathon

7. 760
    − 755

    rings in the Olympic symbol

8. 259
    −243

    balls in a billiard (pool) game

9. 156
    + 144

    yards in the length of a polo field

10. 850
     − 829

    points in a ping-pong match

11. 39
    + 15

    outs in a 9-inning baseball game

12. 92
    − 88

    riders in an Olympic bobsled

13. 263
    + 137

    dimples on a golf ball

Name _____

Noises in the Woods

The campers are hearing sounds in the woods.
What things might be hiding in the woods around them?
You'll find out when you solve the problems.
Follow the color code to color the puzzle pieces.
(Some things might be upside-down!)

$21 \div 3$

$14 \div 2$

$\begin{array}{r} 7 \\ \times 7 \\ \hline \end{array}$

$\begin{array}{r} 3 \\ \times 3 \\ \hline \end{array}$

$36 \div 4$

$\begin{array}{r} 6 \\ \times 8 \\ \hline \end{array}$

$\begin{array}{r} 4 \\ \times 9 \\ \hline \end{array}$

$\begin{array}{r} 7 \\ \times 4 \\ \hline \end{array}$

$40 \div 8$

$27 \div 9$

$\begin{array}{r} 6 \\ \times 6 \\ \hline \end{array}$

$56 \div 7$

$\begin{array}{r} 6 \\ \times 5 \\ \hline \end{array}$

$30 \div 5$

$45 \div 9$

$42 \div 7$

$24 \div 4$

$36 \div 9$

$42 \div 6$

6×4

$81 \div 9$

Name _____

Multiplication & Division Facts

Who Wins the Race?

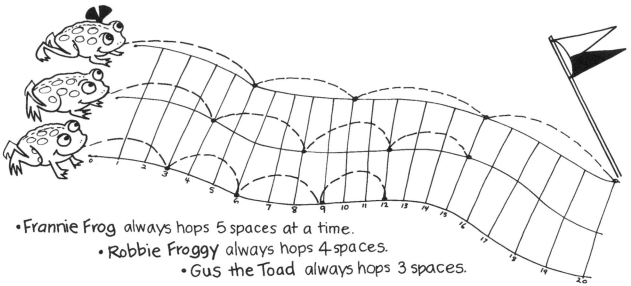

- **Frannie Frog** always hops 5 spaces at a time.
  - **Robbie Froggy** always hops 4 spaces.
    - **Gus the Toad** always hops 3 spaces.

In this race they each hop 4 times, so Frannie wins the race.
Tell who will win each of these races.

Race 1
Frannie   3 hops x 5 spaces =

Robbie   4 hops x 4 spaces =

Gus   6 hops x 3 spaces =

Who wins? _____

Race 2
Frannie   6 hops x 5 spaces =

Robbie   6 hops x 4 spaces =

Gus   3 hops x 3 spaces =

Who wins? _____

Race 3
Frannie   2 hops x 5 spaces =

Robbie   3 hops x 4 spaces =

Gus   4 hops x 3 spaces =

Who wins? _____

Race 4
Frannie   3 hops x 5 spaces =

Robbie   1 hops x 4 spaces =

Gus   2 hops x 3 spaces =

Who wins? _____

Race 5
Frannie   5 hops x 5 spaces =

Robbie   4 hops x 4 spaces =

Gus   3 hops x 3 spaces =

Who wins? _____

Race 6
Frannie   2 hops x 5 spaces =

Robbie   3 hops x 4 spaces =

Gus   2 hops x 3 spaces =

Who wins? _____

Name _____

Skip Counting • Multiplication

Is It Tic-Tac-Toe?

In each row across, one answer is different from the others.

Put a big, red **X** on the different answer.

To win, you must get a line of X's either across, up and down, or diagonally.

A.

2⟌24	6⟌72	9⟌99
8⟌72	4⟌52	4⟌36
7⟌91	3⟌42	8⟌112

Which games are winners? _____

Ladies and Gentlemen!
It's 'Tic-Tac-Toe' by a nose!

FINISH

B.

4⟌24	6⟌66	9⟌54
2⟌44	7⟌49	3⟌66
7⟌84	5⟌20	4⟌48

C.

8⟌160	5⟌80	7⟌112
9⟌108	4⟌72	7⟌126
8⟌72	7⟌98	9⟌81

Name _____

Wild River Ride

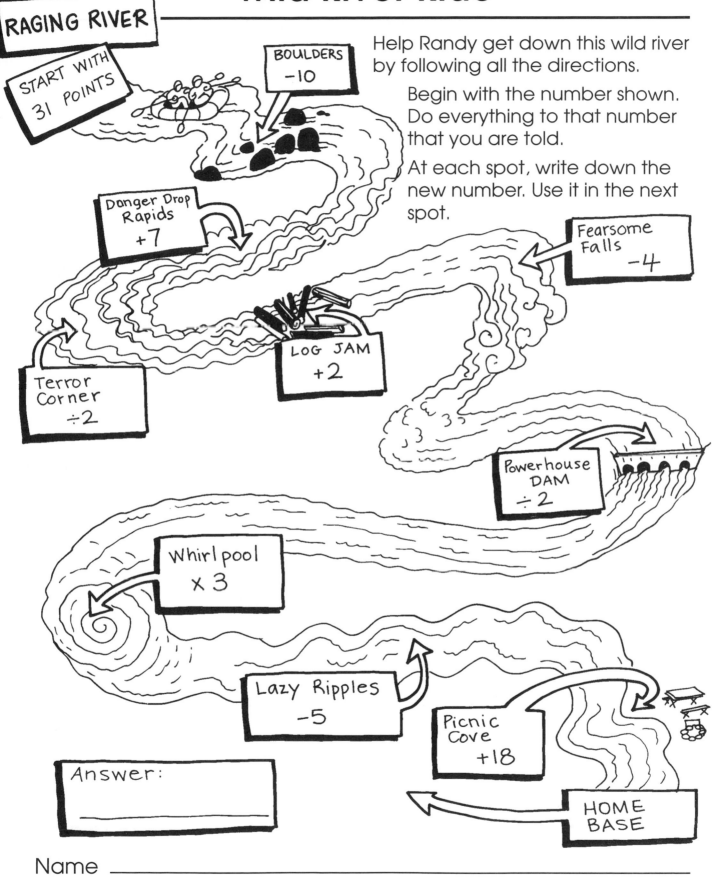

RAGING RIVER

START WITH 31 POINTS

BOULDERS −10

Help Randy get down this wild river by following all the directions.

Begin with the number shown. Do everything to that number that you are told.

At each spot, write down the new number. Use it in the next spot.

Danger Drop Rapids +7

Fearsome Falls −4

LOG JAM +2

Terror Corner ÷2

Powerhouse DAM ÷2

Whirlpool ×3

Lazy Ripples −5

Picnic Cove +18

HOME BASE

Answer:

Name

Hide & Seek

Chester is playing hide & seek, and he is IT.
Help him find the numbers that are hiding.
Find the number for each number sentence. Put it in the box.
You can use a number more than once.

1) ☐ + 10 = 14

2) 6 ÷ ☐ = 3

3) ☐ x 3 = 21

4) 9 − ☐ = 4

5) 5 + ☐ = 11

6) 4 + ☐ = 11

7) 2 x 5 = ☐

8) 24 ÷ 4 = ☐

9) 8 − ☐ = 0

10) 9 x 2 = ☐

11) 6 + ☐ = 12

12) ☐ ÷ 4 = 2

13) 5 x 5 = ☐

14) 8 x ☐ = 8

15) ☐ − 6 = 3

16) ☐ + 5 = 13

Name _____

Number Sentences

Lost in the Cave

A spelunker is someone who explores caves.

These spelunkers are looking for lost signs to put into the number sentences.

Find the right sign for each sentence. Each sign can be used many times.

1. 4 ☐ 7 = 11

2. 3 ☐ 2 = 6

3. 8 ☐ 5 = 3

4. 5 ☐ 3 = 15

5. 6 ☐ 2 = 3

11. 9 ☐ 1 = 9

12. 10 ☐ 2 = 5

13. 5 ☐ 3 = 8

14. 9 ☐ 3 = 3

15. 3 ☐ 3 = 9

6. 4 ☐ 4 = 0

7. 3 ☐ 8 = 24

8. 7 ☐ 2 = 9

9. 14 ☐ 2 = 7

10. 9 ☐ 1 = 10

16. 2 ☐ 6 = 8

17. 5 ☐ 3 = 2

18. 2 ☐ 2 = 4

19. 6 ☐ 6 = 1

20. 10 ☐ 5 = 15

Name _____

Signs for Operations

Which Route?

Help these cross-country runners decide which route to take.

Choose four different colors of crayons or markers. Draw a route for each runner to one of the finish flags. Use a different color for each route.

Add and subtract in your head as you follow each route. Start with the number 8 for each number. Write the number you have at the end of each route.

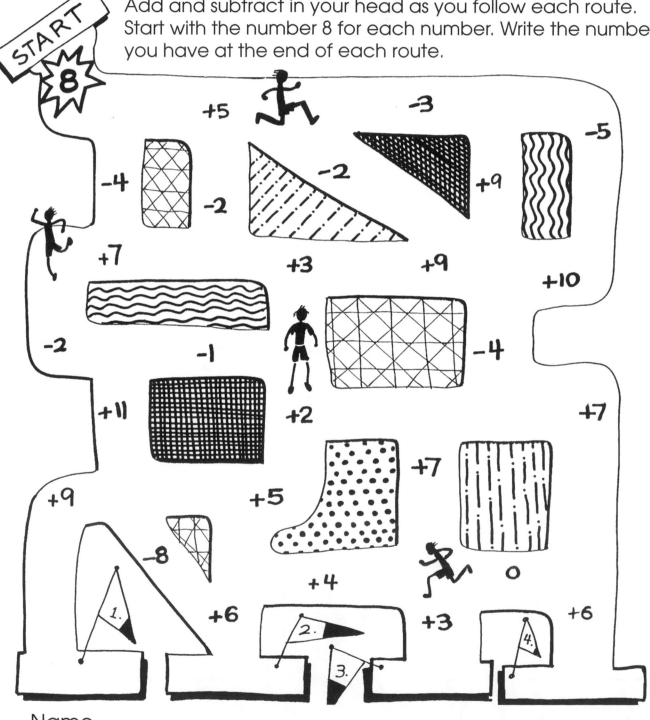

Name _____

Mental Math • Addition & Subtraction

Frisbee™ Fractions

Which Frisbee™ is which?
Write the letter to tell which Frisbee™
matches each description.

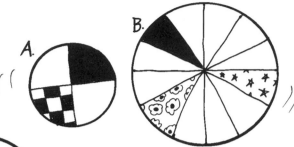

A.

B.

____ 1. $\frac{6}{6}$ dotted

____ 2. $\frac{2}{3}$ striped

____ 3. $\frac{1}{2}$ stars

____ 4. $\frac{1}{4}$ white

____ 5. $\frac{9}{12}$ white

____ 6. $\frac{3}{8}$ dotted

____ 7. $\frac{4}{6}$ white

____ 8. $\frac{1}{12}$ black

____ 9. $\frac{2}{7}$ stars

____ 10. $\frac{1}{1}$ flowered

____ 11. $\frac{1}{3}$ stars

____ 12. $\frac{3}{3}$ black

____ 13. $\frac{1}{2}$ white

____ 14. $\frac{1}{12}$ stars

____ 15. $\frac{1}{7}$ stripes

____ 16. $\frac{1}{8}$ checkered

C.

D.

E.

F.

G.

H.

I.

J.

K.

L.

M.

N.

Name _____

Skateboard Tricks

Adding and subtracting fractions is as easy as riding a skateboard!
You just need to know the trick. When the denominators are the same,
just add or subtract the numerators!

Find the answer for each skateboard fraction problem.

Then color the skateboards.

Follow the coloring directions in the box.

1. 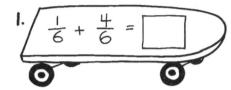 $\frac{1}{6} + \frac{4}{6} =$ ▢

2. 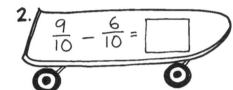 $\frac{9}{10} - \frac{6}{10} =$ ▢

3. 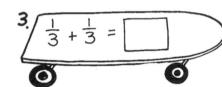 $\frac{1}{3} + \frac{1}{3} =$ ▢

4. 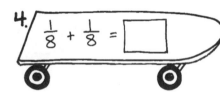 $\frac{1}{8} + \frac{1}{8} =$ ▢

5. 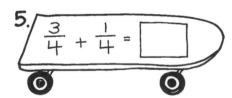 $\frac{3}{4} + \frac{1}{4} =$ ▢

6. 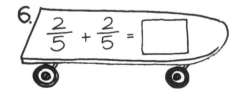 $\frac{2}{5} + \frac{2}{5} =$ ▢

7. 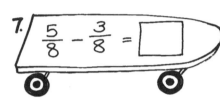 $\frac{5}{8} - \frac{3}{8} =$ ▢

8. 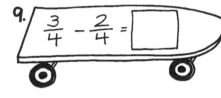 $\frac{5}{5} - \frac{1}{5} =$ ▢

9. 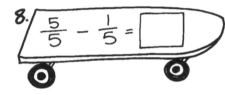 $\frac{3}{4} - \frac{2}{4} =$ ▢

10. 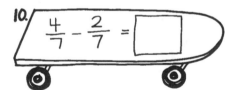 $\frac{4}{7} - \frac{2}{7} =$ ▢

11. 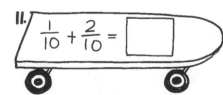 $\frac{1}{10} + \frac{2}{10} =$ ▢

12. 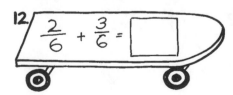 $\frac{2}{6} + \frac{3}{6} =$ ▢

Look for the answer. Then color or decorate the skateboard as the chart says.

$\frac{2}{8}$ purple

$\frac{3}{10}$ green

$\frac{5}{6}$ orange

$\frac{4}{5}$ yellow

$\frac{1}{4}$ silver

$\frac{2}{3}$ red

$\frac{2}{7}$ gold

$\frac{4}{4}$ blue

Name _____

Lunch on the Mountaintop

Equivalent fractions
name the same amount
of something.

$\frac{1}{2}$ of a sandwich is the same amount as $\frac{2}{4}$ of it.

So we say that $\frac{1}{2}$ is **equivalent** to $\frac{2}{4}$. Write $\frac{1}{2} = \frac{2}{4}$.

These mountain climbers have stopped for lunch.
Look at the food they are eating.
Write fractions that are equivalent to each other.

1. Tuna and Sprout Sandwich

$$\frac{1}{2} = \frac{}{4}$$

2. Whole wheat pizza

$$\frac{4}{6} = \frac{}{3}$$

3. Low fat Swiss cheese

$$\frac{2}{6} = \frac{}{3}$$

4.

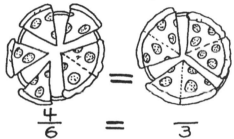

Mega "C" Soda

$$\frac{2}{8} = \frac{}{4}$$

5. Chocolate Energy Squares

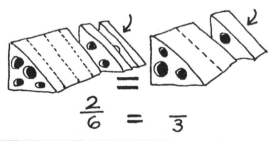

$$\frac{3}{6} = \frac{}{2}$$

6. Health Nut Loaf

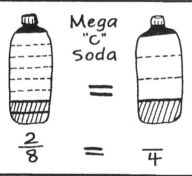

$$\frac{1}{2} = \frac{}{8}$$

Name _____

Equivalent Fractions

Lost Skates

A **decimal** is a fraction with tenths.

You can write a decimal number as a fraction or a mixed numeral.

The decimal one-tenth (.1) is the same as the fraction $\frac{1}{10}$.

The decimal 3.5 means the same as the mixed numeral $3\frac{5}{10}$.

These skaters have each lost a skate.

Draw a line from each skater to the skate that has the matching fraction or mixed numeral. (There is an extra skate that matches no one!)

Watch Out!

This scuba diver has come face-to-face with something scary under the water. What is it?

Follow the dots to find out. Connect the dots from the smallest to the largest decimal number shown.

82.3

66.3

99.9

88.8

57.6

41.3

4.6

5.7

7.5

4.4

29.3

10.9

4.9

24.5   21.2

6.3   3.7

26.0

9.5

16.3

4.2

22.6   2.9

2.1

3.0

1.4

2.5

1.8   0.4   0.1

1.1   START

0.9

0.6

Gack!

Name _____

Ordering Decimals

Field Day Math

Field Day is an exciting day for all the kids at Walker School.

Every student needs to know the time of the events.

The schedule is posted on the fence.

Use the Field Day Schedule to solve the problems on the next page (page 301).

I'm here for the Hop, Skip, and Jump Contest

FIELD DAY — WALKER SCHOOL

TIME	FIELD 1	FIELD 2
9:00 A.M.	Sign-ups	Sign-ups
9:30 A.M.	3-Legged Race	Water Balloon Toss
9:45 A.M.	100 Yard Potato Sack Hop	Softball Throw
10:00 A.M.	4-Person Relay Races	Bubble Gum-Blowing Contest
11:00 A.M.		Frisbee™ Tournament
11:30 A.M.	Hop, Skip, & Jump	
12:00 P.M.	Lunch	Lunch
1:00 P.M.	Teacher-Kid Softball Game	Bike Rodeo
3:15 P.M.	Squirt Gun Target Shoot	Watermelon-Eating Contest
4:00 P.M.	Award Ceremony (Ribbons) and Barbecue	

Name _____

Use with page 301.
Time • Problem Solving

Field Day Math, cont.

Use the Field Day Schedule on page 300.

1. Gracie gets to the field at 9:20 A.M. Does she have time to sign up for an event? _____

2. Trudy has a ballet class at 5:00 P.M. Can she compete in the watermelon-eating contest? _____

3. Chad wants to toss water balloons and be on a relay team. Which will he do first? _____

4. Name 2 events that take only 15 minutes.

   _____ and

   _____

5. Name the event that takes 1 hour.

   _____

6. Steve looks at his watch. It is 11:30 A.M. How many minutes are there until lunch? _____

7. Maggie rides to Field 2 at 1:30 P.M. What's going on when she gets there? _____

8. What time will the Frisbee™ tournament end? _____

9. What happens at the same time as the softball throw?

   _____

10. How much time is allowed for the softball game? _____

11. After lunch, Pete and Abe run home to get squirt guns. What time do they need to get back for the target shoot? _____

12. How much time does the schedule allow for relay races? _____

13. Al's friend Margie wants him to run the 3-legged race with her. He gets to Field 1 at 9:40 A.M. Is he early, late, or on time? _____

14. Erik wins a blue ribbon in the bike rodeo. What time will he go to get his award? _____

Name _____

Sara's Sports Schedule

Sara is busy with many sports. She has to keep a schedule.
Each clock tells what time it is when Sara arrives at one of the events.
For each problem, tell if Sara is on time.

Soccer Practice	Monday 6:30 P.M.	Chess Club	Tuesday 5:15 P.M.
Ski Meet	Saturday 11:00 A.M.	Bowling Team	Thursday 1:45 P.M.
Dance Lessons	Tuesday 2:45 P.M.	Batting Cage	Thursday 4:20 P.M.
Tennis Match	Friday 4:10 P.M.	Ice Skating Practice	Thursday 4:20 P.M.

Is she on time?

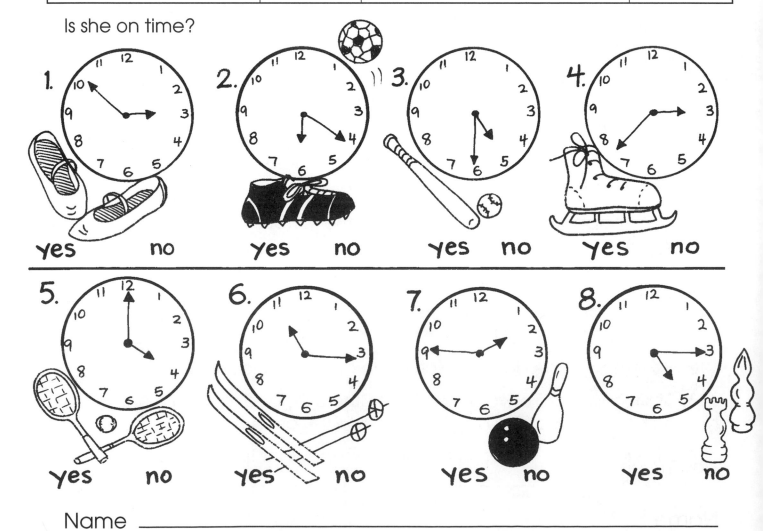

1. yes   no

2. yes   no

3. yes   no

4. yes   no

5. yes   no

6. yes   no

7. yes   no

8. yes   no

Name _____

A Pocketful of Coins

Gabe is very hungry at the soccer game.
He is buying food with the money in his pockets.
Count the coins to find how much each treat costs.

1.

How much? _____

2.

How much? _____

3.

How much? _____

4.

How much? _____

5.

How much? _____

6.

How much? _____

7.

How much? _____

8.

How much? _____

Name _____

Meet Me at the Snack Bar

During the game, Tammy and Tracy work at the snack bar.
Help them make the correct change for each customer.

MENU

ICE CREAM......75¢
POP CORN......25¢
FRENCH FRIES..$1.00
PIZZA......$1.25
GUM......10¢
SODA POP......60¢
JUICE......85¢
MILKSHAKE......$1.50

---

1. **Ice Cream**

   You give $ 1.00

   Cost   – _____

   Change

2. **Pizza**

   You give $ 2.00

   Cost   – _____

   Change

3. **2 packs of gum**

   You give   50 ¢

   Cost   – _____

   Change

4. **Juice**

   You give $ 1.00

   Cost   – _____

   Change

5. **Soda & French Fries**

   You give $ 2.00

   Cost   – _____

   Change

6. **Milkshake**

   You give $ 5.00

   Cost   – _____

   Change

7. **Popcorn**

   You give   50 ¢

   Cost   – _____

   Change

8. **French Fries**

   You give $ 5.00

   Cost   – _____

   Change

Name _____

Cheers for the Team

Every team needs fans! Sports wouldn't be as much fun without them. Solve these problems about the fans at the Championship Swim Meet.

1. 35 fans were cheering for the Dolphins. 46 fans cheered for the Sharks. How many fans were cheering?

   _____

2. Carlos went to buy a snow cone from the snack bar. It cost 40¢. He had 25¢. How much more does he need?

   _____

3. Anna's mom brought hats for all 7 people in their family. Anna and Danna dropped theirs under the bleachers. How many hats were left?

   _____

4. The pool has 4 rows of bleachers with 12 spaces in each row. How many fans can fit in the bleachers?

   _____

5. Lily watched the swimmers line up for the relay. There were 5 teams, each with 4 swimmers. How many swimmers are racing in all?

   _____

6. Angie brought jelly beans for her friends in the stands. She has 100 to share among 3 friends and herself. How many jelly beans will each girl get?

   _____

Name _____

APPENDIX

CONTENTS

Language Arts Skills Test

PART ONE: READING

Read the following poem, and then answer the questions.

Ernie stepped in quicksand
Even though the sign was there.
He walked right into the middle
Though the sign told him, "Beware!"

The sand was filled with water,
Which turned it into muck
All wet and thick and gooey,
Poor Ernie was out of luck!

His feet sank in up to the knees
He tried to run on through.
He grabbed and pulled and hollered,
But the quicksand was like glue.

We all went out to find him.
Poor Ernie was up to his ears.
We threw him a rope and dragged
  him out,
And he's lived for years and years!

---

1. A good title for this poem would be
   a. Ernie's Walk
   b. Foolish Ernie
   c. All About Sand

2. Where did Ernie step into the quicksand?
   a. the edge
   b. the river bottom
   c. the middle

3. How many people went to look for Ernie?
   a. No one
   b. One person
   c. Many people

4. What word in stanza #3 is a synonym for **yelled?**
   _____

5. What did the sign tell Ernie?

   _____

6. What did Ernie do after he sank into the quicksand?

   _____

7. Write three words the poem used to describe the quicksand.

   _____

   _____

   _____

8. What kind of a person do you think Ernie was?

   _____

Name _____

Look at each pair of sentences. Write C in front of the cause. Write E in front of the effect.

9. ____ The ship was tossed around wildly.
   ____ A terrible hurricane crossed the ocean.

10. ____ The airport was surrounded by heavy fog.
    ____ No airplanes could take off yesterday.

11. ____ The volcano erupted again last week.
    ____ The sky is filled with ash.

12. ____ We explored the island on motorbikes.
    ____ No cars are allowed on the island.

13. This limerick is mixed-up!
    Number the lines in the correct order.
    ____ So why was he giggling
    ____ A certain young man from France
    ____ And shaking and wiggling?
    ____ It's because he was covered with ants!
    ____ Was always too bashful to dance.

Read the paragraph, and answer the questions.

Frannie started up the helicopter motor. She shouted to Felix, "Are you ready?" "Yes!" he hollered. "Let's take off!" And off they went, flying over the bridge. Then Felix had an idea. "Let's try flying under the bridge!" he shouted.

14. What do you think will happen next?

   _____

   _____

15. Find a pair of synonyms in the story. _____ , _____

16. Find a pair of opposites. _____ , _____

17. What did Frannie start? _____

Name _____

Finish the sentences.

18. **Wet** is to **rain forest** as **dry** is to _____ .

19. **Morning** is to **evening** as **day** is to _____ .

20. **Submarine** is to **airplane** as _____ is to **above.**

21. **Child** is to **children** as _____ is to **geese.**

Read the passage, and answer the questions.

Yum

A long time ago in the jungle, a big, fierce lion caught a tiny mouse for a snack. Just as the lion was about to gobble up the mouse, the mouse cried, "Oh please! Please! Don't eat me! If you let me go, I promise to come back and help you some day!" Now the lion thought that was pretty funny that such a tiny thing could help him, the king of the jungle! While he was laughing, the mouse escaped and ran away.

Many days later, the big, powerful lion, was caught in a tricky trap set by some lion hunters. The mouse was far away, but he heard the lion's painful roar. He ran quickly through the jungle and found the trapped lion. "Here I am to help you!" cried the mouse. This time, the lion did not laugh. He needed all the help he could get! The tiny mouse gnawed the ropes off the lion. In no time at all, the lion was loose again. From that day on, the lion and the mouse were best friends.

22. How did the mouse escape from the lion? _____

23. When did this story take place? _____

24. What word describes the trap? _____

25. What word describes the lion's roar? _____

26. What word means the same as **mighty?** _____

27. What title would you give to this? _____

28. This story is a fable. A fable teaches a lesson. What lesson does this teach?

_____

_____

Name _____

Read the passage, and answer the questions.

In 1980, Mt. St. Helens, in Washington, erupted three times in two months. The first blast was 500 times as powerful as an atom bomb. The volcano caused 60 deaths. It caused three billion dollars in damage.

A volcano is an opening in the surface of the Earth. Gases and melted rock erupt through the opening. There are over 500 active volcanoes in the world today. Some volcanoes are slow and quiet, but many are very violent. The big explosions do a lot of damage.

Here is an example of the harm a volcano can do. A volcano on an island in Indonesia killed 2000 people in 1883. The next day, the mountain collapsed. This killed 3000 more people. The collapse of the mountain caused a huge tidal wave in the ocean. That wave crashed onto other countries and killed another 31,000 people.

29. When did Mt. St. Helens erupt? _____

30. How many active volcanoes are there in the world today? _____

31. Is it true that all volcanoes erupt violently? _____

32. What was the cost of the eruption at Mt. St. Helens?

_____ people and _____ dollars

33. How many deaths were caused by the tidal wave? _____

34. What is the main idea of this passage? _____

_____

_____

35. What do you think the author's purpose was in writing this passage?

_____

_____

_____

_____

Name _____

PART TWO: SPELLING

Find the correct words in each row. Circle them.

36. dolar   zipper   hugging   gost

37. puddle   garadge   million   laugh

38. afraid   lemmon   appear   sumer

39. graph   quizes   cotton   friend

Circle the correct spelling.

40. absent   abcent

41. krayon   crayon

42. sise   size

43. jiraffe   giraffe

Write the correct contraction for each pair of words.

44. did not _____

45. she will _____

46. they are _____

47. I have _____

48. **Circle the words that have one or more silent letters.**

bottle   **rhyme**   dough   *shhhhh*

lumpy   **lamb**   ghost

bridge   halo   liver

wrap   **lonesome**

know   sword

Choose a pair of vowels from the hat to spell each word correctly.

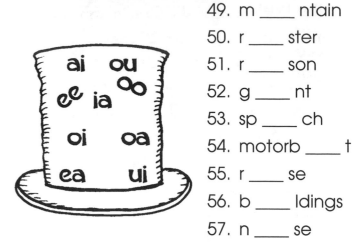

ai   ou   ee   ia   oo   oi   oa   ea   ui

49. m _____ ntain

50. r _____ ster

51. r _____ son

52. g _____ nt

53. sp _____ ch

54. motorb _____ t

55. r _____ se

56. b _____ ldings

57. n _____ se

Write the correct ending on each word: *er, ar,* or *or*

58. col _____

59. doll _____

60. nev _____

61. flav _____

62. coll _____

63. ladd _____

Write the correct ending on each word: *y* or *ey*

64. penn _____

65. reall _____

66. vall _____

67. monk _____

68. hon _____

69. cit _____

Write the plural form of each of these words. Write the whole word.

70. watch _____

71. quart _____

72. candy _____

73. box _____

74. donkey _____

75. mouse _____

76. tooth _____

77. family _____

78. goose _____

Name _____

Spelling Skills Test

79. **Circle the words on the trash can that are spelled correctly.**

garbige   judge

brige   cabbege

fudge   hedge

ridge   garadge

ledge

80. **Circle the words on the rock that are spelled correctly.**

tryed   wishd

caught   rubed

worryed   slipped

grabbed   getted

keeped   enjoyed

Write the past tense of each of these words. Write the whole word.

81. eat _____

82. hop _____

83. find _____

84. hurry _____

Add *ing* to each word. Write the whole word.

85. leap _____

86. hide _____

87. fly _____

88. swat _____

Name _____

Add the suffix or ending. Write the whole word. Spell it right!

89. hot + er = _____

90. scare + y = _____

91. tiny + est = _____

92. care + less = _____

Choose a prefix from the poster to add to each word. Write the whole word.

tri   dis   un
re   sub
pro
mis   super

93. angle _____

94. write _____

95. tie _____

96. marine _____

97. take _____

98. Mimi chose some wrong words when she wrote her story.
Circle the wrong words.

Polly road along on an old hoarse threw the woulds. The hoarse tripped and lost a shoo in the creak. Polly fell off. Did she brake her tow?

99. Which of the bee's words are correct? **Circle them.**

none   once   choclat
people   forty   ocean
wheather   opin   voice
trubble

This menu has some wrong spellings. Write each food again, spelling each word correctly.

• tomatoe sause

• suger cookies

• cheese pissa

• lettice salid

• bannanna pie

• hamburglers

100. Which words are compound words? **Circle them.**

bedspread   homeless
disturb   campfire
nightgown   argument
reward   fingernail

107._____

108._____

109._____

110._____

111._____

112._____

Circle the word in each group that is spelled wrong.

101.   syrup   success   fussy
        Friday   stranger   sience

102.   surprise   sixtey   possible
        friend   messy   sentence

103.   moter   doctor   cotton
        mystery   double   tomato

104.   chocolate   around   vegetable
        different   Lincoln   memary

105.   squirrel   squeak   quake
        questun   Africa   quietly

106. **Circle the animal names that are spelled correctly.**

giraffe   ant   eagel

turtel   goose   monky

rooster   parrot   raccoon

Find the word that is spelled wrong. Write it correctly.

_____ 113. Cassie's friends were quiet mad at her.

_____ 114. Felix can't remember witch path to take.

_____ 115. Bruno already tired to open that door.

I ca'nt rember if I put jelley on my sammich.

116. **Write this quote again. Spell all the words correctly.**

_____

_____

Name _____

117. Circle the words that can be nouns.

    friendly   Mrs. Clown
    afternoon   suddenly
    trick   gobbled
    Friday   laughter
    merry-go-round

118. Circle the words that are proper nouns and should be capitalized.

    easter   mexico
    teacher   boston
    thursday   school
    texas

119. Circle the words in the magician's hat that can be verbs.

swing   leaping   roar
clown   laugh
magic   tricks
flying   tricked
    music
grabbed   slowly

Draw a box around adjectives that describe nouns in these sentences.

120. Seven silly little clowns ate four bags of cotton candy.

121. Don't go near that fierce lion with the large teeth!

122. Which baby elephant has the broken toe?

123. Jennifer held her breath as she walked slowly across the thin, high wire.

Draw a box around the adverb that tells how, when, or where.

124. The tiger ate his lunch hungrily.

125. Four trapeze artists practice their tricks daily.

126. Circle the signs below that have complete sentences.

Elephants do daring tricks!

The acrobat doing a dangerous act.

Where is the roller coaster?

Crocodiles hiding in the water.

See the Amazing Fire-Eater!

FROM THE TOP OF THE FERRIS WHEEL.

CAN SHE JUGGLE 10 THINGS?

Name _____

127. **Underline the sentence below that is a statement. Put a box around the sentence that is a question. Put a check mark in front of the sentence that is an exclamation.**

    a. Can you ride a unicycle?

    b. Never put your hand in the tiger's cage!

    c. It is a good idea to be friendly to the gorillas.

Circle the numbers of the sentences that have CORRECT punctuation.

    128. Don't look down!

    129. Which bear is good at dancing.

    130. Did you try the giant hot dogs with grilled onions?

    131. The juggler dropped a toaster on his head yesterday.

    132. That is not a very good idea?

133. **Circle the subject of the sentence.**

    Two brave clowns jumped on the pirate ship this morning.

134. **Circle the subject of the sentence.**

    A nervous Gino put his head in the lion's mouth.

135. **Circle the predicate of the sentence.**

    The monkeys climbed all over their barrel.

136. **Circle the predicate of the sentence.**

    Chester, grab those balloons before they float away!

137. **Circle the letters in Allie's envelope that should be capitalized. Add the missing punctuation.**

allie clown
112 fun street
central city iowa

        abby apricot
        2222 laughter lane
        cow's ear illinois 60001

Name _____

138. **Circle the letters in Allie's letter that should be capitalized. Add the missing punctuation.**

dear abby

you won't believe the news the carnival came
to our town last Thursday molly and i rode the
roller coaster seven times we bought cotton
candy four times guess what happened when
I went to see the circus acts they invited me to
be in the show they gave me the job of fire-eater
it isn't all that hard—just a little hot

          love

          allie

Make a contraction from each of these pairs of words.

139. we will   _____

140. they are   _____

141. will not   _____

142. **Circle the letters on the poster that should be capitalized. Add the missing punctuation.**

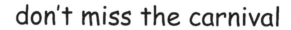

don't miss the carnival

see the most amazing things

we have clowns acrobats and jugglers

eat delicious treats

you can play lots of fun games

there are 25 great rides

thursday october 15

central city iowa

Name _____

143. Draw a line through the idea in this story that is not necessary.

You won't believe what happened on the Pirate Ride today! Four visitors fell overboard! Three pirates had to walk the plank, and the mechanical shark sank. Everything was going wrong. Just then the circus show started. The sails fell down, too. Luckily, all the visitors thought these things were part of the ride. They laughed and laughed and said, "This is the best ride we've taken yet!"

144. Circle the title that would be best for the above story.
   a. Time to Walk the Plank   c. Trouble on the Pirate Ride
   b. The Mechanical Shark   d. Trouble at the Carnival

145. Choose one clown. Circle the one you chose. Imagine what this clown is like and what he or she might do, wear, or say!

Give the clown a name. _____

Write 6 words that describe what you imagine this clown to be like.

   1. _____   4. _____

   2. _____   5. _____

   3. _____   6. _____

Write a sentence telling something the clown might do.

_____

_____

_____

Name _____

Social Studies Skills Test

PART ONE: SOCIAL STUDIES

1. Circle the states.
   Texas   Florida
   Kansas   Asia
   Chicago

2. Circle the cities.
   Colorado   San Francisco
   Boston   Mexico

3. Circle the countries.
   Canada   Seattle
   Germany   Guatemala

4. Which of the U.S. states below is farthest north?
   Montana
   Colorado
   Alaska

5. Which of the U.S. states below is farthest south?
   Ohio
   Florida
   Tennessee

Use the map to answer the questions.

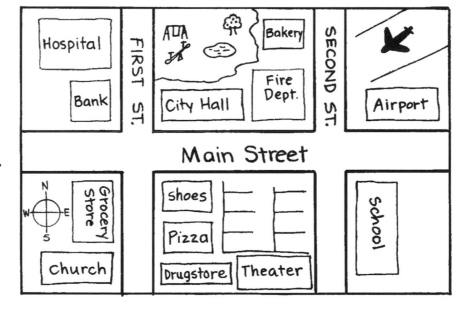

6. What direction is the park from the airport? _____

7. Is the school on First Street? _____

8. Which one is not on Main Street?   bank   drugstore   parking lot

9. How many blocks is it from the hospital to the airport? _____

10. What store is west of the shoe store?
    grocery store   pizza shop   drugstore   bakery

Name _____

Circle the correct answer.

11. Which country is not a neighbor of the United States?

   Mexico   Canada   India   Costa Rica   Haiti

12. Which country is in South America?

   Canada   Russia   Bolivia   Germany

13. Which country is in Europe?

   France   Panama   China   Australia

14. Which country is in North America?

   Japan   United States   Ireland

15. Which part of the U.S. government makes the laws?

   the president   the Supreme Court   the Congress

16. Which happened first?

   the first airplane was flown   the first person stepped on the moon

17. Which happened last?

   Washington   Kennedy   Lincoln
   was president   was president   was president

18. Which building is not in Washington DC?

   the Statue of Liberty   the Capitol Building   the Lincoln Memorial

Look at the grid. Write the location of each American symbol or monument.

_____ 19. flag

_____ 20. Statue of Liberty

_____ 21. eagle

_____ 22. White House

_____ 23. pilgrim

_____ 24. fireworks

_____ 25. Liberty Bell

_____ 26. Washington Monument

Name _____

PART TWO: MAP SKILLS & GEOGRAPHY

Look for these parts of the map. Write the letter for each one next to its name.

_____ 27. title

_____ 28. key

_____ 29. scale

_____ 30. compass

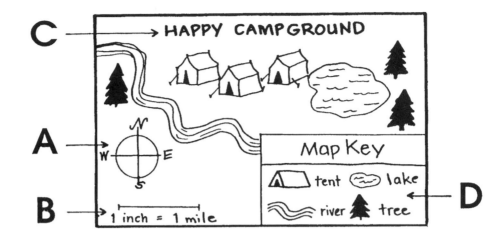

Use the map to answer the questions.
Write N, S, E, or W in each blank.

31. The town is _____ of the airport.

32. The river is _____ of the town.

33. The lake is _____ of the river.

34. The town is _____ of the lake.

35. The airport is _____ of the lake.

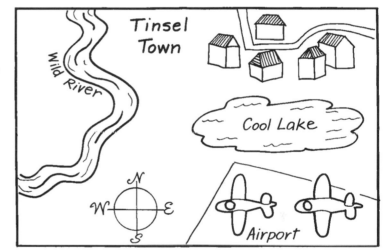

36. Circle the state that is in the western part of the United States.

    New York   Florida   Michigan   California

37. Circle the state that is in the southern part of the United States.

    California   Colorado   Florida   Maine

38. Circle the state that is in the eastern part of the United States.

    Texas   New Jersey   Arizona   California

Name _____

Use the maps to find the hemispheres for these continents and oceans. Write E for Eastern, W for Western, and B for both.

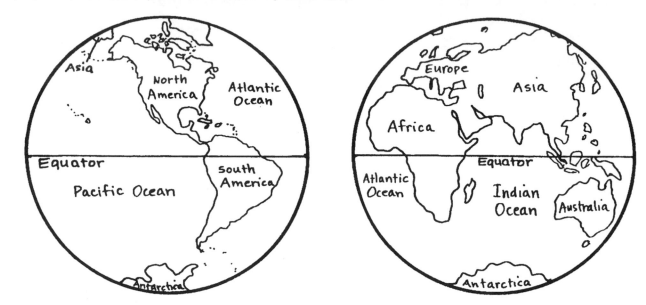

_____ 39. Africa   _____ 40. The Atlantic Ocean   _____ 42. Europe

                          _____ 41. South America   _____ 43. Asia

44. Circle the word that is NOT a continent.

Asia   Africa   Texas   North America   Australia

45. Circle the word that is NOT a state.

Iowa   Pennsylvania   Kansas   Boston   Georgia

46. Circle the word that is NOT a country.

France   India   Chicago   Mexico   Canada

47. Circle the country that is on the northern border of the United States.

Alaska   Germany   Canada   Montana   Mexico

48. Circle the country that is a neighbor to the south of the United States.

Japan   Mexico   Canada   China   Russia

Name _____

Map Skills & Geography Test

Use the grid to help you find things on the picnic table.

_____ 49. Where is the 🍎 ?

_____ 50. Where is the 🐜 ?

_____ 51. Where is the 🧁 ?

_____ 52. Where is the 🥪 ?

```
      1    2    3    4
```

Use the map to answer the questions.

_____ 53. How many rabbits are in the north area of the park?

_____ 54. What area has the least rabbits?

_____ 55. What area has 40 rabbits?

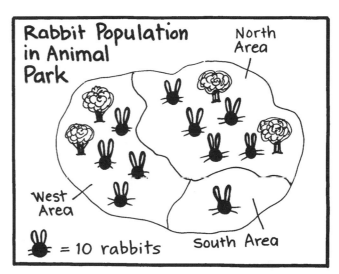

Rabbit Population in Animal Park

North Area

West Area

South Area

🐰 = 10 rabbits

Write the word that matches the definition.

_____ 56. tells distances on a map   west

_____ 57. land surrounded by water   continent

_____ 58. opposite of east   ocean

_____ 59. a large body of land   scale

_____ 60. a large body of water   title

_____ 61. tells what a map is about   compass

_____ 62. tells directions on a map   island

Name _____

Science Skills Test

Circle the correct answer or answers.

1. Which things are part of the circulatory system? A B C D

Write the letter of the word that matches each definition.

2. _____ break in a bone   a. fracture

3. _____ a muscle or joint stretched too far   b. cavity

4. _____ a body's reaction to something like pollen   c. allergy

5. _____ an illness   d. disease

6. _____ hole caused by decay in a tooth   e. sprain

Circle the correct answer.

7. Which is the ribcage?
   A   B   C   D

Write the letter of the word that matches each definition.

8. _____ a crack in the Earth's surface   a. atmosphere

9. _____ a large mass of ice that moves   b. fault

10. _____ when a volcano explodes   c. eruption

11. _____ the layer of air around the Earth   d. lava

12. _____ melted rock that flows from a crack in the Earth e. glacier

Circle the correct answer or answers.

13. Which one travels around the sun?
    A   B   C

14. Which is a peninsula?
    D   E   F

Name _____

15. Which shows the molecules in a gas?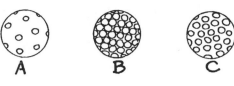

16. Which swimmer is on the crest of the wave?

17. Which does this picture show?
     A. freezing   B. evaporation   C. melting

18. The radius, ulna, and humerus are bones in the
     A. arm   B. leg   C. back

19. The tibia, fibula, and femur are bones in the
     A. ankle   B. arm   C. leg

20. Which one of these is caused by germs?
     A. a bruise   B. an infection   C. a fracture

_____

21. Which cloud is a cumulonimbus?

_____

22. Which machine is an inclined plane?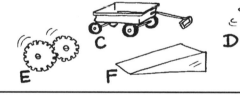

_____

23. Which machine is a pulley?

_____

Write the letter of the matching word.

24. ____ a push or a pull   a. vibrate

25. ____ to move back and forth   b. pitch

26. ____ the way sound travels   c. melt

27. ____ a change from a solid to a liquid   d. waves

28. ____ the highness or lowness of a sound   e. force

Name _____

Math Skills Test

PART ONE: NUMBER CONCEPTS & RELATIONSHIPS

Look at this picture to answer the questions below.

Circle the correct answer.

1. The snake is _____ in the line.   fourth   first   third   second   fifth

2. Is the bird fourth in line?   yes   no

3. Which is second in line?   snake   rat   turtle   frog   bird

Fill in the numbers that are missing from the skip counting.

4. 25, 30, 35, _____, _____, 50   5. 100, 90, 80, _____, 60, _____

Write the numeral for each number.

_____ 6. forty-seven   _____ 8. three hundred twenty-six

_____ 7. six hundred ten   _____ 9. seven thousand two hundred sixteen

For problems 10–12, circle the answers.

10. Which words match this numeral?   **440**

    a. four hundred fourteen   d. four hundred forty
    b. four hundred forty-four   e. four thousand, four hundred
    c. four hundred four

11. Which words match this numeral? **6,207**

    a. six hundred twenty-seven   c. six thousand, two hundred seven
    b. six thousand, two hundred seventy   d. six thousand twenty-seven

12. Which number is two million?   a. 20,000   c. 2,000   e. 0,000,000
                         b. 200,000   d. 2,000,000   f. 2,000,000,000

13. Write this number in words. **59** _____

14. Circle the odd numbers: **74 101 55 3,003 66 929 1,000 15**

Name _____

Number Concepts & Relationships Skills Test

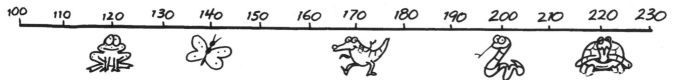

100   110   120   130   140   150   160   170   180   190   200   210   220   230

Use the number line to answer questions 15–17. Write the answer on the line.

15. Is the baby alligator at 150 on the number line? _____

16. Which animal is at a number 60 greater than the butterfly? _____

17. Which animal is at a number that is about 100 less than the turtle? _____

18. **Circle the largest number:**   35,623   5,999   24,900   25,800   9,000

19. **Circle the smallest number:**   10,000   927   729   2,900   777

Write the correct symbol (< or >) in the box.

20. 222 ☐ 202   21. 634 ☐ 643   22. 5,005 ☐ 5,050

23. Write these numbers in order   237   333   273   193   103
    from smallest to largest: ____   ____   ____   ____   ____

24. Write these numbers in order   72   67   39   36   94
    from largest to smallest: ____   ____   ____   ____   ____

Write these numbers:

_____ 25. 9 ones and 7 tens   _____ 27. 8 hundreds and 6 ones

_____ 26. 4 hundreds, 3 tens, 9 ones   _____ 28. 2 thousands and 5 hundreds

29. Look at the beaver's sign.

_____ Which number is in the hundreds place?

_____ Which number is in the tens place?

Write the expanded numbers. *Example: 523 = 500 + 20 + 3*

30. 416 = _____   31. 7,520 = _____

Write the number.

32. 500 + 90 + 3 = _____   33. 3,000 + 20 + 5 = _____

Name _____

In 34-36, finish each pattern. Write or draw what will come next.

34.  _____

35. 2, 5, 8, 11, 14, _____

36. AB, BC, CD, _____

Look at the line of bugs to answer questions 37–39. Write a fraction for each answer.

_____ 37. What fraction of the creatures have spots?

_____ 38. What fraction of the creatures have 8 legs?

_____ 39. What fraction of the creatures have wings?

_____ 40. Write a fractional number to show how much pizza has NOT been eaten.

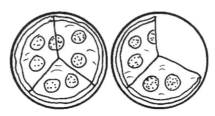

Write a fractional number to match the words:

_____ 41. five sixths

_____ 42. twelve and seven eighths

_____ 43. twenty-two and four ninths

44. Circle the words that match this number: $10 \frac{3}{7}$

    a. thirteen sevenths

    b. ten and seven thirds

    c. ten thirds

    d. ten and three sevenths

45. Circle the greatest amount.	$\frac{1}{10}$	$\frac{1}{2}$	$\frac{1}{4}$	$\frac{1}{12}$
46. Circle the greatest amount.	$7.90	$9.70	$9.69	$6.99
47. Which is about $5 more than $12?	$12.70	$19.50	$17.20	$7.00

Name _____

Write the numbers.

_____ 48. What is 10 > 450?

_____ 49. What is 2 < 500?

_____ 50. What is $\frac{1}{2}$ of 100?

51. **Circle the number that does not belong in this group.**   **35   405   275   500   115**

52. Is this number sentence true?   **200 + 88 < 300**   Yes   No

53. Is this number sentence true?   **60 – 10 = 30 + 30**   Yes   No

54. Is this number sentence true?   **100 + 200 > 900 – 600**   Yes   No

Write the answers on the lines.

_____ 55. If Ollie takes these coins out of the jar, how much money will be in his hand?
6 nickels and 4 pennies

_____ 56. If Ollie takes these coins out of the jar, how much money will be in his hand?
5 dimes, 1 nickel, and 3 pennies

_____ 57. If Ollie takes these coins out of the jar, how much money will be in his hand?
1 quarter and 3 dimes

58. Allie practices tennis every day.

On Monday, she hit 325 balls.
On Tuesday, she hit 412 balls.
On Wednesday, she hit 352 balls.

On which day did she hit the least number of balls? Write your answer. _____

59. Samantha Skunk does many push-ups every day.

The number she did today has these digits in it: 4   8   2
The largest number is in the ones place.
The smallest number is in the tens place.

What is the number? Write your answer. _____

Name _____

PART TWO: GEOMETRY, MEASUREMENT, & GRAPHING

Write the letter of the figure that matches each of the terms below:

_____ 60. point

_____ 61. line segment

_____ 62. parallel line segments

_____ 63. angle

_____ 64. triangle

Write the letter of the figure that matches each of these:

 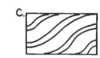

_____ 65. square

_____ 66. hexagon

_____ 67. triangle

_____ 68. circle

_____ 69. rectangle that is not a square

Find the perimeter of each of these figures.

_____ 70.

_____ 71.

_____ 72.

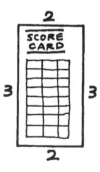

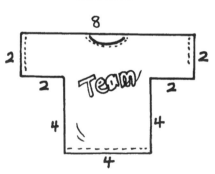

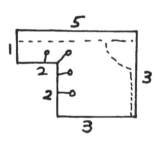

Tell how many square units are in each figure.

_____ 73.

_____ 74.

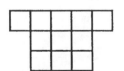

Name _____

Geometry, Measurement, & Graphing Skills Test

Tell how many cubic units are in each figure.

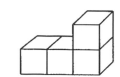

_____ 75.

_____ 76.

Circle the unit that would be best for measuring each of these.

77. juice in the glass ——————— 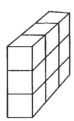 ——————— cup   gallon

78. water in the pool ——— ——————— pints   gallons

79. weight of cap ——————— ——— kilograms   grams

80. weight of weight lifter — ——————— kilograms   grams

81. weight of bug ——————— ——— ounces   pounds

82. height of a building — ——————— meters   centimeters

83. length of your thumb ——— ——— inches   feet

Circle the unit that is biggest.

84.   quart   cup   pint   gallon
85.   kilometer   centimeter   meter
86.   gram   kilogram
87.   yard   foot   inch

Write the time that each clock shows.

_____ 88.

_____ 89.

Name _____

90. Which clock shows 6:50?

A. 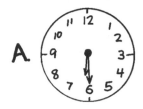 B. 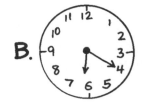 C.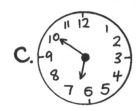

Fill in the blanks with the correct numbers.

91. _____ cups = 1 quart

92. _____ grams = 1 kilogram

93. _____ inches = 1 foot

94. _____ centimeters = 1 meter

**Use the graph
to answer the questions.**

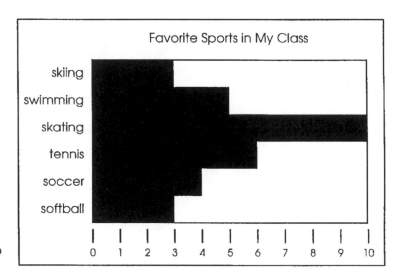

_____ 95. Which sport has
6 votes?

_____ 96. How many votes
are for skating?

_____ 97. Which sport has 1 less
vote than swimming?

_____ 98. Which 2 sports got the
same number of votes?

Use the graph to answer the questions.

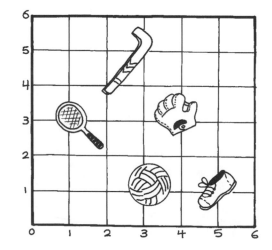

_____ 99. Write the
location of the .

_____ 100. What is at (4, 3)?

_____ 101. Where is the ?

_____ 102. Where is the ?

_____ 103. What is at (1, 3)?

Name _____

Geometry, Measurement, & Graphing Skills Test

104. Circle all the odd numbers.

3   5   2   30   16   31

105. Circle all the even numbers.

7   21   10   100   14   47

Write the answers.

_____106. In the number 473, which number is in the tens place?

_____107. In the number 115, which number is in the ones place?

_____108. In the number 716, which number is in the hundreds place?

_____109. In the number 2816, which number is in the hundreds place?

_____110. Round 56 to the nearest ten.

_____111. Round 73 to the nearest ten.

_____112. Round 228 to the nearest ten.

_____113. Round 472 to the nearest hundred.

Write the missing numbers in the number sentences.

114. $5 + 7 =$ _____

115. $3 +$ _____ $= 7$

116. $6 + 9 =$ _____

117. $5 +$ _____ $= 12$

118. $18 - 9 =$ _____

119. _____ $- 6 = 5$

120. $17 -$ _____ $= 9$

121. $13 - 6 =$ _____

122. $15 -$ _____ $= 6$

Solve the problems.

123. $\begin{array}{r} 403 \\ + 192 \\ \hline \end{array}$ 124. $\begin{array}{r} 6911 \\ + 1044 \\ \hline \end{array}$ 125. $\begin{array}{r} 295 \\ - 62 \\ \hline \end{array}$

Name _____

_____126. Write a fraction that tells what part is checkered.

_____127. Write a fraction that tells what part is checkered.

_____128. Write a fraction that tells what part is striped.

_____129. Write a fraction that tells what part has flowers.

_____130. Write a fraction that tells what part is checkered.

Write the missing numbers in the number sentences.

131. 3 x 6 = _____

132. 4 x _____ = 20

133. _____ x 6 = 42

134. 9 x 3 = _____

135. 4 x 8 = _____

136. 6 x _____ = 36

_____¢137. Count the coins. Write how much money is shown.

_____¢138. Count the coins. Write how much money is shown.

139. Circle the number that is the largest.

   111   101   10   110

140. Circle the number that is the largest.

   4.5   4   1.4

Solve the problems.

141.   17
        29
     + 12

142.   101
       75
    + 11

Name _____

SOCCER SCORES

TEAM	GOALS
Grizzlies	7
Eagles	2
Lions	5
Panthers	9
Cougars	6

143. Which team has the lowest score?

    A. Cougars

    B. Eagles

    C. Lions

144. Which team scored more than the Grizzlies?

    A. Lions

    B. Cougars

    C. Panthers

Write in the missing numbers in the number sentences.

145. $28 \div 4 =$ ☐

146. $18 \div 9 =$ ☐

147. $40 \div 8 =$ ☐

148. $21 \div 3 =$ ☐

149. $36 \div 4 =$ ☐

150. $35 \div 7 =$ ☐

Solve the problems.

151.
$$\begin{array}{r} \$\ 42.66 \\ -\ 13.21 \\ \hline \$ \end{array}$$

152.
$$\begin{array}{r} 55¢ \\ -\ 10¢ \\ \hline ¢ \end{array}$$

153.
$$\begin{array}{r} \$10.00 \\ +\ 12.16 \\ \hline \$ \end{array}$$

154. Which mixed numeral shows how much pizza is left? Circle the answer.

    A. $1\frac{2}{3}$ B. $\frac{1}{3}$ C. $1\frac{1}{3}$

Solve the problems.

155.
$$\begin{array}{r} 2176 \\ +\ 944 \\ \hline \end{array}$$

156.
$$\begin{array}{r} 66 \\ -19 \\ \hline \end{array}$$

157.
$$\begin{array}{r} 910 \\ -\ 66 \\ \hline \end{array}$$

158.
$$\begin{array}{r} 232 \\ \times\ 4 \\ \hline \end{array}$$

159.
$$\begin{array}{r} 65 \\ \times\ 7 \\ \hline \end{array}$$

160.
$$\begin{array}{r} 22 \\ \times\ 6 \\ \hline \end{array}$$

161. $4\overline{)52}$

162. $6\overline{)84}$

Name _____

Skills Test Answer Key

1. b
2. c
3. c
4. hollered
5. Beware
6. He tried to run, he grabbed, he pulled, and he hollered. Allow any of these.
7. Any 3 of these: muck, wet, thick, gooey, glue
8. Answers will vary. Possibly careless
9. E, C
10. C, E
11. C, E
12. E, C
13. 3, 1, 4, 5, 2
14. Answers will vary.
15. hollered and shouted
16. over and under
17. the helicopter motor
18. desert
19. night
20. below or under
21. goose
22. He ran away while the lion was laughing.
23. a long time ago
24. tricky
25. painful
26. powerful
27. Answers will vary.
28. Answers will vary—something about each person having something to offer, no matter how small.
29. 1980
30. over 500
31. no
32. 60, 3 billion
33. 31,000
34. Volcanoes can be very destructive.
35. The author wanted to teach about volcanoes and tell how destructive they can be.
36. zipper, hugging
37. puddle, mllllon, laugh
38. afraid, appear
39. graph, cotton, friend
40. absent
41. crayon
42. size
43. giraffe
44. didn't
45. she'll
46. they're
47. I've
48. bottle, rhyme, dough, lamb, ghost, bridge, wrap, lonesome, know, sword
49. ou
50. oo
51. ea
52. ia
53. ee
54. oa
55. ai
56. ui
57. oi
58. or
59. ar
60. er
61. or
62. ar
63. er
64. y
65. y
66. ey
67. ey
68. ey
69. y
70. watches
71. quarts
72. candies
73. boxes
74. donkeys
75. mice
76. teeth
77. families
78. geese
79. judge, fudge, hedge, ridge, ledge
80. caught, slipped, grabbed, enjoyed
81. ate
82. hopped
83. found
84. hurried
85. leaping
86. hiding
87. flying
88. swatting
89. hotter
90. scary
91. tiniest
92. careless
93. triangle
94. rewrite
95. untie or retie
96. submarine
97. mistake or retake
98. road, hoarse, threw, woulds, hoarse shoo, creak, brake, tow
99. none, once, people, forty, ocean, voice
100. bedspread, campfire, nightgown, fingernail
101. sience
102. sixtey
103. moter
104. memary
105. questun
106. giraffe, ant, goose, rooster, parrot, raccoon
107. tomato sauce
108. sugar cookies
109. cheese pizza
110. lettuce salad
111. banana pie
112. hamburgers
113. quite
114. which
115. tried
116. I can't remember if I put jelly on my sandwich.
117. Mrs. Clown, afternoon, trick, merry-go-round, Friday, laughter
118. Easter, Mexico, Boston, Thursday, Texas
119. swing, leaping, tricks, tricked, roar, laugh, grabbed, flying, clown
120. Seven, silly, little, four, cotton
121. fierce, large
122. baby, broken
123. thin, high
124. hungrily
125. daily
126. Elephants do daring tricks!
See the Amazing Fire-Eater!
Where is the roller coaster?
Can she juggle 10 things?
127. a. box around it
b. √ in front
c. line under it
128. Circled
129. Not circled
130. Circled
131. Circled
132. Not circled
133. Two brave clowns
134. A nervous Gino
135. climbed all over their barrel
136. grab those balloons before they float away
137. Allie Clown
112 Fun Street
Central City, Iowa
Abby Apricot
2222 Laughter Lane
Cow's Ear, Illinois
60001
138. Dear Abby,
You won't believe the news! The carnival came to our town last Thursday. Molly and I rode the roller coaster seven times. We bought cotton candy four times. Guess what happened when I went to see the circus acts? They invited me to be in the show! They gave me the job of fire-eater. It isn't all that hard—just a little hot!
Love, Allie
139. we'll
140. they're
141. won't
142. Don't miss the carnival!

See the most amazing things!

We have clowns, acrobats, and jugglers.

Eat delicious treats. (or !)

You can play lots of fun games.

There are 25 great rides. (or !)

Thursday, October 15

Central City, Iowa

143. Just then the circus show started.
144. c
145. See that student has completed all sections of the question.

Social Studies Skills Test

1. Texas, Kansas, Florida
2. San Francisco, Boston
3. Canada, Germany, Guatemala
4. Alaska
5. Florida
6. west
7. no
8. drugstore
9. 2
10. grocery store
11. India
12. Bolivia
13. France
14. United States
15. the Congress
16. the first airplane was flown
17. Kennedy was president
18. the Statue of Liberty
19. A, 3
20. A, 1
21. B, 3
22. B, 1
23. C, 3
24. C, 1
25. A, 2
26. C, 2
27. C
28. D
29. B
30. A
31. N
32. W
33. E
34. N
35. S
36. California
37. Florida
38. New Jersey
39. E
40. B
41. W

42. E
43. B
44. Texas
45. Boston
46. Chicago
47. Canada
48. Mexico
49. B, 4
50. B, 2
51. C, 3
52. D, 2
53. 50
54. South
55. West
56. scale
57. island
58. west
59. continent
60. ocean
61. title
62. compass

Science Skills Test

1. a & c
2. a
3. e
4. c
5. d
6. b
7. d
8. b
9. e
10. c
11. a
12. d
13. b
14. d
15. a
16. d
17. c
18. a
19. c
20. b
21. b
22. f
23. b
24. e
25. a
26. d
27. c
28. b

Math Skills Test

1. third
2. no
3. turtle
4. 40, 45
5. 70, 50
6. 47
7. 610

8. 326
9. 7,216
10. d
11. c
12. d
13. fifty nine or fifty-nine
14. 101, 55, 3,003, 929, 15
15. no
16. snake
17. frog
18. 35,623
19. 729
20. >
21. <
22. <
23. 103, 193, 237, 273, 333
24. 94, 72, 67, 39, 36
25. 79
26. 439
27. 806
28. 2,500
29. 2, 0
30. 400 + 10 + 6
31. 7,000 + 500 + 20
32. 593
33. 3,025
34. Upside down mushroom with 3 spots
35. 17
36. DE
37. $\frac{2}{5}$
38. $\frac{1}{5}$
39. $\frac{3}{5}$
40. $1\frac{2}{3}$
41. $\frac{5}{6}$
42. $12\frac{7}{8}$
43. $22\frac{4}{9}$
44. d
45. $\frac{1}{2}$
46. $9.70
47. $17.20
48. 460
49. 498

50. 50
51. 500
52. yes
53. no
54. no
55. 34¢
56. 58¢
57. 55¢
58. Monday
59. 428
60. B
61. C
62. A
63. E
64. D
65. E
66. F
67. B
68. A
69. C
70. 10
71. 28
72. 16
73. 13
74. 11
75. 4
76. 9
77. cup
78. gallons
79. grams
80. kilograms
81. ounces
82. meters
83. inches
84. gallon
85. kilometer
86. kilogram
87. yard
88. 12:25
89. 4:45
90. C
91. 4
92. 1000
93. 12
94. 100
95. tennis
96. 10
97. soccer
98. skiing and softball
99. (3, 1)
100. mitt
101. (2, 4) or (3, 5)
102. (5, 1)
103. racquet
104. 3, 5, 31
105. 10, 100, 14
106. 7
107. 5
108. 7
109. 8

110. 60
111. 70
112. 230
113. 500
114. 12
115. 4
116. 15
117. 7
118. 9
119. 11
120. 8
121. 7
122. 9
123. 595
124. 7955
125. 233
126. $\frac{2}{4}$
127. $\frac{3}{5}$
128. $\frac{3}{6}$
129. $\frac{2}{8}$
130. $\frac{2}{5}$
131. 18
132. 5
133. 7
134. 27
135. 32
136. 6
137. 80¢
138. 21¢
139. 111
140. 4.5
141. 58
142. 187
143. B
144. C
145. 7
146. 2
147. 5
148. 7
149. 9
150. 5
151. $29.45
152. 45¢
153. $22.16
154. A
155. 3120
156. 47
157. 844
158. 928
159. 455
160. 132
161. 13
162. 14

Skills Exercises Answer Key

page 21
1. shoes
2. luggage
3. pillow
4. atlas
5. clock
6. binoculars
7. journal
8. camera, film
9. telephone

pages 22–23

Main ideas will be something along these lines:
1. The icebergs are very large.
2. We are looking for a panda but have not seen one yet.
3. Bullfighting is terrible to watch.
4. It is very hard to learn how to throw a boomerang.

pages 24–25
1. 3
2. 2
3. 2
4. Sahara
5. Loch Ness
6. submarine
7. The Great Wall
8. The Everglades

page 26

Check to see that student has drawn a path that follows this order:
Shoe Store, Calendars & Cards, Sunglass Hut, Popcorn Corner, Jewelry Store, Shirts & Shorts, Toys and Games, Food Court, Travel Shop.

page 27

Check to see that student has drawn the items in the correct squares on the grid.

page 28
1. Sticker of Brazil drawn on bag #4.
2. Percy Penguin written on tag of bag #2.
3. Lu Sing written on tag of bag #5.
4. Sticker for Hawaii drawn on bag #1.
5. Frannie Frog written on tag of bag #3.
6. Dolly Dimples written on tag of bag #6.

page 29
1. See that student writes Jenny Jinx on the yacht ticket.
2. hot air balloon
3. George Gonzo
4. no
5. Las Vegas
6. Peru
7. blimp
8. airplane

page 30

Pedro is the only one who was not somewhere else at that time. Other answers will vary.

page 31

Incorrect words and phrases:
Alligators (there is only one alligator), rainy day, has her camera out, Raindrop, Bill's, four, five, gorilla, alligators, two black panthers, there are no umbrellas

page 32
1. Norlisk (coldest town)
2. 1 week
3. Greenland
4. Russia
5. Petronas Towers
6. 3 days
7. $1200
8. Norlisk (coldest town)

page 33
1. 5
2. Venezuela
3. Yosemite Falls
4. Tugela Falls
5. Sutherland Falls
6. gold
7. 1970

page 34
1. Pacific
2. Ecuador
3. Some of the animals are not found anywhere else in the world.
4. Answers will vary.
5. very few
6. giant land iguanas and sea iguanas
7. volcanoes

page 35
8. Galley
9. Answers will vary— perhaps a mouse or rat

page 36
1. meteors
2. meteoroids
3. meteorites
4. They burn up.
5. 500
6. blazing
7. outer space
8. thousands

page 37
1. Bermuda
2. proof
3. disappear
4. seventy
5. planes
6. none

page 38
1. 20 francs
2. whipped cream cake
3. strawberry and mocha
4. 3 lemon custards
5. whipped cream cake
6. caramel cream

7. 28 francs
8. Answers will vary.

page 39
1. murky, black, cold
2. 30 feet
3. lurking
4. Loch Ness
5. Scotland
6. darkness
7. Answers will vary.

page 40
1. Nerv S. Knight
2. Dewey U. Swim
3. Great-Great-Aunt Florence Frog
4. Chef Barbie Q.
5. O. Watta Suit
6. Queen Ima Ruler
7. Ben Caught
8. Professor Pancake
9. Sing A. Long
10. A. Jester

page 41

C—Frannie brought new wooden shoes.
E— Frannie had huge blisters on her toes.
C—The hotel ran out of apples.
E—The chef baked berry pies.
C—Another tourist sat on Frannie's camera.
E—Frannie had no pictures of Holland.
C—The tulip gardens are in full bloom.
E—Thousands of visitors have come to Holland.
C—The bus to Amsterdam had a flat tire.
E—Frannie arrived late at her hotel.
C—Frannie ate four pounds of Dutch chocolate.
E—Frannie spent two days in bed sick.

page 42

A. 1
B. 1
C. 3
D. 1
E. 1
F. 2

page 43

A. 3, 2, 1, 4, 5
B. 2, 4, 3, 5, 1
C. 5, 1, 3, 4, 2
   Also accept 5, 1, 4, 3, 2

page 44

A. 2, 7, 3, 5, 1, 6, 4
B. 3, 2, 4, 1, 7, 5, 6

page 45

Answers will vary. Check to see that student additions are reasonable to fit with story.

page 46

1. I liked Ed, my elephant guide.
2. We visited the Hippo Mud Spa.
3. I took a quick dip in Lake Makat.
4. I flew over Ngorongoro Crater.
5. I camped in the fig trees near the Lerai Forest.
6. Answers will vary—something about fishing or rafting on the river.

page 47

Answers will vary. See that student expresses some purpose the author had—such as to teach something about making a mummy.

page 48

elephant—Omaha
kangaroo—Australia
porcupine—Germany
moose—Spain
lizard—Peru

8. The bear is going to Tahiti.

page 49

helicopter—Mr. Dog
sports car—Miss Cat
airplane—Aunt Frannie
motorcycle—Mr. Rabbit
bookmobile—Mrs. Bear

1. the airplane
2. the sports car
3. Mr. Dog

page 50

Answers will vary. See that student has reasonable predictions based on information in story and picture.

page 51

Answers will vary.

page 52

Answers will vary.

page 53

Answers will vary.

page 54

Answers will vary.

page 55

1. bored
2. excited
3. selfish
4. helpful
5. grumpy
6. frightened

page 56

Opinions
1. Hawaii is wonderful.
   I was pretty silly-looking.
   The food here is wonderful.
2. My hotel is a bit dumpy.
   I think it is also overpriced.
   The hotel staff is not friendly, and there are too many mosquitoes!
   The beach is the best part.
3. It is amazing!
   I thought the view was beautiful.

Facts
1. It lasted one hour.
   They serve meals all day.
2. It costs $100 a day because it is on the beach.
3. Today I took a helicopter tour over the volcanoes of Hawaii.
   There are many active volcanoes in Hawaii.
   The tour lasted 3 hours.
   The helicopter pilot was from Singapore.

page 57

1. Answers will vary.
2. Great-Great-Grandpa Leonardo
3. Answers will vary.

page 58

1. . . . nose turned into icicle
   . . . fingers became ice cubes and broke off
   . . . shadow froze
   . . . drops of mist turned to snowflakes
   . . . milk came out as ice cream
   . . . words froze
   . . . stick crawled away
2. Answers will vary.

page 59

Answers will vary.

page 60

1. rowdy
2. polite or kind
3. refuse
4. not allowed
5. shrieking
6. deposit

page 61

1. insisted
2. slick

3. massive, monstrous
4. droopy, lonely
5. sticks that look like wishbones
6. ailing
7. ghostly, white

page 62

pairs of synonyms are:
destroy-ruin
weary-tired
wild-savage
prevent-stop
simple-easy
rapid-speedy
frighten-scare
steal-rob

page 63

1. a
2. b
3. a
4. b
5. c
6. a
7. b
8. a
9. b
10. b

page 64

1. b
2. a
3. c
4. a
5. b
6. a
7. c
8. b
9. b

page 65

1. grab
2. grand
3. reserve
4. gang
5. whole
6. more
7. country
8. take
9. stay
10. smile

page 66

hungry-eating as tired-sleeping
lawyer-courtroom as doctor-hospital
fingers-typing as feet-climbing
grumpy-happy as nervous-relaxed
monkeys-monkey as mice-mouse
cold-freezing as warm-hot

page 67

Words to circle—
    Opposites to write
bad—good
worst—best
incomplete—complete
late—early
easily—hard
none—all
sooner—later
won't—will
yesterday—tomorrow
cold—warm
midnight—noon
night—day
warm—cool
terrible—nice or good or
    wonderful
don't—do
less—more

page 68

Answers will vary. See
    that student has used
    a different and correct
    meaning for each
    word.

page 69

1. Circle all s sounds.
2. Circle beginning f
    sounds.
3. Circle ch sounds and
    t sounds in tasty
    truffles.
4. Circle p sounds.
5. Circle s sounds.
6. Circle c sounds.
7. Circle w sounds.
8. Circle all n sounds
    and the kn.
9. Circle all t sounds.
10. Circle the h sounds.

page 70

Ralph's red rocks are:
phonics, geography,
phrase, graph,
photograph
Fulbright's blue rocks are:
daughter, though, laugh,
tough, frighten, high,
ghost

page 71

1. afternoon
2. breeze

3. doorknob
4. freezer
5. knee
6. oversleep
7. goose or geese
8. outdoors
9. choosy or cheesy
10. drool
11. rooster
12. squeeze
13. bloom
14. foolish
15. speech
16. cool
17. steep or stoop
18. queen
19. raccoon
20. baboon
21. tooth or teeth
22. peek
23. loose
24. cartoon
25. school
26. balloon
27. cocoon

page 72

Path should connect
these words (not
necessarily in this order).
The exact path a student
chooses will vary.
about
fountain
cousin
ground
mouth
thought
sound
blouse
bought
shout
round
should
house
yours
scout

page 73

Words to be circled are:
1. coach
2. boast
3. coast
4. groaned
6. charcoal
10. load
12. oak

13. road
14. moaning
15. loan
16. toaster
19. throat
20. loaf
21. moat
23. motorboat
24. poach

page 74

The trail should connect
these points (words) in
this order:
Clue #1 – Check student
    maps to see that the
    trail begins at Cape
    Fear.
Clue #2 – early
Clue #3 – beard
Clue #4 – easy
Clue #5 – searching
Clue #6 – stealing
Clue #7 – bread
Clue #8 – seasons
Clue #9 – earthworm
Clue #10 – breathe
Clue #11 – weather
Clue # 12 – beach
    X should be on or
    near the word beach.

page 75

Down
1. raining
2. aunt
3. mail
4. glue
6. noise
8. frown
10. suit
11. soil
12. blue
Across
4. giant
5. buildings
7. point
9. raise
13. flows
14. tail

page 76

1. or
2. er
3. er
4. er
5. er

6. or
7. er
8. or
9. ar
10. or
11. er
12. ar
13. or
14. or
15. er
16. ar
17. or
18. er
19. er
20. or
21. er
22. er
23. er
24. or

page 77

1. age words:
    garbage
    garage
    courage
    manage
    cabbage
2. adge words:
    badge
3. edge words:
    ledge
    hedge
    pledge
4. idge words:
    bridge
    ridge
5. udge words:
    fudge
    judge
    budge

page 78

1. ey
2. y
3. y
4. y
5. y
6. ey
7. ey
8. y
9. y
10. y
11. y
12. ey
13. y
14. ey
15. y

Skills Exercises Answer Key

16. ey
17. y
18. y
Color these starbursts
yellow:
2, 3, 4, 5, 8, 9, 10, 11,
14,16, 17, 18
Color these purple:
1, 6, 7, 12, 13, 15

page 79

Cross out these words.
   never, liver, halo,
   wishes, cola, gasping,
   slippery, lumpy,
   whisper, whine
(Students may argue that
whisper, whine, and
slippery do have silent
letters—these answers,
therefore, may be
counted either way.)

page 80

1. s
2. es
3. es
4. es
5. s
6. es
7. s
8. es
9. es
10. s
11. es
12. s
13. s
14. es
15. s
16. s
17. es
18. es
red, yellow, or blue: 1, 5,
7, 10, 12, 13, 15, 16
orange, purple, or green:
2, 3, 4, 6, 8, 9, 11, 14, 17,
18

page 81

Kite # 1 should have
these words written on
the lines of its tail:
   teeth
   wolves
   knives
   women
   geese

feet
mice
Kite # 2 should have
these words written on
the lines of its tail:
   armies
   babies
   candies
   cities
   spies
   countries
   navies
   ladies
   families
   ponies
   bakeries
   parties
Kite # 3 should have
these words written on
the lines of its tail:
   keys
   valleys
   donkeys
   turkeys
   monkeys

page 82

1. grabbed
2. shouted
3. jumped
4. flshed
5. hurried
6. climbed
7. smelled
8. chewed
9. cooked
10. stirred
11. rubbed
12. tried
13. followed
14. wished
15. denied
16. sniffed
17. worried
18. slipped
19. rested
20. trimmed
21. robbed
22. enjoyed
23. laughed

page 83

1. slid
2. left
3. kept
4. shook
5. bit

6. ate
7. chose
8. built
9. taught
10. caught
11. found
12. lost
13. saw
14. hid

page 84

1. leaping
2. waving
3. laughing
4. swatting
5. screaming
6. gripping
7. opening
8. hollering
9. running
10. squeezing
11. writing
12. stirring
13. hiding
14. climbing
15. worrying

page 85

1. sweeter, sweetest
2. tastier, tastiest
3. bigger, biggest
4. grumpier, grumpiest
5. fuller, fullest
6. greater, greatest
7. stickier, stickiest
8. hotter, hottest
9. fluffier, fluffiest
10. taller, tallest

page 86

A. submarine
B. describe
C. untie
D. mistake
E. bicycle
F. antigerm
G. explain
H. minivan
I. triangle
J. rewrite
K. internet
L. impolite
M. preview
N. disobey
O. nonfat
P. semicircle

page 87

1. scary
2. actor
3. different
4. tropical
5. lonely
6. careless
7. friendliness
8. troublesome
9. famous
10. shiniest
11. frighten
12. likable
13. fancier
14. selfish
15. forgetful
16. friendship

page 88

1. choose
2. pale
3. groan
4. so
5. fur
6. see
7. toe
8. paws
9. ants
10. sense
11. prints
12. road
13. shoe
14. berry

page 89

Words from story that
should be circled and re-
written (The words do not
need to be in this order):
board—bored
wood—would
meat—meet
write—right
ate—eight
creak—creek
weight—wait
knot—not
threw—through
beet—beat
maid—made
tale—tail
eye—I
knight—night
pare—pair
buy—by
their—there

page 90

A. water
B. finger
C. rain
D. bed
E. sand
F. shoe
G. any
H. sea
I. home

page 91

1. night: nightmare, overnight, nightgown, nighttime, nightlight
2. out: campout, outside, outdoors, knockout, without
3. camp: campfire, campground, campsite
4. light: sunlight, lighthouse, flashlight, daylight, lightweight
5. under: underwater, underground, underline, underpants
6. down: sundown, downtown, downstairs, downpour
7. book: bookworm, bookstore, bookcase, cookbook
8. snow: snowflake, snowman, snowball, showshoes
9. door: outdoor, doorstep, doorbell, doorway
10. sun: sunlight, sundown, sunburn, sunset, sunflower

page 92

1. you're
2. I've
3. won't
4. she'd
5. let's
6. weren't
7. who'll
8. wasn't
9. what's
10. we're
11. we'd
12. didn't
13. it'll
14. couldn't
15. that's
16. you'll
17. they're
18. can't
19. he'll
20. doesn't

page 93

1. Which
2. tired
3. quiet
4. dessert
5. weather
6. from
7. except
8. through
9. carton
10. recipe
11. colors
12. diary

page 94

1. Please put garbage in the barrel.
2. Be careful with matches.
3. Watch out for falling rocks.
4. No shouting allowed in forest!
5. Broken bridge may be dangerous!
6. Loud noises bother the animals.
7. Beware! The blueberries are poison.
8. Tonight's forest walk is canceled.

page 95

TOP, left to right:
Could you give me your exact address, please?
That's impossible! I don't live anywhere.
Oh, you just don't want anyone to bother you.
BOTTOM, left to right:
Go straight to bed without your supper.
Why? Did I do something wrong?
Yes, you ate my favorite pumpkin pie that I had been saving for weeks!

page 96

1. helped; skipped
2. talked; tripped
3. leaped; begged
4. trimmed; yelled
5. popped; trotted
6. crawled; jumped
yellow: cup 1, 2, 3, 6; saucer 4, 6
green: cup 4, 5; saucer 1, 2, 3, 5

page 97

1. lucky, purple, big—30 points
2. six, good—20 points
3. new, striped, important—30 points
4. first, nice, smooth, steady—40 points
5. Four, noisy, teenage—30 points
6. second, highest—20 points
7. big, pink, cotton—30 points
8. long, winning—20 points
Zelda's score was 220 points.

page 98

1. larger
2. biggest
3. taller, shorter
4. largest
5. longer
6. shorter
7. widest
8. littlest
9. redder
10. silliest

page 99

1. slowly
2. soon
3. down
4. Carefully
5. ahead
6. tightly
7. never
8. frequently
9. deeply
10. Soon
11. Suddenly
12. rapidly
13. safely
14. Tomorrow

page 100

Ribbons around 2, 4, 6, 7
See that student has correctly fixed the run-ons.

page 101

All bubbles are exclamations except:
Save a bone for an old sea dog.
Just take one more step.
There's a ship on the horizon.
I am so scared of heights.

page 102

1. S—The balancing elephant
   P—is wearing a rather strange costume!
2. S—The clown
   P—juggles only one ball.
3. S—Only one bear
   P—was invited to be in the show today.
4. S—The other four elephants
   P—lost their costumes.
5. S—Ellie
   P—can stand on a ball with one foot for three minutes.
6. S—The galloping horse
   P—pays no attention to the lady on his back.
7. S—Clyde's pants
   P—need some more patches.
8. S—The audience
   P—wonders what is under the clown's hat.

9. S—A rather silly little hat
   P—sits on the bear's large head.
10. S—The center circus circle
    P—has four acts going on today.

page 103

Answers will vary. See that students have formed 10 complete sentences.

page 104

1. Bubbles rides the giraffe on Fridays and Saturdays.
2. Do you like all that loud music?
3. Chester held onto a ring and rode standing up last June.
4. This ride has an elephant, a giraffe, and a unicorn.
5. Reach for the ring!
6. Ulysses likes to ride on the unicorn on Tuesdays.
7. Is this carnival open on Thanksgiving?
8. Does the carnival travel to Chicago, Illinois?

page 105

Look out below! The trapeze clowns have a tricky act. They do twists, turns, and breath-taking flips. Is there anything they are afraid to do? They never fall, but watch out when they add the flying elephants to their act!

page 106

See that student has chosen dull words and replaced them with interesting words.

page 107

Punctuation may vary. Some sentences may be seen as exclamations or statements.
Dear Ulysses,
I miss your smiling face. I would have written sooner, but I've been tied up. The life of a famous contortionist can be knotty! Did you hear my news? I've added a trick to my act. You should see me do a double loop with a knee twist!
Come and see me in Florida.
Your clown pal,
                      Pretzel

pages 108–109

See that student has written an appropriate title for each passage.

page 110

See that student has completed all sections with reasonable questions.

page 111

See that student has written an adequate letter with some detail.

page 112

See that student has given logical, clear, sequential directions that match the map.

page 113

See that student has given logical, clear, sequential directions.

pages 114–115

Irrelevant sentences are:
1. All the balloons fly into the air.
2. The monkey ate a bag of peanuts.
3. Cookie washed her dishes.
4. Chester visited the elephants yesterday.

pages 120–121

Check map to see that student has written names of missing states: Alaska, Arizona, Arkansas, Alabama, Florida, Oregon, Oklahoma, Ohio, Tennessee, Texas
1. Answers will vary. Check map for accuracy.
2. Check map to see that student has located cities correctly.
3. Answers will vary. Check map for accuracy.
4. Hawaii
5. Answers will vary. Check map for accuracy.

pages 122–123

1. Colorado
2. Connecticut
3. Indiana
4. Kansas
5. Nevada
6. Maine
7. North Carolina
8. New York
9. New Jersey
10. Hawaii

page 124

1. willow ptarmigan
2. forget-me-not
3. Sitka spruce
4. Juneau
5. Yukon River
6. Mt. McKinley
7. Barrow
8. Fairbanks
9. Alaska
10. Aleutian

page 125

Answers will vary. Check for accuracy.

pages 126–127

Check to see that student draws a route that goes to each country listed in 1–19. The party is in Puerto Rico!

page 128

1. mountain
2. valley
3. plateau
4. river
5. lake
6. bay
7. peninsula
8. island
9. beach
10. plain
11. ocean

page 129

Eastern Hemisphere:
  Africa, Asia, Europe, Australia, Antarctica
Southern Hemisphere:
  South America, Africa, Australia, Asia, Antarctica
Western Hemisphere:
  North America, South America, Antarctica, Asia
Northern Hemisphere:
  North America, South America, Europe, Asia, Africa

page 130

1. c
2. a
3. b
4. c
5. b
6. b
7. c
8. c
9. a
10. b
11. c
12. b

page 131

Cities (green):
  Chicago, London, Moscow, Mexico City, Tokyo
States (blue):
  Kansas, Vermont, Florida, Arizona, Hawaii, Texas
Countries (red):
  Brazil, Egypt, Israel, Spain, India, Korea
Continents (yellow):
  Asia, Antarctica, Europe, South America, Africa

page 132

Answers will vary. Check to see that answers are correct.

page 133

1. A, 3
2. D, 1
3. D, 2
4. C, 1
5. A, 4
6. B, 1
7. A, 1
8. B, 2
9. D, 4
10. C, 3
11. B, 4
12. C, 4

pages 134–135

Answers will vary.

page 136

Check to see that flags are colored accurately.

7 red stripes
6 white stripes
13 stars

7 red stripes
6 white stripes
50 stars

page 137

1. c
2. b
3. b
4. b
5. c
6. c
7. a

page 138

1. 100
2. the first railroad
3. yes
4. 1927
5. yes
6. yes
7. 1869
8. Armstrong

page 139

Answers will vary.

page 140

A. 4
B. 5
C. 3
D. 9
E. 8
F. 2
G. 6
H. 10
I. 1
J. 7

page 141

Answers will vary.

pages 142–143

1. Pennsylvania Avenue
2. Pennsylvania Avenue
3. a and c
4. a and b
5. b and c
6. Constitution
7. Independence
8. Answers will vary.

page 144

1. Scotland
2. Italy
3. England
4. Belgium
5. Ireland
6. Wales
7. Norway
8. Germany

page 145

1. Chicago
2. New York
3. 1¹/2 million
4. 3¹/2 million
5. San Diego
6. Houston
7. 7¹/2 million
Answers will vary.

pages 146–147

Addresses will vary.
Planet: Earth
Galaxy: Milky Way
Check to see that student answers are correct.

page 148

1. 10
2. the Icebergs
3. 30
4. 15
5. 30
6. Ingrid

page 149

1. 6
2. 4
3. 4
4. 5
5. 6

page 150

1. 30 miles
2. 20
3. 40
4. 20
5. 30

page 151

Connect these boxes with a line to these landforms.
fish boat—bay
motorboat—lake
snowshoes—mountain
tractor—plain
gold pans—river
trees—plateau
log cabin—valley
lightbulbs—lighthouse

pages 152—153

1–3. Check to see that student has traced, colored, and drawn pictures according to the instructions.
4. North America
5. South America
6. Antarctica
1–2. Check to see that student has colored the hemispheres accurately.
3. Western
4. Northern
5. Eastern
6. Southern
7. Eastern
8. Northern
9. Eastern and Western

page 154

Check to see that student has colored each area accurately.

page 155

Check to see that student has traced or colored each area accurately.

page 156

RED—Hal Horse—California, Ohio, Colorado, New Hampshire, Montana, Alabama, Pennsylvania
GREEN—Gail Snail—San Francisco, Albuquerque, Dallas, Albany, New Orleans, Boston, Nashville
BLUE—Gilbert Gull—United States, Peru, Japan, India, Great Britain, Australia

page 157

1. Texas
2. Louisiana
3. Michigan
4. Florida
5. New Jersey
6. Hawaii
7. Oklahoma
8. Alaska

pages 158–159

1. Red—Missouri
2. Green—Pennsylvania, Louisiana, Massachusetts
3. Orange—Florida
4. Purple—Arizona
5. Blue—Wisconsin
6. Yellow—Texas
7. Pink—California
8. Brown—Utah
9. Red—South Dakota
10. Green—Washington
11. Blue—New York
12. Yellow—Tennessee
13. Purple—Connecticut
14. Orange—Ohio

pages 160–161

1, 3–8. See that student has drawn and traced things accurately.
2. 5
9. Gulf of Mexico
10. Columbia
11. Ohio
12. Kansas City

13. Albuquerque
14. Galveston
15. Rio Grande
16. Chicago

Check to see that student has drawn a route by water from the Gulf of Mexico to Boston Harbor.

page 162
1. California
2. Arizona
3. Arizona
4. California
5. New Mexico
6. east
7. Utah
8. Colorado
9. Colorado
10. 5

page 163
1. 2030
2. 1615
3. 2690
4. 1480
5. 1040
6. 890
7. Seattle and Boston
8. Chicago and Washington, DC

page 164
1. no
2. no
3. yes
4. 10
5. 12
6. yes
7. no
8. yes
9. yes
10. Wild West Waterworks

page 165
1. A, 2
2. D, 8
3. F, 5
4. C, 2
5. B, 7
6. C, 5
7. treasure chest
8. whale

page 166
1. D, 4; C, 6; and B, 7

2–10. Check to see that student has drawn worms in correct spots.

page 167
1–6. Check to see that student has drawn items in correct spots.
7. bridge

page 168
1–4. Check to see that student has drawn flowers in correct spots.
5. B, 3
6. E, 4
7. E, 2
8. C, 2

page 169
1. no
2. 6
3. no
4. D, 4; D, 5; E, 4; E, 5
5. C, 3
6. A, 4; A, 5; B, 4; B, 5

page 170
1. Green Lakes District
2. 70
3. Green Lakes District
4. 50
5. Big Trees Area
6. 40

page 171
1. African ostrich
2. brown hyena
3. black rhino
4. cheetah
5. Moroccan gazelle
6. African elephant
7. gorilla
8. lemur
9. white rhino

page 172
1. Argentina
2. Peru or Argentina
3. Venezuela or Argentina
4. Chile, Peru, Columbia, Uruguay, or Argentina
5. Uruguay, Argentina, Brazil, or Columbia

6. Brazil
7. grain, coffee, sheep, or fish
8. oil
9. Brazil
10. Brazil

page 173
1. Kalgoorlie
2. Cairns
3. eastern
4. middle
5. Perth
6. 46 inches a year
7. 59 inches a year

page 174
1. Sugarplum
2. 10 miles
3. 57
4. yes
5. yes
6. Sweet Town
7. 20
8. Route 1

page 175
Across
1. key
4. ocean
7. road
8. Island
10. sea
11. peninsula
12. west
13. poles
Down
2. equator
3. continent
5. scale
6. hemisphere
9. bay
10. states

pages 176–177
Directions: NE, NW, NE, E, SW, SE
1–6. Check to see that Ferris wheel, clown tent, and ticket booth are colored.
4. trailer parking or hay truck
5. no
6. yes
7. yes
8. no
9. yes

10. no

page 178
Check to see that student has included title, key, scale, symbols, and a place for the stamps to be lost.

page 179
Answers will vary. Check to see that student has included map title, compass rose, key, signature, and date.

page 183
Check to see that student has finished the pictures and labeled the parts.

page 184
1. skull
2. collarbone
3. humerus
4. breastbone
5. ribs
6. shoulderblade
7. backbone
8. pelvis
9. kneecap
10. femur

page 185
Circulatory—blood, vein, aorta, heart, vessel
Skeleton-Muscle—ribs, backbone, shoulder blade, humerus, tibia, sternum, kneecap, pelvis, femur, skull, fibula, radius
Digestive—intestines, esophagus, saliva, stomach
Respiratory—lungs, trachea, diaphragm
Nervous—brain, nerves, spinal cord, nerve endings
Senses—eyes, tongue, nose, ears, skin
The body part is a skull.

page 186
1. disease
2. cavity
3. fracture

4. pinkeye
5. sprain
6. bruise
7. infection
8. allergy
9. arthritis
10. strain

page 187
1. mouth
2. lungs
3. skeleton
4. heart
5. tongue
6. knee
7. elbow
8. muscle
9. brain
10. ankle
11. blood

page 188
Matching pictures
1—E
2—A
3—F
4—B
5—D
6—C

page 189
1. animals
2. lines
3. hands
4. signs
5. crossing

page 190
Answers may vary. Discuss possibilities with students.

Healthy foods:
- peas
- carrots
- vegetarian pizza
- spaghetti sauce
- orange juice
- fruit
- milk
- carrot juice
- eggs
- yogurt
- bananas
- vegetables
- turkey
- tomatoes

page 191
1. T
2. T
3. F
4. T
5. F
6. F
7. F
8. F

page 192
Bob — Blue path—to Earth
Bill — Red path—to moon
Bo — green path—to Jupiter
Bev — yellow path—to Mars
Barb — purple path—to sun

page 193
1. earthquake
2. lava
3. ash
4. shakes
5. fault
6. tremor
7. crack
8. erupts
9. volcano
10. crust

pages 194-195
Check to see that pictures are drawn in appropriate places.

page 196
Answers may vary somewhat.
1. earthquake—fast
2. lightning—fast
3. volcano—fast
4. wind—fast (or slow)
5. fire—fast
6. people & machines—fast
7. moving water—slow

page 197
ocean words to follow:
salt water—waves—shells—jellyfish—starfish—crabs—sand—kelp—shipwrecks—currents—sharks—whales

page 198
1. surfer, sailboat
2. otter
3. umbrella
4. sailboat
5. treasure chest
6. lobster
7. anchor
8. diver

page 199
solid—definite shape—close together molecules—picture of ring—definite size—"solid"

liquid—definite size—molecules farther apart—picture of rain—no definite shape—can be poured—"liquid"

gas—picture of balloon—molecules farthest apart—no definite shape—no definite size—"gas"

page 200
1. solid to liquid
2. liquid to solid
3. liquid to gas
4. gas to liquid
5. evaporate
6. freeze
7. condense (or evaporate) depends on explanation of what is happening
8. melt
9. melt
10. condense

page 201
1. air
2. atmosphere
3. evaporate
4. condense
5. water
6. oceans

pages 202-203
1. cumulonimbus

2. cirrus
3. stratus
4. cumulus
5. fog

page 204
1. tornado
2. sunny
3. rain
4. hot
5. windy
6. blizzard
7. lightning
8. dry

page 205
Some missing forces:
wind—tree, kite, water, sailboat, leaves
people—rake, jump rope, wagon, pogo stick, ball, swing, ping pong
dog or other animal—girl

page 206
lever— screwdriver opening paint can
inclined plane— ramp to house
screws— screws in wood, door knob
wedge— axe and wedge in wood
wheel & axle— bike
pulley— clothesline

page 207
1. sound made by small sound waves
2. sound made by big sound waves
3. a loud sound that is not pleasant
4. the highness or lowness of a sound
5. moving back and forth
6. the way sound travels

page 208
1. thermometer
2. heat
3. degree
4. warmer
5. melt
6. expand
7. explode

8. sun
9. fuel
10. boil

page 209
1. a
2. b
3. a
4. b
5. c
6. a
7. c
8. b

page 215
Answers 1, 2, 3, 4, 6, 7, 8, 9, and 10 may vary slightly from those listed. Cars stretch over space, and therefore are not at one specific mark on the number line. Give student credit for answers close to these:
1. 270
2. 300 and 320
3. 50
4. 210
5. 3
6. 250
7. 120 and 130
8. 340
9. 380
10. 350
11. 79
12. RED—Car # 3
13. GREEN—Car # 10
14. ORANGE—Car # 79

page 216
A. four thousand nine hundred
B. six hundred twenty
C. two thousand
D. seventy-seven
E. nine hundred ninety
F. ten thousand
G. three hundred thirty-three

page 217
Check student page to see that:
all ODD numbers are colored green, purple, or blue: 201, 607, 35, 611, 159, 169, 253, 5,255, 8,887
all EVEN numbers are colored red, orange, or yellow: 70, 870, 2,020, 5,142, 3,430, 9,902, 702
1. 403
2. 792 or 972
3. 8,001
4. 756 or 576

page 218
1. 700,000 (D)
2. 1,000,000 (C)
3. 4,000,001 (K)
4. 3,000,000,000 (I)
5. 61,000 (J)
6. 2,666 (E)
7. 6,885 (H)
8. 42,000 (L)
9. 28,888 (G)
10. 1,001 (A)
11. 9,000,000,000 (F)
12. 9,999 (B)

page 219
5 "greater than" problems
6 "less than" problems
A. <
B. <
C. =
D. <
E. <
F. >
G. >
H. >
I. <
J. =
K. <
L. >
M. >

page 220
1. water mite diver (or water mite)
2. coiled vorticella dancer (or coiled vorticella)
3. stento swimmer (or stento)
4. walking bean high jumper (or walking bean)
5. cyclops water hopper
6. water flea
7. stento
8. cyclops water hopper
9. walking bean
10. water mite
11. coiled vorticella
12. wheel animal
11. yes
12. chair and towel

page 221
1. c
2. 40
3. 843
4. Big Sissy
5. 120
6. Alfy
7. c
8. 228

page 222
1. 3265
2. 6261
3. 2359
4. 8045
5. 6372
6. 6421
7. 1070

page 223
Across
A. 89
B. 746
E. 3555
G. 4002
H. 5736
J. 2109
L. 9870
N. 135
Down
A. 8665
C. 6032
D. 90,007
F. 5702
I. 620
J. 2483
K. 99
M. 7170
N. 16

page 224
1. 4,263
2. 1,810
3. 9,246
4. 7,221
5. 231
6. 5,202
7. 300 + 20 + 9
8. 600 + 70 + 8
9. 500 + 90
10. 1,000 + 500 + 70 + 2
11. 4,000 + 400 + 70 + 7
12. 2,000 + 800 + 30 + 1

page 225
Wrong bubbles are these listed below.
Corrected answers are included.
B. 8,032
C. 1,400
E. 402
H. 9,001
K. 69

page 226
Check to see that student has designed the fourth butterfly to contain 4 stripes across the middle and a set of four dots on each of the 4 corners of the wings. Check student drawings to see that the patterns are completed with these things in the empty spaces:
1. a triangle in first space (same size as others shown); small circle in second space
2. 3 upside down mushrooms
3. a ladybug with 1 spot
4. numbers 40, 41
5. fly facing to right of page
6. cute, kite

page 227
1. $\frac{2}{3}$
2. $10\frac{4}{5}$
3. $5\frac{3}{4}$
4. $\frac{1}{4}$
5. $\frac{3}{4}$
6. $\frac{2}{4}$
7. $5\frac{6}{10}$
8. $\frac{8}{3}$

9. $\frac{10}{2}$

10. $2\frac{2}{4}$

11. $2\frac{3}{2}$

12. $3\frac{1}{4}$

page 228

1. $\frac{4}{6}$ or $\frac{2}{3}$

2. $\frac{3}{6}$ or $\frac{1}{2}$

3. $\frac{2}{6}$ or $\frac{1}{3}$

4. $\frac{1}{6}$

5. $\frac{1}{6}$

6. $\frac{5}{12}$

7. $\frac{3}{12}$ or $\frac{1}{4}$

8. $\frac{2}{12}$ or $\frac{1}{6}$

9. $\frac{2}{3}$

10. $\frac{1}{2}$

11. $\frac{1}{4}$

12. $\frac{2}{4}$ or $\frac{1}{2}$

13. $\frac{1}{4}$

14. $\frac{2}{3}$

page 229

Answers on 3, 4, 5, and 8 may vary, depending upon how student "reads" the picture.

1. $\frac{13}{14}$

2. $\frac{1}{14}$

3. $\frac{5}{14}$

4. $\frac{4}{14}$ or $\frac{2}{7}$

5. $\frac{10}{14}$ or $\frac{5}{7}$

6. $\frac{1}{14}$

7. $\frac{4}{14}$ or $\frac{2}{7}$

8. $\frac{1}{14}$

9. $\frac{1}{14}$

10. $\frac{1}{14}$

page 230

Check student pages to see that the proper amounts are colored:

1. $2\frac{2}{3}$

2. $3\frac{1}{5}$

3. $3\frac{5}{6}$

4. $1\frac{7}{8}$

5. $2\frac{2}{5}$

Students should write these answers:

6. $2\frac{2}{4}$ or $2\frac{1}{2}$

7. $1\frac{9}{12}$ or $1\frac{3}{4}$

page 231

top of page:
Her score is c.

1. $16\frac{5}{9}$

2. $10\frac{2}{3}$

3. $45\frac{1}{2}$

4. $22\frac{5}{6}$

5. $12\frac{2}{5}$

6. $18\frac{8}{9}$

7. $8\frac{1}{7}$

8. $25\frac{2}{3}$

9. $5\frac{16}{20}$

10. $12\frac{3}{4}$

11. $15\frac{6}{8}$

12. $10\frac{1}{6}$

13. twenty and four fifths

14. ten and one sixth

15. nine and three fourths

16. two and one third

page 232

Top question: $\frac{1}{4}$ of the race is left.

1. $\frac{6}{8}$

2. $1\frac{9}{10}$

3. $1\frac{1}{2}$

4. $10\frac{1}{2}$

5. $\frac{1}{2}$

6. >
7. >
8. <
9. >
10. =
11. >
12. <
13. <
14. >
15. >

page 233

A. four fifths
B. two thirds
C. Freddy
D. $\frac{7}{9}$
E. no
F. $22\frac{3}{4}$
G. three sevenths
H. the singers

page 234

1. 2 quarters, 1 dime
2. 2 dimes, 2 pennies
3. 5 nickels
4. 1 quarter, 1 dime, 1 nickel, 1 penny
5. 1 quarter, 1 penny
6. 2 quarters, 5 dimes
7. yes
8. 4 quarters; yes OR 3 quarters, 1 nickel; no OR 3 quarters, 1 dime; yes
9. 80¢
10. 34¢

page 235

1. 80¢
2. 70¢
3. 99¢
4. 22¢
5. 78¢
6. $1.10 or 110¢
7. Ara
8. 9 nickels or nickels
9. 3 quarters, 1 dime
10. 4 dimes, 2 pennies
11. Ollie
12. Ara

page 236

1. Swamp Soccer Game
2. Frog Leap Finals or Dance Contest
3. Water Ski Races
4. yes
5. Trampoline Tournament
6. Swampy River Swim Meet
7. Dance Contest
8. about $28 (Allow any estimate close to this.)
9. High Dive Show
10. Water Ski Races
11. no
12. yes

page 237

The numbers in these dreams make sense. These should be colored blue: 3, 7, 8, 10, 11, 12, 13

The numbers in these dreams do NOT make sense. These should be colored orange: 1, 2, 4, 5, 6, 9

page 238

1. 5.4
2. 14.6
3. 11.4
4. 9.7
5. 1.5 or 14.6
6. 15.0
7. Any one or all of these: 2.4, 4.2, 8.5, 10.3, 12.6, 13.8
8. 1.0 or 6.0 or 15.0
9–15. Check student drawings for the items listed in these problems

page 239
1. 398
2. 502
3. 12,000
4. 2
5. 29
6. 76
7. 610
8. 431
9. 298
10. 50
11. 5,003
12. 40

page 240
1. F = 88 + 50
2. 200 − 150 = B
3. A = 320 − 17
4. F + A = 441
5. T = 4 x 250

page 241
These sentences should be marked with a T as true: 1, 2, 3, 4, 7, 8, 12, 13, 16, 17, 18, 20

page 242
1. a. $\frac{3}{10}$
   b. $\frac{4}{10}$ or $\frac{2}{5}$
   c. $\frac{3}{10}$
2. a. $\frac{5}{25}$ or $\frac{1}{5}$
   b. $\frac{3}{25}$
   c. $\frac{10}{25}$ or $\frac{2}{5}$
   d. $\frac{7}{25}$
3. a. $\frac{10}{24}$ or $\frac{5}{12}$
   b. $\frac{3}{24}$ or $\frac{1}{8}$
   c. $\frac{6}{24}$ or $\frac{1}{4}$

page 243
This is a difficult concept. Students may have varying answers that they can support with argument. Discuss these answers with students.
1. 2 red socks
2. 1 yellow, 1 green, 1 white sock

3. 3 purple socks
4. 2 orange socks
5. 5 blue socks
6. 3 blue socks
7. 2 black, 2 red socks

pages 244–245
Answers will vary. Examine student pictures to see that they have followed directions.

page 246
1. ft
2. mi
3. in.
4. in.
5. in.
6. ft
7. in.
8. in.
9. in.
10. ft
11. ft
12. ft

page 247
1. m
2. cm or m
3. m or km
4. cm
5. m
6. cm
7. m
8. cm
9. cm
10. m

page 248
A. 40 ft
B. 140 ft
C. 40 ft
D. 24 ft
E. 90 ft
F. 120 ft

page 249
1. 70 in.
2. 25 in.
3. 40 in.
4. 170 in.
5. 140 in.

page 250
Answers are estimates. They may vary.
1. 2
2. 7
3. 2

4. 8
5. 12
6. 12
7. 55
Josie: about 23

page 251
1. 14
2. 12
3. 18
4. 11
5. 28
6. 27
7. 3
8. trampoline
9. diving board
10. T-shirt
11. no

page 252
1. 8
2. 16
3. 4
4. 17
5. 5
6. 11

page 253
1. lb or t
2. lb
3. oz
4. lb
5. oz
6. lb or oz
7. oz
8. t
9. oz
10. lb

page 254
1. g
2. g
3. g
4. kg
5. kg
6. g
7. g
8. kg
9. kg
10. g
11. kg
12. kg
13. g
14. g

page 255
1. gallons
2. gallons

3. gallons
4. gallons
5. cups
6. gallons

page 256
1. 11:30
2. 2:50
3. 3:50
4. 1:00
5. 8:10
6. 9:40
7. 10:45
8. 4:35

page 257
1–4. Cactus Cath
      1 min. 30 sec.
   Wild Wanda
      2 min. 15 sec.
   Annie O.
      3 min. 30 sec.
   Barb 3 min.
5. Annie O.
6. no
7. 2 min.

pages 258–259
1. 15 seconds
2. 28 lb
3. 15°; warmer
4. 16 cups
5. 1 ft, 4 in.
6. 5 in.
7. 30 sq. units

page 260
1. Jake
2. Tuesday
3. 36
4. 16
5. Thursday
6. Wednesday and Friday
7. Jake and Tilly
8. Jake
9. Tuesday

page 261
1. 30
2. 10
3. Cabbage Throw
4. Broom Balance
5. Nose Wiggling & Banana Peel Jump
6. 15
7. 100

page 262
1. 12
2. bruises
3. 2
4. 14
5. black eye
6. frostbite
7. 10
8. 20
9. broken bones
10. 4

page 263
Check student graphs to see that amounts are colored correctly.

page 264
1. skate
2. apple
3. bat
4. no
5. (2, 4)
6. (3, 1)
7. duck
8. notebook
9. no
10. soccer shoe
11. (7, 12)
12. (5, 6)

page 265
She is jumping over a dinosaur.

pages 266–267
1. ant
2. salt
3. yes
4. cake
5. yes
6. no
7. knife
8. bananas
9. apple
10. yes
11. melon
12. yes
13. spoon
14. (7, 6)
15. ant
16. nothing
17. ant
18–20. Check student drawings.
20. the cake

page 268
Check student maps to see that they've found the trail.

page 269
He's riding a bucking beetle.

page 270
Across
4. congruent
6. degree
7. minute
9. square
Down
1. segment
2. hour
3. quart
5. triangle
8. area

page 273
1. 239
2. 106
3. 99
4. 422
5. 340
6. 200
7. 9
8. 110
9. 908

page 274
A large ocean liner

page 275
Even numbers : 12, 22, 50, 66, 72, 86, 100, 444; 8 even numbers
Odd numbers: 9, 13, 27, 33, 39, 75, 103, 999, 2947; 9 odd numbers

page 276
1. George
2. sky diver
3. no
4. 18
5. yes
6. eighth
7. gymnastics
8. Chen
9. seventh
10. 81

page 277
1. 763,002
2. 497

3. 19,058
4. 414
5. 24,263
6. 9,100
7. 4,907
8. 1267

page 278
Down
1. 262
2. 1000
3. 9130
4. 716
6. 19
9. 312
10. 421
11. 295
12. 903
13. 286
15. 17
Across
1. 29
4. 7000
5. 211
7. 30
8. 96
9. 304
11. 20
13. 22
14. 51
16. 88
17. 39

page 279
1. 16 .... pattern is x 2
2. 11, 19 .. pattern is + 4
3. 7 .... pattern is – 4
4. 12 .... pattern is + 1, + 2, + 3, + 4
5. 8, 5 ...... pattern is –1

pages 280-281
1. >
2. =
3. >
4. <
5. >
6. <
7. <
8. <
9. >
10. >
11. >
12. =
13. <
14. =
15. >
16. <

pages 282-283
1. longer
2. shorter
3. shorter
4. longer
5. shorter
6. shorter
7. more
8. less
9. less
10. more
11. more
12. more
13. less
14. more
15. more

page 284
1. 30
2. 70
3. 690
4. 600
5. 1,800
6. 900
7. 7000
8. 3,000
9. 5,000
10. 12,000

page 285
1. 6
2. 7
3. 4
4. 4
5. 8
6. 4
7. 2
8. 3
9. 8

page 286
Terry
  A. Wrong 114
  C. Wrong 120

Kerry
  E. Wrong 791

Mary
  J. Wrong 16
  L. Wrong 481

Barry
  N. Wrong 395
  O. Wrong 275

Most right? Kerry

page 287

1. 22
2. 9
3. 25
4. 2491
5. 14
6. 26
7. 5
8. 16
9. 300
10. 21
11. 54
12. 4
13. 400

page 288

deer, bat, owl, bear, rabbit

page 289

Race 1
Frannie 15
Robbie 16
Gus 18 Winner

Race 2
Frannie 30 Winner
Robbie 24
Gus 9

Race 3
Frannie 10
Robbie 12 Tie
Gus 12 Tie

Race 4
Frannie 15 Winner
Robbie 4
Gus 6

Race 5
Frannie 25 Winner
Robbie 16
Gus 9

Race 6
Frannie 10
Robbie 12 Winner
Gus 6

page 290

A. 12 - 12 - 11
9 - 13 - 9
13 - 14 - 14
Tic Tac Toe — yes

B. 6 - 11 - 6
22 - 7 - 22
12 - 4 - 12
Tic Tac Toe — yes

C. 20 - 16 - 16
12 - 18 - 18
9 - 14 - 9
Tic Tac Toe — no

page 291

21 - 28 - 14 -
16 - 12 - 6 -
18 - 13 - 31
Answer: 31

page 292

1. 4
2. 2
3. 7
4. 5
5. 6
6. 7
7. 10
8. 6
9. 8
10. 18
11. 6
12. 8
13. 25
14. 1
15. 9
16. 8

page 293

1. +
2. x
3. −
4. x
5. ÷
6. −
7. x
8. +
9. ÷
10. +
11. x
12. ÷
13. +
14. ÷
15. x
16. +
17. −
18. x or +
19. ÷
20. +

page 294

Answers will vary.

page 295

1. E
2. C
3. Γ
4. H
5. B
6. L
7. D
8. B
9. M
10. G
11. J
12. I
13. F
14. B
15. M
16. L

page 296

1. $\frac{5}{6}$ —orange
2. $\frac{3}{10}$ —green
3. $\frac{2}{3}$ —red
4. $\frac{2}{8}$ —purple
5. $\frac{4}{4}$ —blue
6. $\frac{4}{5}$ —yellow
7. $\frac{2}{8}$ —purple
8. $\frac{4}{5}$ —yellow
9. $\frac{1}{4}$ —silver
10. $\frac{2}{7}$ —gold
11. $\frac{3}{10}$ —green
12. $\frac{5}{6}$ —orange

page 297

1. $\frac{2}{4}$
2. $\frac{2}{3}$
3. $\frac{1}{3}$
4. $\frac{1}{4}$
5. $\frac{1}{2}$
6. $\frac{4}{8}$

page 298

$3.3 = 3\frac{3}{10}$ (D)

$4.2 = 4\frac{2}{10}$ (I)

$.8 = \frac{8}{10}$ (A)

$6.5 = 6\frac{5}{10}$ (E)

$5.2 = 5\frac{2}{10}$ (B)

$1.1 = 1\frac{1}{10}$ (G)

$.6 = \frac{6}{10}$ (F)

$1.9 = 1\frac{9}{10}$ (C)

page 299

The picture is of a shark.

pages 300-301

1. yes
2. yes
3. Water Balloon Toss
4. (any two) Potato Sack Hop, 3-Legged Race, Water Balloon Toss, or Softball Throw
5. Bubble Gum–Blowing Contest
6. 30 min.
7. Bike Rodeo
8. 12 P.M.
9. Potato Sack Hop
10. 2 hr. 15 min.
11. 3:15 P.M.
12. $1\frac{1}{2}$ hr.
13. late
14. 4:00 P.M.

page 302

1. no
2. yes
3. no
4. yes
5. yes
6. no
7. yes
8. yes

page 303

1. 30¢
2. 75¢
3. 60¢
4. 55¢
5. 11¢
6. 35¢
7. 20¢
8. 51¢

page 304

1. $ .25
2. $ .75
3. $ .30
4. $ .15
5. $ .40
6. $ 3.50
7. 25¢
8. $ 4.00

page 305

1. 81 fans
2. 15¢ more
3. 5 hats
4. 48 fans
5. 20 swimmers
6. 25 jelly beans